D0076908

FROM CLINIC
TO CLASSROOM

FROM CLINIC TO CLASSROOM

Medical Ethics and Moral Education

Howard B. Radest

PRAEGER

Westport, Connecticut
London

Library of Congress Cataloging-in-Publication Data

Radest, Howard B., 1928–
    From clinic to classroom : medical ethics and moral education /
Howard B. Radest.
        p. cm.
    Includes bibliographical references and index.
    ISBN 0–275–96194–X (alk. paper)
    1. Medical ethics.   2. Moral education.   I. Title.
    R725.5.R33   2000
    174'.2—dc21   99–37525

British Library Cataloguing in Publication Data is available.

Library of Congress Catalog Card Number: 99–37525
ISBN: 0–275–96194–X

First published in 2000

Praeger Publishers, 88 Post Road West, Westport, CT 06881
An imprint of Greenwood Publishing Group, Inc.
www.praeger.com

Printed in the United States of America

The paper used in this book complies with the
Permanent Paper Standard issued by the National
Information Standards Organization (Z39.48–1984).

10 9 8 7 6 5 4 3 2 1

For

Rita

and

Nora, Robert, Jes, and Emma

and

Karen, Michael, Brendan, Kara, and Colin

Contents

Preface

I begin with a confession, and I know that isn't a good way to start. But here goes. Nearly ten years ago, I retired as director of the Ethical Culture Fieldston School in New York City and also as dean of The Humanist Institute. But I quickly found out that retirement need not be—ought not be—abdication. So I now serve as ethics consultant and ethics committee chair at a small local hospital (less than 100 beds). I also teach a course or two each year in medical ethics at one of the smaller branches of my state university. Of course, I try to keep up with the thinking of my colleagues by reading the literature, by attending conferences and seminars, and by using the Internet. Nevertheless, things move very quickly in biomedical ethics, and the news does not always reach this corner of South Carolina in timely fashion. So I am often surprised. That, I suppose, helps to keep me interested. It also warns me against hasty conclusions.

What follows in the chapters below, then, is a reflection "from the trenches," as it were. I have tried to say as clearly and as completely as I can what I have observed over the years in the classroom as a teacher and administrator, and in the clinic as an ethicist (although I'm not sure I like the pretensions of that title). Without, I hope, indulging in mock humility or in Socratic irony, I have a deep sense of what I do not know. In fact, the more time I spend in the field, the less satisfied I am.

To be sure, as a philosopher, I am tempted by the conceptual side of issues like confidentiality, organ transplant, managed care, physician-assisted suicide, and the rest of the biomedical ethics agenda. I enjoy working with ideas, so I'm also tempted to enter the argument between autonomy and community, principalism and casuistry, justice and caring. But a biomedical literature that expands daily already pays attention to these, and does it very well. So why, then, multiply words? In looking backward from my new vantage point, it struck me that biomedical ethics and moral education might offer insights to one another. Hence "thinking with cases."

When clinic and classroom address one another, ethical philosophy benefits, too. Issues, problems, concepts, and methods are found in richer dimension. The typical arguments between various ideologies and theories—for example, between the right and the good, virtue and process, universalism and particularism—are reshaped by attention to events and persons. Of course, in this turn to experience, I carry out the pragmatist's program: to address, as John Dewey put it, the "problems of men" and not the "problems of philosophers." In other words, I understand my own prejudice or hope that I do. But perhaps it is a useful prejudice.

In developing this book, I have tried to minimize reliance on specialized language. I'm sure I did not succeed, in part because the subject matter itself has its necessary technicalities, in part because I have grown used to the vocabularies of clinic and classroom. I have also tried to keep the structure of the argument, if not the details, direct and simple. Summing it up, "thinking with cases" can be analyzed into the following elements: the happening, the story, the case, the practice community, and the relationships among these. "Thinking with cases" can also be understood by looking at the players in the clinical and the classroom situations, the teller and the told-to, and how each of these is pluralized as new voices are invited and old voices reconstructed. Indeed, the word "players" is deliberate, because theater turns out to be a useful metaphor for what goes on. Finally, "thinking with cases" can be understood as criticism of ethical approaches that evade moral realities in the name of abstractions like duty, principle, and rule. The outcome is a connection between ethics and aesthetics, between judgment and art. Of course, I could not resist exploring a byway or two that interested me.

Many people and many places have guided my thinking. My onetime colleagues in the Ethical Culture Fieldston School, and particularly in its Ethics Department, surely reminded me over and over again that ethics without attention to actual persons living through actual events is pointless. Students in the various grades from kindergarten through high school kept verifying this insistence on particularity. My colleagues in The Humanist Institute, many of them engaged in community building and community leadership, reinforced the message and corroborated my worries about a moral atomism run wild as in the notion of autonomy. They were also a critical audience for the ideas I was trying out in preparation for this book, as were members of the South Carolina Philosophical Association and of the Association for Moral Education. Students at the University of South Carolina-Beaufort instructed me as well. Many of them struggle to work out decent and productive lives while earning a living, raising a family, and studying for degrees. To talk with them about the "right and the good" is, for example, an experience in the thickness and complexity of moral discourse.

All of this came to a point of reformulation as I worked with physicians, nurses, counselors, clergy, and administrators in the clinical setting. The messages of students, teachers, and colleagues reinforced each other and finally focused for me in the epistemology of "thinking with cases."

Naturalism and pragmatism are welcoming philosophies. So the themes of this book also owe much to existential and feminist ideas and to a philosophy of caring. Human beings are "situated," shaped by and shaping the actual and finite world around them. Of course, I knew that students, teachers, colleagues, and caregivers had constructed my culture and located my place in it. At the same time, I did not pay sufficient attention to what this meant philosophically, morally, and pedagogically. The clinic was then a form of reminder and connection; the classroom, a scene of potency.

As I look back, I realize how many people have readied my experience, so many that to name them all is simply not possible. My colleague at the University of South Carolina, Gordon Haist, however, needs special mention. He served as a special reminder that there is indeed a necessary place for abstraction and reason in the midst of phenomena. He was a counterweight to a moral tangibility that, in its detail and passion, can overwhelm intelligibility.

Friends and family have given me dimension, too; touched my ideas even if, at times, only indirectly. So for my children, Robert and Nora, Michael and Karen, and grandchildren, Brendan, Emma, Jes, Kara, and Colin an acknowledgment that what and who and where I am, and how I think, is an outcome of their being. Finally, for more than forty-seven years, I have been "situated," as feminists say, by my wife, Rita—friend, critic, supporter, and adviser. Her love, care, and patience have made my work possible. Her appreciation has made it rewarding.

To all of them—teachers, students, leaders, clergy, caregivers, friends, and family—my deepest gratitude.

CHAPTER 1

Doing and Undoing Ethics

THINKING WITH CASES

Most of us, most of the time, try to take ethics seriously and are troubled when we fall short of what we think we ought to do. But, at the same time, our ideas and feelings are unfocused, and that, of course, increases our sense of discomfort. Morality just doesn't seem to do the work it's supposed to do when we need it most. Of course, this doesn't stop us from naming villains and heroes and boasting of our own sense of virtue. In fact, our boasts grow louder just when their dependability becomes more questionable. In this setting, philosophers, preachers, and pundits only add to the moral noise around us. And, to be sure, denial in one form or another is always an available strategy. Dissonance then pervades the ordinary moral situation and not simply moments of crisis.

To be sure, we get by often enough to avoid moral insanity. But our anger at others and our increasing alienation from others betray a certain cynicism and reveal our insecurities. Moral discomfort grows. We are, as John Dewey reminded us some decades ago, still afflicted by a "quest for certainty," and nowhere more than in the moral life. Disappointed in that search, as we must be, we scarcely know how to grasp, let alone decide between, conflicting and conflicted demands like "be successful" and "be cooperative," be "loving" and "be competitive," be "honest" and be popular. In our public lives, too, we reach moral dead ends, and with greater and greater frequency these days. The endless debates about "big" issues like abortion and affirmative action are a metaphor for what is happening.

Consequently, moral silences show up everywhere. The disappearance from the moral agenda of issues of social justice confirms our retreat to moral indifference. The turn inward to self-help strategies and the conversion of intimacy into technique confirm our moral blindness.[1] The relief with which we seize upon this or that moral fad on the one hand and the rapidity with which we surrender to a fundamentalist temptation on the other reveal our moral uncertainties.[2] Civil discourse fails, and communities fragment into separated enclaves. Our institutions are torn between traditionalists and modernists. Thus the interminable arguments in the university about the "canon." We become propagandists more than scholars, choosing up sides in answer to the question: What is the basis of teaching and learning? Is it "Western" or "global," patriarchal or feminist, classic or contemporary, and on and on. Thus, too, the nostalgia for the family of yesterday where every person knew his or her place—if it ever really existed—and for "family values" where the moral rules were clear and dependable. Everywhere we look, there are signs of the failures of moral common sense.

Like so many of us, I, too, am frustrated by our moral inadequacies, whether found in the self, the academy, the church, or the polis. And like so many of us, I continue to live by a commonsense morality for want of something better, and to teach ethics as I have been taught. At the same time, I come to feel more like a museum curator than a moralist. The claim of ethics to be a "practical" discipline takes form, then, as philosophic irony when it is not trapped by cynicism.[3] Of course, the story of our historic search for a usable ethics, like any good story, is still worth telling. In the telling we learn how ought-worlds have responded to events in their day and place. We also learn that, blinded by claims of universality and eternity, this temporality is often left implicit, and even denied. To be sure, today's chapter in that story—is it the final chapter—is still in the making. For some of us it can only be written in the language of the past, as in "virtue" theory,[4] and for others in the language of criticism or of moral law. For still others, it cannot be written at all. If emotivists and postmodernists are to be believed, ethics is as dead as Zarathusthra's god. In this confusion, we make a virtue of necessity by turning the disarray of anarchy into the virtue of diversity, the arbitrariness of moral habit into the virtue of individuality. But that isn't good enough. We realize that what is put before us today, in popular or in scholarly form, does not do the trick. At the same time, we hope that the career of ethics is not ended. Of course, I sometimes wonder if this is only an act of faith or, perhaps, of desperation.

It is in this troubling context that I reflect on my experience as an "ethicist" in a clinical setting. Like Stephen Toulmin in his classic essay, "How Medicine Saved the Life of Ethics,"[5] I've learned that biomedical ethics can take us beyond desperation. For some years now, I have been

working with a group of doctors, nurses, social workers, hospital administrators, clergy, and lawyers to develop a program of medical ethics in
our community and to build ethics committees in our two local hospitals.
In developing this project, I have participated in case and policy reviews.
Along the way, too, I have taught the subject at the university to a mixed
collection of clinicians, and to ordinary students simply interested in exploring the subject. I have come to appreciate the wider import of the
literature of biomedical ethics, a literature that has really emerged only
in the past several decades. From time to time, I have been invited to
speak to general and to professional audiences on the subject, and have
been struck by the interest and the concern that it evokes, no doubt
because none of us is untouched by matters of birth, life, and death,
health and sickness. Most important of all, I have become aware of how
rapidly and dynamically the field is changing. As Edmund Pellegrino
wrote:

When I entered medical school 50 years ago, medical ethics was, as it had been
for centuries, solely the domain of the profession, protected from the mainstream
of cultural change and framed in seemingly immutable moral precepts. This is
the way medical ethics also appeared 30 years ago when I began to study, teach,
and observe the field. If there was anything that seemed impervious to the metamorphosis we felt all of medicine to be undergoing, it was its ancient ethical
framework.
  Today, that framework is under the severest strain in its long history.[6]

At the same time that this rapid change goes on, solutions in practice
have to be found. Patients, their families, and their doctors simply cannot
wait at the bedside or in the examining room for the final resolution of
the moral puzzles we philosophers love to pose. The luxury of postpone-
ment is seldom available. Nor can ambivalence remain unresolved. The
imperative of solution while the "foundations are shaking" seems to me
particularly apt in a world of evolving moral dissonance. So I ask myself
if there might be clues to a more general and usable moral model in the
experience of biomedical ethics.
  Looking back on my work with nurses, doctors, social workers, clergy,
administrators, patients, and their families, I realize that a lifelong interest
in ethics and in moral education is being reshaped. Philosophically and
practically, epistemological and moral commitments are being subverted.
I have had to reexplore moral concepts like dignity and autonomy and
justice. But while that exploration went on, I have also had to participate
in recommendations for action in actual cases where terms like these had
reference and yet their meanings remained unsettled. As this experience
has evolved, my assumptions for teaching ethics and for doing ethics have
changed. Once upon a time, and not so long ago, I believed that medical

ethics was simply an "applied" field. I invoked Plato or Aristotle, Kant or Mill, and ethical theories, principles, and rules drawn from the historic discipline. These, I thought, would be usable in analyzing, judging, and deciding the moral questions raised in clinical practice and in shaping health-care policy. So, for example, in designing a yearlong orientation and training seminar as a preliminary to establishing the hospital ethics committees, I began with a review of alternative ethical theories, and the participants seemed to expect me to. Application of these, after all, while not simply mechanical, was still only problem-solving while the tough conceptual questions were being dealt with elsewhere.

Pretty soon, however, I realized that there was an expectation of concreteness among the participants that did not appear in the same way in my classroom experiences. On the first evening we met, I recall one of them—a clergyman who served as a volunteer hospital chaplain—sharing with us the problem of withdrawing treatment from a patient with a terminal illness. The discussion grew complicated and rich in ways that were not typical of academic dialogue. Of course, just about all students want to know the "cash value" of what they are learning. But what I was hearing was not simply an echo of the cry for "relevance" that we used to hear in the 1960s. Although our seminar would start out with concepts, citations from the literature, analytic exercises, and the inevitable problem-posing examples, one or another participant would, sooner or later, begin a sentence with "I had a case that . . ." Pretty soon, details were being explored, alternative diagnoses and treatments were being offered, questions of ought and ought not were being raised. Inevitably, too, one such recollection would trigger another.

At first, I was politely impatient. After all, the anecdote is an old temptation in ethics as everywhere else, and demonstrates little beyond itself. The wealth of detail seemed to conceal the moral issues. So I would try to bring the group back to the point—to my point—but was only temporarily successful in doing so. Pretty soon, another case would be brought up and another round of remembrances triggered. Often, there was a real-time discussion. A case would be introduced about something happening or going to happen even as we were meeting. The ever present pagers and beepers were reminders that matters medical did not stand still. And, more often than not, the clinical stories referred to choices between life and death, to choices someone, somewhere was actually facing as we talked.

My new colleagues were polite enough, to be sure, and tolerant. But they were telling me of their urgencies and they were asking me to demonstrate how moral principle and moral theory connected realistically to the examining room and the hospital bed. Nor was this mere curiosity or some quirk of style. They really cared about the moral decision, and they were really puzzled. As I learned to listen to what was being said, I realized that to call it anecdotalism was inadequate to the richness of shared detail and shared memory, to the effort at connection between cases, and to the concern for defensible outcomes that would instruct the future and not just serve the present. I was learning that doctor and nurse and social worker perceived through a lens of tangibility and thought with ideas that came to them embedded in specific situations. The ways in which they knew and judged always led back to something that had happened or was happening in the hospital or examining room. An exchange of words for words, as in the typical ethics discussion or an assessment of moral coherence or an assignment of specifics to general categories, did not satisfy. Our seminars, just about always, developed toward the questions, "But what shall I do?" or "But what should I have done?" Subsequent monthly workshops for hospital staff members moved in a similar direction. And informal discussions in the corridors corroborated the existence of a way of thinking and understanding.

At first, I remained skeptical. I put the demand for tangibility down to the natural impatience of very busy and overworked people—understandable to be sure, but not likely to lead to ethical insight. More cynically, I was not unmindful of the fact that neither insurance companies nor Medicare provide payment for time spent in reflection on biomedical ethics. Moreover, the "right" and the "good" could all too easily disappear in the complexity of events. The focus on the case could obscure the need to develop ways of responding to the next one and the next one after that, could obscure the need for some kind of moral structure and moral methodology. On reflection, however, I realized that much more was going on than mere opportunism or than a disharmony of professional styles. There was a gulf between my impatience with this urgency to get to the "bottom line" in the way of practical guidelines, and the clinicians' impatience with a philosopher's habit of always finding another question to be explored. In that gulf, however, was the latent possibility of an amended or reconstructed moral epistemology and moral pedagogy. I came to realize its presence when I caught on that, as David Rothman put it:

Perhaps the most remarkable feature of clinical decision making is the extraordinary reliance on a case-by-case approach. No two patients, after all, are exactly alike; symptoms do not appear in the same pattern in the course of disease, and the results of tests do not always fall unambiguously into one category or another. Thus, medicine is as much art as science, and the clinical anecdote becomes highly relevant to treatment decisions.[7]

At the same time I was learning this lesson, I began to suspect that the possibility of other ways of doing ethics was implicit in the biomedical approach and that new perspectives on problems of moral judgment,

objectivity, and knowledge were opening up. It seemed possible, at least
intuitively, to avoid being trapped in the case without deserting it. That,
after all, was what biomedical ethics was all about. The pragmatist's
phrase the "lived experience" came to mind more than once as I listened
to and reflected on what was being reported around the table. Motivating
the question "What shall I do?" was a passion for the reality of the particular event and a respect for the unique features of person and situation.
At the same time, uniqueness was embedded in comparability. The next
event always lurked in the background. To be sure, this passion for the
event was hidden by the cloak of professionalism, the language of medicine, which served as much to conceal as to reveal, but the passion was
there! As a nurse expressed it in a recent collection of poems and stories:

> I like talking about patients
> as if they aren't real, calling them
> "the fracture" or "the hysterectomy."
>
> It makes illness seem trivial . . . [8]

The institutional and practical status of doing ethics and being an
"ethics consultant" in the clinical situation was a puzzle, too. So, just like
those who began developing biomedical ethics two decades ago, I stum-
bled upon a difference of understanding that initially stood in the way
of effectiveness. I had assumed, without thinking too much about it, a
distinction between moral theory and clinical practice that invited the
notion, as I have said, that medical ethics was only another applied field
of study. The "ethicist" would bring theory to the table, where the clinician would use and apply it. But that turned out to be untruthful to the
experience. Forced by attention to the "case," practice and idea interacted
with consequent changes in both and, more significantly, the people and
the institutional structures involved interacted with consequent changes
in them as well. As James F. Childress, who, along with Tom Beauchamp,
worked out the original "principled" approach to medical ethics some
years ago, writes:

Many principlists have used the metaphor of *application*, as in *applied ethics*,
but most would concede that this metaphor is misleading if taken too literally.
Few principlists take a mechanical or deductive view of application as critics sometimes suggest . . . but, as the discussion of lying and deception suggested, . . . [we]
incorporate exceptional cases through deepening the meaning of the principles
or rules by a process that is very close to specification. . . . And many principlists
recognize that particular case judgments may modify our interpretation of principles and rules.[9]

A separation between theory and practice has too often been taken for granted. Ironically, I was encouraged in that assumption by my clinical colleagues and by much of the literature that addresses biomedical ethics. Most of it reads as if theory and application were normative categories.[10] That, of course, is not surprising, given the intellectualist bias we have all inherited from the Greeks, the isolation of *techne* from *theoria*, of artisan from philosopher, and the class and status implications of these distinctions. At the same time, these cultural and conceptual assumptions not only are problematic but in fact make doing ethics all the more difficult.[11]

While my academically driven perspective looked to the distinction between "pure" and "applied" knowledge, my medical colleagues perceived a different distinction, the distinction between "professional" and "layman." I identified expertise with theoretical knowledge. They identified it with the arts and specialties of medicine. It was to take me some time to untangle the two, not quite successfully, in my own mind and also, not quite successfully, in the minds of my clinical colleagues. The traditions of medical consultation, after all, were deeply rooted in practice. The idea of an ethics *specialist*, then, did not come as a surprise, although what such a specialist was supposed to do was something of a mystery. So, without being entirely aware of its implications, I found myself the ethics specialist. I was expected to bring ethical "expertise" to bear on the medical situation just as other specialists were invited in when the case was complicated or difficult or unusual. But, unlike the clinical specialist, a different sociology was at work in the background, and it was not a medical sociology. So while the medical consultant is typically an authoritative adviser on diagnosis and treatment to the attending physician, I took my task to be philosophic dialogue. My intervention was tentative and participatory. I was asking questions and making suggestions rather than offering authoritative recommendations. My presence stirred frustration and even, at times, polite but genuine anger. I did not meet expectations.

To this problem of different professional sociologies and different professional histories was added the clinical habit of calling in specialists only in difficult circumstances. This was further complicated by the fact that we presume anyone and everyone can do ethics. So ethical judgments in medicine, as elsewhere, rely on an intuitive morality, rely on time-honored maxims. The medical norm is a phrase taken out of context from the Hippocratic Oath, "First, do no harm." More recently, "autonomy" has become a term of art. But most of the time, these norms are invoked not to make the moral decision but to explain and justify it when challenged. It is not surprising, then, that the ethics "consult" is delayed until the moment of crisis. More often than not, it is invited when it is too late to make moral sense. For example, we would be called in when a conflict between family members deciding about withdrawing treatment had already reached a point where antagonism had replaced conversation. By then little could be done to resolve a situation that had had plenty of time to evolve toward moral impasse. Given the in extremis nature of the moral setting, let alone the sense of urgency that was always present, the clinical situation is frustrating for everyone. So what to do, how to do it, and who is to do it are caught in ambiguity. The ethics "specialist" is, finally, invited and resented, consulted and ignored.

I could not help but compare my clinical experience with my teaching experience. For example, in a university class on medical ethics—as is true in the business ethics and legal ethics that I also teach—I would begin with a "quick and dirty" review of ethical inquiry. Of course, these days I would incorporate feminist ethicists like Carol Gilligan and Nel Nodding. And in a global and multicultural setting, Eastern traditions like Buddhism and Native American traditions like the legal code of the Iroquois would be included, too. Then, like my colleagues elsewhere, I would work with students to apply alternative ethical theories like deontology, utilitarianism, and intuitionism to examples in order to see how things came out. My interest was in refining theory rather than in developing insight into issues posed by actual cases. My classroom examples were designed to be instrumental to the understanding of theory. Similarly, I would try to encourage students to identify the principles at work—that is, in medical ethics to look for "nonmaleficence" or "beneficence" or "utility" or "justice," to cite the four principles that have become standard in "principlist" approaches to the field.[12] The cases we chose were edited, as it were, in order clearly to present instances where principles were at work. Bringing these to the surface surely had its usefulness, permitting critical analysis and exposing actual and pseudomoral conflicts. At the same time, it became evident that, like the maxims of commonsense morality, theories were not used in advance of the event in the making of moral decisions.

As I compared these different experiences, I found myself asking whether there was in the clinical experience a model for the ethics classroom: the tangibility of the case, the attention to detail, the urgency of decision, the responsibility for consequences, the demand for assessment, the ability to connect across the details. The clinical situation also suggested a critical apparatus and a concern for outcomes. Thus, it revealed the inadequacies of the classroom ethical situation. Whatever its other problems, the clinical situation clearly connected thought and act, unavoidably connected thought and act.

At the same time, I asked myself how the classroom could serve the needs of clinical ethics. There are cognitive sensitivities and resources in ethical theory that thinking with cases can all too easily ignore. The press of time and decision can be an excuse and not just a motive. Indeed, it is possible to deny that a given case even has a moral dimension. I have heard it said more than once that this case presents only medical or technical issues and not moral ones. Of course, implicit moral judgments were being made all the time, but they were hidden, even suppressed. And, particularly, as newer clinical issues are posed—around death and dying, the uses of technology, the question of access to treatment, the availability of organ transplants—the embeddedness of medicine in the detail of the case can all too easily lead to an uncritical moral conservatism.

In short, the clinic cannot replace the classroom—medicalizing ethics, as it were. But, as a physician-educator wrote:

The larger question, however, remains problematic. *Do we know how to educate physicians (or anyone else) so that they will act ethically.* . . . There are many suggestions on how to "make" physicians ethical. Emphasizing good role models is one. Selecting students who demonstrate sensitivity to human needs is another. Providing experiences in classroom and on the wards in which careful moral reasoning is emphasized has also been recommended. Simply telling medical students and residents a fundamental truth, that central events in the life cycle such as pregnancy, birth, and death are not only medical moments, is a start.[13]

The academicism of the classroom and the insularity of the clinic are barriers. But the foundations are shaking, and this is opportunity as well as anxiety. So the question: How, then, might medical ethics serve as a model for moral education, and why is it worth exploring?

DISSONANCE

But first a look back. It would be a comfort if moral dissonance were only a teacher's puzzle, only an academic puzzle.[14] Then we could blame the spaces between moral idea and moral action on a failed pedagogy or on a student's immaturity. If only we could learn how to be better teachers or to wait patiently until our students finally grew up, the puzzle would resolve itself. But that just isn't the case. There seem to be unavoidable spaces in human experience between what we "know" is morally right or morally good and what we "do" about it. These persist whether we are young or old, naive or sophisticated. Indeed, as life grows more and more complicated—as we marry and raise children, become citizens and go to work, and even as we learn more and more—the spaces increase in number and grow in size.

This is not the place for a personal confession, and in any event, the details wouldn't be all that interesting. But I can surely recall moments when my acts denied my moral values and I knew it even as it was happening. To be sure, when challenged by a troubled conscience, I would find excuses, alibis, justifications, and explanations. But these, more often than not, only confirmed my skill at invention and my ability to hide from myself. If this experience is at all typical, then I am not alone. For example, like every teacher, I have known students who did brilliantly in ethics talk or who scored high on assessments like he or she "works and plays well with others." But many of these "good students" cheated or lied or played the truant. A connection between thought and act just wasn't being made. And I have known colleagues with a superb grasp of moral theory who in their conduct forgot that ethics is as ethics does.

In reply, the argument is often made that ethics is not a cookbook discipline. At its best, it offers possibilities for naming the good and guidelines for their application, or else, after the fact, it serves as an evaluative instrument. Ethics is not, nor is it intended to be, constructive or predictive. But it strikes me that this austere and purist view of ethics is just a little bit like isolating scientific ideas from the laboratory and artistic creativity from canvas and stone. In other words, what song can the tone-deaf really sing? Once again, a culture that isolates *theoria* and *techne* is at work. To be sure, in matters of public policy, a utilitarian calculus is used. Assessing costs and benefits is the way we put it these days. But all too often decisions are made on other grounds—economic, political, technical—while the moral cost and benefit seem only an afterthought, often only a bit of window dressing. So if knowing the good is only retrospective and tells us little or nothing about doing the good in the actual event, then what is knowing the good really good for?

There are so many other moral spaces. It is not unusual to find one kind of moral practice among friends and another among strangers, one kind of moral practice when being observed and another when hidden. At the same time, the ethicist claims to transcend location, self-interest, and bias. Ethical values are supposed to hold whether anyone is watching or not. Moral spaces also appear in moral consciousness, in the dissonance between will and feeling, between intention and motive. So it is that I may think the right thing and even do the right thing, and yet not really be present to either. I can, as it were, go through the moral motions, intellectually and practically. I lack moral authenticity, lack integrity in the sense of wholeness. I lack moral passion.

I have little doubt that what is true of me is true of most of the rest of us, except perhaps for that rare and saintly breed which reminds us of moral possibility and which reminds us, too, by its rarity, of what is not likely to happen. This does not mean that we need resign ourselves to being the wicked and sinful creatures of some religious moralities. In fact, that inevitability of sin would really solve the ethical problem, explain why we are moral failures. Little moral thought would need to be done because it had already been done. The moral task becomes descriptive, legislative, or psychological. We would have to learn how to overcome our stubbornness, our resistance to what is good and good for us. Failing in that task, we would be judged and punished, whether in this life or in some putative next one. But the more likely fact is that we are well-intentioned but conflicted creatures. Our moral knowledge is imperfect at best. Our actions simply don't fit with what we know or think we know.

Unlike ants and bees, we are able to choose and to change, "condemned to be free," as Jean Paul Sartre put it. Never has this been more so than in our own age, when ways of doing have become globalized. At times, then, the moral situation seems like moral anarchy. The sheer diversity of our moral universe invites a certain moral numbness. Plenty is sooner or later an opiate. Once, perhaps, in a smaller and more intimate world, the moral spaces could be bridged by more or less reliable and believable codes and practices, and so by effective moral habits. But that is less and less likely for us. At the same time, nostalgia should not blind us to the facts of yesterday, to slavery and exploitation and Caesarism. Moral dissonance, for all its dramatic evidence today, is not a modern invention. After all, one of the first recorded murder stories is to be found in the Hebrew Scripture. And it was Thomas Hobbes in the seventeenth century who described our lot as "nasty, brutish, and short." Even in an allegedly simpler era, moral spaces appeared and saintliness was a rarity. Else, how account for Socrates' still unanswered question, "Can ethics be taught?"[15] Or for Augustine's sense of sin? Regret, confession, and atonement are perennial in our moral vocabulary.

And yet, choosing is unavoidable and change needs to be possible. So unless the moral life be only a seeming, a pointless moral game, we must find out how better to choose—how, in other words, really to do moral education without expectations of perfection. That has been the human assignment in every culture, in every society. Thus, the myth of Eden and the forbidden fruit of the knowledge of good and evil, the princely Siddhartha and the suffering world. Moral spaces, however, are perennial, too. Their existence tells us that we never will finally learn how to do ethics well. Perfection remains elusive, and yet the moral judgment must be made and the moral decision taken. And, in the modern condition, the multiplying spaces between thought and act tell us of a special urgency when the ability to destroy is so magnified and its likely victims so numerous. Holocaust and Hiroshima are, after all, the modern metaphor. At the same time, the human story tells us not to expect too much. Keeping arrogance at bay, moral spaces close and open but do not vanish.

Moral experience is a puzzle and moral education is its stumbling interpreter. We know that it is easy to learn a moral language. The child learning to speak can echo the moral rules and prohibitions of his or her place and time, can be successfully catechized. But it's not as easy for child or for adult to figure out what that moral language means, although, again, we early on grow facile in putting new words in place of old, in playing the moral dictionary. It's even tougher to learn how to make moral judgments and decisions. And it's hardest of all to learn how to do things morally, to put our judgments and decisions to work, and to care about doing so.

The spaces between confound us, frustrate us. In response, we retreat to a rough-and-ready folk wisdom. Everyone is supposed to be morally expert, to know right from wrong, or at least to know which moral authority to obey and which to disobey. We are, after all, creatures with a conscience. But moral common sense, useful enough in the ordinary course of living, fails us just when we need it most. There are so many goods to choose from and they run into each other, so many evils to reject, and yet the lesser evil is always a moral possibility. So, making a virtue out of authority, we turn to priests and wise men or, in democratic enthusiasm, to an egalitarian ethicality. Every person, after all, is an authority, is entitled to an opinion, and all opinions are equal. Alternatively, we may claim that knowing is not knowing at all unless it includes doing, acting in the double sense of acting within one's knowledge and acting upon the world. So it is that genuinely to know is not simply to know about but to know how and why, to be engaged in a practice. Helpful as it is to redefine knowing as doing, it still leaves us with the problem of moral spaces. The spaces between moral thought and moral action are, as it were, relocated but not eliminated. Doing takes the moral idea into the world but then, like a stone thrown into a pool of water, doing's boundaries are inevitably blurred. What, then, does doing mean, and where is moral doing to be done? In positivist despair, we deny that morality is any kind of knowledge at all, but only an emotive or linguistic activity, a matter of expressiveness, of feeling, of power, or of custom.[16]

To be sure, for some of us much of the time and for all of us some of the time, the spaces between language, meaning, judgment, and action can be an alibi and even, following Machiavelli's advice to the prince, a strategy for success. The spaces vindicate our helplessness before the immoral. We are enabled to enjoy the appearance of virtue without bothering with its reality. Immorality, we tell ourselves, is only another instance of failed knowledge. And moral ignorance, while regrettable, is not blameworthy. The idea of a moral idea itself becomes a puzzle. In extremis, we play out the drama of guilt and shame, but these, all too often, only fill the moral spaces with sentimentality, often a self-serving sentimentality.

Most of us, most of the time, are not hypocrites. We want to do what we ought to do. But we also want to do other things and cannot do them all. The situation is seldom coherent. We reach the dead end of the moral dilemma where good confronts good, evil confronts evil. Of course we face choices, but rarely between good and evil. Troubled by that fact, we are impelled toward the clear choice between good and evil. There, as is most often the case, that choice is not really available. We invent it. It is not surprising, then, that we use every energy to reduce the moral situation to the either/or of saint and sinner. But the fact is that we are hard pressed to work with this moral habit in the hurly-burly of actual events. Often, too, we face the conflict within, caught by choices between moral values and other values, by loyalties that force us to choose sides where we cannot validate one over another. Moral intuition may take us one way; moral reasoning, another. One authority contradicts another. Little wonder, then, that one outcome is moral blindness, and another, moral numbness. We surrender, and surrendering often enough, we live the double life of moral language and nonmoral conduct.

Hamlet-like, "conscience *does* make cowards of us all." And then, we may add, "Experience makes cowards of us all, too." But neither the likelihood of conflict within nor the temptation to exploit the spaces between names all of the spaces we find between idea and act. There is a sense in which "talk is," in fact, "cheap" and action is costly. Words can be altered without great difficulty; understandings can be interpreted and reinterpreted; judgments can be amended. But commit to the act, and irrevocability is unavoidable. We know that much at least. The moral decision, once enacted, changes the world forever. Neither atonement nor regret can make things other than they have become. The lie once told, the pain once inflicted, the cheating once performed cannot be remade into what they are not. So moral education is not well served by the learning of rules and directives that only help us to parse praise and blame after the fact. Moral reflection, and not just moral habit, is, for all its difficulties, the cue to character. As John Dewey put it:

Deliberation is an experiment in finding out what the various lines of possible action are really like. It is an experiment in making various combinations of selected elements of habits and impulses, to see what our resultant action would be like if it were entered upon. But the trial is in imagination, not in overt fact. The experiment is carried on by tentative rehearsals in thought which do not affect physical facts outside the body. Thought runs ahead and foresees outcomes, and thereby avoids having to wait the instruction of actual failure and disaster. An act overtly tried out is irrevocable, its consequences cannot be blotted out. An act tried out in imagination is not final or fatal. It is retrievable.[17]

Unfortunately, however, this resort to moral imagination both works and does not work. As such, it, too, becomes a moral problem. Unless done in secret—and this defeats the project before it begins—the choice I have made to deliberate on this rather than on that tells me and others what I am contemplating. Deliberation's agenda is already an enactment. The moral reflection is its own problematic. A road misaligned can be realigned, a dollar misspent can be replaced, a law can be repealed. Each of these has its costs, to be sure, but each of these ordinarily permits another go at the world in good faith. However, trust is at stake in the moral situation, and trust is at risk in reflection as in other moral performance.

For example, I reflect on lying. At that moment, I have already put you on notice. So the moral educator is trapped in paradox. Little wonder, then, that the classroom exercise is so often flat, impersonal, and unconvincing. Once I have been lied to by another, he or she continues the liar in the mind's eye, no matter the apology. If I have been lied to often enough, harmed often enough, then lying and hurting become my possession, too; my character, too. The lie remains within me, the suspicion remains within me. Although charity demands forgiveness, it cannot produce forgetfulness. Nor is the liar or the cheat immune to memory. Not for nothing do we call excuse-giving "rationalization"; not for nothing do we imagine the eternities of hell and heaven. These point to the irrecoverable costs of reflection's betrayal and not just to the act's wickedness.

Moral costs, unlike so many other human costs, carry this pain of not forgetting. Of course, the moral situation is not all darkness. The good deed also remains with us, although it is the regret that is more likely to linger. So it is little wonder that we struggle to bridge the spaces and at the same time that we are not sure we can or even want to succeed. It is revealing in this context that so much of our religious life is constructed to judge moral failure and to sustain us in the experience of it. Thus, the rites of Catholicism, the eightfold path of Buddha, the rules of Confucius, the law of the Jews. It is overly simple to interpret these merely as moral directives. They are really ways of making the pain of immorality intelligible and tolerable. Nor is secular ethics immune to this project, although its practitioners often fail to reflect on the reasons and passions that drive our search for an Archimedean point or our denial of its possibility. In a self-revealing moment, we continue to explain and explain and explain why that denial is the only thing that makes moral sense.

Religious or secular, we thus verify, even when we seem most abstract, Nietzsche's comment, "Gradually, it has become clear to me what every great philosophy so far has been: namely the personal confession of its author and a kind of involuntary and unconscious memoir."[18] And, as William James observed on more than one occasion, we exhibit our temperament as much as our character in our philosophies, particularly in our religious and moral philosophies.

Given the situation of spaces and conflicts, of rememberings and forgettings, it is not surprising that we try to reduce moral ideas to principles, moral judgments to rules, and moral decisions to commandments. In that way we think to substitute a moral mechanics or a moral geometry for our failed abilities. This effort, like its mathematical relative, is logical, even beautiful. Sometimes it is useful and comforting. But ultimately, it is empty as Immanuel Kant's "categorical imperative" is empty or as the "golden rule" is empty. For example, unless I know the actual other in his or her place and time, I cannot really determine what I ought to do in response to his or her need. Or, surely, if my soul is at risk, I would want to be burned at the stake in order to be saved from Satan; and if pain is my pleasure, I would want to be hurt in order to enjoy. As Bernard Shaw once quipped, "Do unto others what we would have them do unto us . . . but our tastes may be different."

Moral principles serve, to be sure, as mnemonic devices and as analytic tools, as ways of recalling what was and as ways of taking apart the moral situation after it happens. But the ability of rules and principles to aid in the midst of the moral situation is minimal. We act and then we reflect. Unhappy, we attempt a moral engineering, a derivation of rules from principles or acts from ideas, but this, too, falters in the event. Principles, we learn painfully, are not self-enacting. In desperation, the "realist" in us, that in us which knows that the spaces are tempting, deadly, and unavoidable, dismisses theory and principle and moral rules for a primitive practicalism. Rules of prudence like "Honesty is the best policy" come to dominate our moral common sense. Yet these kinds of rules fail us, too, just when bridging the spaces becomes urgent, just when the gap is widened by conflict, by contradiction, and above all by ambiguity.

This commonsense practicalism works only as long as the moral situation is stable and recognizable. It is internalized as habit, and thus we can act on it when facing standard moral difficulties. Luckily, then, we are often better than our talk. Most of us do not reflect, but we do tell the truth and keep our promises. We are helpful and not hurtful. But there are horror stories, too, not least of all when practicalism leads us into mistaken simplification or just plain moral blindness. The moral certainty of common sense expects us to condemn the unexpected other, the alien other. Yet another moral space appears, the space between the righteous and the damned. Moral fanaticism is thus latent in each of us, fed by moral habit and the desperate wish to reduce complexity to simplicity and ambiguity to clarity. Moral education stumbles again as it confirms the righteous in their righteousness.

There are times, too, when being moral is just too costly. The things we value morally compete with the things we value socially or politically or economically or aesthetically. We want to be moral, but we also want to be wealthy, successful, popular. A little reflection shows, however, that yet another moral space overtakes us. Our moral location is revealed in the ways we order our choices. Yet these preferences are even more deeply embedded than common sense, even more deeply hidden from us. A moralistic moral education misses this broader reach. So it is not surprising that we divide our moralities along the lines of privacy and

publicity, behaving one way with family and friends, another way in business or work, and yet another as citizen. We build up moral walls. At the
same time, breaching the walls is unavoidable. That is why we work so
hard to find excuses for ourselves and why we feel shame at our moral
failures, whether public or private.

It seems easier to be the amoral political animal, the efficient, merely
efficient, competitor, the aesthete, the social success, the lover. But the
walls do not really shut these things away from each other. The divided
conscience is its symptom. Pacifying it, even with illusion, is its cure—at
least as long as the illusion persists. Ironically, the moral spaces owe their
existence to the nonspatial character of experience, and so to the fearful
and threatening qualities of experience that has no walls, only unreal and
finally unbelievable boundaries. I suppose it is because we cannot finally
turn memory off, turn connections off. Maybe, as some of the newer
biologists claim, we are, as it were, "hardwired" to be "moral animals."[19]
Or maybe, in a way, the Scottish moralists of the eighteenth century were
right when they spoke of a "moral sense."[20]

But depending on intuitions can often be disastrous. Common sense
is trapped by nuance. We cannot be sure that what looks like, feels like,
common sense does in fact represent a *moral* intuition. Not so long ago,
for example, the common sense of the matter held that blacks or women
were somehow less than human, and so less entitled to be treated as
human beings than whites or men. Moral intuition can be a name for our
biases. We may be born with a moral sense as we are born with lungs
and heart. In fact, we probably are born with a capacity for morality, but
we are not equipped with its content, or else how account for the moral
variety the species exhibits. Just as taste can lead to McDonald's ham-
burger or to haute cuisine, so moral capacity can lead to fanaticism or
indifferentism and everything in between.

As John Dewey put it in struggling to describe the connections among
science, art, and ethics:

Shelley said, "The great secret of morals is love, or a *going out of our nature* and
the identification of ourselves with the beautiful which exists in thought, action,
or person not our own. A man to be truly good must imagine intensely and
comprehensively." What is true of the individual is true of the whole system of
thought and morals in thought and action. While perception of the union of the
possible with the actual in a work of art is itself a great good, the good does not
terminate with the immediate and particular occasion in which it is had. The
union that is presented in perception persists in the remaking of impulse and
thought. The first intimations of wide and large redirection of desire and purpose
are of necessity imaginative. Art is a mode of prediction not found in charts and
statistics, and it insinuates possibilities of human relations not to be found in rule
and precept, admonition and administration.[21]

Add to all of this the fact that the moral imagination has its spaces, too—now social spaces, for we must be able to find out whose imagination it is. We cannot act as if position—family, gender, time, place, culture, society—made no difference. We cannot escape the fact of ego in community. So we cannot be sure that even the cultivated moral intuition is genuinely our own or genuinely moral. Wherever we look, then, the moral situation is clouded by doubt. But since moral doubt is most threatening of all—we grow accustomed to probabilities and uncertainties just about everywhere else—we often suppress it by denying that the situation presents a moral question at all. We transform the situation, reducing its problems to technique or economics or psychology. These days, in a typically American move, we sublimate our discomfort by reducing the moral to the legal. Finally, the spaces that appear in all these varied guises turn the moral situation into frustrating experience.

INSTABILITY

In the presence of dissonance, the moralist works out variations on the theme of is and ought. Hopefully—at least that is the intention— strategies of order and intelligibility can be discovered in the distinction. To begin with, there would seem to be, after all, only a finite number of moral ideas around.[22] As Alfred North Whitehead once remarked with only minor exaggeration, "All philosophy is only a footnote to Plato and Aristotle." Moreover, ought-worlds are simpler and more manageable than the confusing unpredictability of events and persons living in time and space and culture. Of course, there are many different ways of doing ethics: idealism, deontology, casuistry, teleology, emotivism, pragmatism, existentialism, natural law, virtue theory, and so on. Moral ideas are developed and amended, and new insights appear. But the family resemblance between one idealism and another, one deontology and another, one teleology and another, one virtue ethics and another is clear enough. Thus, ought-worlds and their history invite us into a familiar moral neighborhood. They have their well-known inhabitants—like Plato and Aristotle, St. Thomas and Kant and Mill, and their contemporary descendants—and their well-known arguments. Even the ought-worlds of Laotzu, of Confucius, of Buddha—the West's discovery of the rest of the moral world—do not force us onto alien ground. Ought-worlds invite coherent moral discourse. All that is lost is detail!

Strangely, for many ought-worlds, I do not exist and events do not exist. Terms like "person" and "event" are to be found in their languages, of course. But these are abstract persons without blood or sinew or biography, and these are abstract events without time, location, or history. Intention and choice have their place, too, but a moral psychology is not the same as an empirical psychology. For ought-worlds, moral ideas may be derived by reason alone or received from community or from God.[23] Alternatively, they may arise, as the naturalist and pragmatist would have it, from experience. But all too soon, even for the naturalist, experiences are left behind in favor of *experience*, in favor of yet another move into ought-world. Like "history" or "reason," "experience" comes to lack the tangibility of the event, becomes an ontological or procedural category.

To be sure, ought-worlds are not only moral science fiction, although they are at least that. Ethics is supposed to be "practical" in a way that physics or astronomy or mathematics does not have to be. But moral practicality, too, has its actual and its abstract meaning. So, in their own special way, ought-worlds are intended for use in assessment of what "is." They appear in judgments on the acts we perform and on their consequences, and more generally in evaluations of what we are and do. The way that religions tell the moral story is revealing. Thus, for Christian ethics, the world is inherently immoral, or society is inevitably immoral, or man is by nature immoral. "In Adam's fall we sinned all," as the old church hymn goes. For Jews, the eternal statute rules. Others—for example, Platonists in the West, Hindus in the East—embed ought-worlds in ontology and devalue the world that is, on epistemological and not just on moral grounds, as appearance or illusion. Morals become forms of ultimate realization, pathways away from the actual and toward what really is and not simply what appears to be.

In a more secular mood, alternatively and less ambitiously, ethics is a critical discipline. "Ought" and "is" announce a division of labor. The world is to be evaluated, enhanced, or completed by the attachment of moral idea, intention, and judgment to event. An action is thus morally qualified. It no longer simply is; it means. The situation as lived through does have its moral work to do. It may stimulate our attention to a moral puzzle, a moral discomfort, but the moral idea is, as it were, never determined by it. In fact, we are told, it is a dangerous error to try to bridge the space between "ought" and "is." To do so is to commit the "naturalistic fallacy," to reduce "ought" to "is," thus hiding our moral biases behind transcendental reasons and prevented from locating and assessing our actual motives. Of course, an idealist goes the other way and reduces "is" to "ought"—commits, if you will, the idealist fallacy. In fact, it should be possible to arrive at moral ideas without any direct reference to actual events at all,[24] much as a theoretical physicist may speculate mathematically about possible worlds without reference to experimental data and certainly without reference to biography and history. In a sense, an ought-world is the creature of a Kantian strategy. It responds to the question "What must the world be like for moral judgment to be possible?"

From this point of view, it is simply an unfortunate complication—an ontological accident—that the human beings who do morals are biological, psychological, and social animals. It would be morally convenient if they were only rational beings but, sadly, they aren't. If it were so, the confusions of taste and interest and bias would not befog the situation. So, for want of anything better, we essay a moral world where we can think as if rationality were all. Thus the story from Platonism to Kantianism and, in its own contrary way, modern positivism. The validity of the moral idea arises, then, simply from its coherence with other moral ideas. For those more empirically minded, it emerges from a thought experiment stimulated by an experienced discomfort. And, for those with a historical temperament, moral ideas are authoritative because of their location and use in a particular cultural or religious narrative. Often, however, this particularity is denied in favor of a claimed universality, a kind of moral imperialism. There were, after all, "Greeks and barbarians." Typically, then, moral authority is accompanied by some kind of hidden ethnocentrism or ideocentrism. Even the moral liberal, playing the game of toleration, assumes an implicit authority by granting permission to differ to lesser breeds. More recently, as in postmodernism and multiculturalism, indifference proclaims the equivalence of all moral ideas, which is the same as saying there are no moral ideas at all.

Moral ideas are typically separated from their roots and taken seriously because of some claimed transcultural validity or transnatural revelation or transempirical justification. Failing that, we are left with descriptions but without norms. For ought-worlds, then, the moralized situation is only another instance of the application of theory to practice. Even the consequentialist, despite an attention to outcomes, imports an implicit moral dualism, converting theory to instrument, perhaps, but not threatening its status as theory. Or else, in a burst of nominalist enthusiasm, moral ideas are merely linguistic conveniences. Ethics becomes the study of yet another language. If, in fact, some moral ideas come into being and others pass away, it is because they are more or less attractive, just as some arts come into being and others pass away because they are more or less attractive. To be sure, moral attractiveness is not only an intellectual or aesthetic exercise. It derives its legitimacy but not its validity from the relevance—real or only claimed—of an ought-world picture to some is-world experience or other. Taste and fittingness become implicit categories of moral selection.

Tutored by an idealist tradition, a moral idea that doesn't work out is a surprise in the same way that a Euclidean theorem that doesn't work out is a surprise. Typically, then, we look for *our* mistakes; in ethics, at greater cost, we look for *our* moral failures. Seen from the ought-world, the immoral act leads us to the failings of the agent and not to the inadequacies of the idea. Even a naturalistic ethic rooted in John Dewey's "funded experience," for example, is conveyed by theories, principles, and rules, although with a tentativeness not found among rationalists and

idealists. Embedded in our habits, these take on a certain permanence
even for the skeptic and the radical. That means uprooting them is difficult and rare.[25] Thus, the typical classroom ethics discussion begins and
ends in the same place, and only rarely does anything like conceptual
change take place, let alone change in feeling or behavior. The naturalist
does expect principles and rules to evolve and change; they are always
on trial as much as we are. But, when it is encrusted by authority and
time, even the naturalist is tempted to lose sight of the mundane roots
of principle. So it is not surprising that the moral common sense of idealist and naturalist, of conservative and liberal, more often than not con-
verges around a common set of moral directives and moral virtues. Hence
the "surprising" fact that atheist and theist, radical and conservative, tend
to agree about things like the virtue of truth-telling and the vice of lying
and, in a democratic society, the dignity of persons. In turn, the moral
enterprise becomes anthropological, sociological, or psychological without admitting it. The convergence itself becomes something to be explained and evaluated.

The philosophic spaces between ought-world and is-world confound
the moral educator. "Can we teach ethics?" becomes a biographical and
not simply a pedagogical question. Of course, it is possible to inculcate
a set of rules, just as we teach someone to walk or speak a language or
use a multiplication table. With an appropriate mix of reward and punishment, we can develop what we come to call moral character in ourselves
and others so that we consistently enact whatever virtues count for us.
In that way, we come to identify people by their reputation as truthful,
as having integrity, as trustworthy, as courageous, and so on. By this we
mean that, by and large, we can expect them to respond to the moral
situation in certain ways and not in others and, most important of all, to
respond as we do. And this conventionality works well under stable conditions where moral situations look enough like each other to allow for
the effective use of moral habits, and where moral habits lead us to behaviors just like those of our communal fellows. In this setting, we do not
look too closely at our virtues and vices. We reinforce them without validation. We transform principles and virtues into commandments. Thus,
we give them a special force by sacralizing them in religious or secular
guise, as "God's will" or as the "democratic way of life" or as the "demands of history." Moral reflection, however, stirs the suspicion that the
cloak of universality or cosmology or ideology hides what is at bottom
only arbitrary.

The moral situation is not stable even in times when change is not as
rapid and as massive as in our own. Communities evolve and authorities
shift. At the same time, explanation and justification come to a halt before
statements like "That's just the way things are" or "That's just the way
we do things" or "You'll know better when you grow up." But we are a

stubborn lot and demand our reasons. When halted by prohibition, the retreat to authority or to absolute, we are resentful and rebellious. The moral story, then, is filled with instances of denial and refusal. And depending on the storyteller, these instances of resistance become in our eyes, but only after the fact, moments of godlike achievement—the surprising arrival of the moral genius—or satanic destruction.

In our experience today, however, instability overcomes conventionality. We meet so many different and contradictory kinds of character in so many different and contradictory kinds of settings. Patriarchal societies face feminist challenge; societies elevate youthfulness or, conversely, old age to ideal; hierarchical societies and pastoral societies are submerged by technologies. Moral habits become less and less effective. In business, we learn that a "bribe" in some places is a "tip" in others, and a legitimate source of "income" in still others. In politics, friend and enemy are quickly interchangeable. In family life, mobility turns intimacy into distance. As we come to live in nonlocal situations, as we come to live in our world, standard judgments decreasingly apply. The moral emperor wears no clothes. Ought-worlds struggle to keep their simplifications and fail. Spaces open up between "is" and "ought" in yet another way.

NOTES

1. For a discussion of this theme, see Howard B. Radest, *Humanism with a Human Face* (Westport, Conn.: Praeger, 1996), chapters 6 and 7.

2. Ibid., chapter 3, I describe this experience with respect to postmodernism, fundamentalism, and the New Age.

3. See Richard Rorty, *Contingency, Irony, and Solidarity* (Cambridge: Cambridge University Press, 1989).

4. For the best and most insightful example of this approach to ethics, see Alisdair MacIntyre, *After Virtue* (Notre Dame, Ind.: University of Notre Dame Press, 1981).

5. The essay (1982) is reprinted in J. R. DeMarco and R. Fox, eds., *New Directions in Ethics* (Boston: Routledge and Kegan Paul, 1986).

6. Edmund D. Pellegrino, "The Metamorphosis of Medical Ethics," *Journal of the American Medical Association*, Vol. 269, No. 9 (March 3, 1993), p. 1158.

7. David J. Rothman, *Strangers at the Bedside* (New York: Basic Books, 1991), p. 7.

8. Courtney Davis, "What Nurse Likes," in Courtney Davis and Judy Schaeffer, eds., *Between the Heartbeats* (Iowa City: University of Iowa Press, 1995), p. 50.

9. James F. Childress, "The Normative Principles of Medical Ethics," in Robert M. Veatch, ed., *Medical Ethics*, and second edition (Boston: Jones and Bartlett, 1997), p. 38. See also note 10.

10. Typically, most textbooks in medical ethics invite the presumption that it is an applied field. For example, as recently as 1994, Tom Beauchamp and James Childress begin their chapters with moral concepts, such as autonomy, and then show how it is used to analyze and judge situations. See Tom L. Beauchamp and

James F. Childress, *Principles of Biomedical Ethics*, fourth edition. New York: Oxford University Press, 1994. The text I use in teaching the subject opens with an extensive chapter titled "Moral Principles, Ethical Theories and Medical Decisions: An Introduction." Students very quickly discover that the situations which pose moral issues overwhelm the abstractness of theory. Ronald Munson, *Intervention and Reflection*, fifth edition (Belmont, Calif.: Wadsworth, 1996).

11. It is interesting to note that my experience (like that of others trained in academic disciplines) almost recapitulates the development of biomedical ethics as a field of study and action. For a discussion of this relevant history, see Albert R. Jonsen, *The Birth of Bioethics* (New York: Oxford University Press, 1998), chapter 10.

12. It was Beauchamp and Childress, in the 1st ed. of *Principles of Biomedical Ethics* (1983), who introduced this way of approaching medical ethics, although now, less than fifteen years later, the idea of "principlism" has been radically criticized as overly theoretical and abstract.

13. Terry M. Perlin, *Clinical Medical Ethics: Cases in Practice* (Boston: Little, Brown, 1992), pp. 58–59.

14. In this essay, I will use "moral" and "ethical" interchangeably to refer to the processes involved in distinguishing between good and evil, right and wrong. I trust that the context in which these terms appear will make clear the different features of moral and ethical activity to which I am referring, for instance, to ethics as a philosophic discipline, to morals as socially sanctioned preferences, to conscience as the attribution of right and wrong in the act or contemplated act, and so on.

15. Like so many others, I have struggled with this question. I published a "progress" report under the title *Can We Teach Ethics* (New York: Praeger, 1989), and this essay is a return to that theme from another—and for me, promising—angle, a consequence of experience with clinical and biomedical ethics.

16. I can still recall, as a student, reading A. J. Ayer's *Language, Truth and Logic* (London: Oxford, 1936) with its positivism and its dismissal of ethics along with metaphysics and aesthetics. In one sense it was a relief, since even then, though only implicitly, the failings of moral knowledge were not merely a subject of argument but a felt betrayal. I don't know whether the anger I recall was at Ayer for his brutality or at his targets for their inadequacy.

17. John Dewey, *Human Nature and Conduct*, in *The Collected Works* (Carbondale: Southern Illinois University Press, 1988), Vol. 14, *Middle Works*, pp. 132–133.

18. Friedrich Nietzsche, *Beyond Good and Evil* (1886), trans. by Walter Kaufmann (New York: Vintage Books, 1966), p. 13.

19. See, for example, Robert Wright, *The Moral Animal* (New York: Pantheon Books, 1994); Edward O. Wilson, "The Biological Basis of Morality," *The Atlantic Monthly*, Vol. 281, No. 4 (April 1998), pp. 53–70.

20. See Adam Smith, *The Theory of Moral Sentiments* (1759) (New York: Hafner, 1948).

21. John Dewey, *Art as Experience, The Collected Works* (Carbondale: Southern Illinois University Press, 1987), Vol. 10, *Later Works*, pp. 351–352.

22. For a description of the moral universe that still serves, see C. D. Broad, *Five Types of Ethical Theory* (New York: Harcourt Brace, 1930).

23. Several moral strategies illustrate this point. Plato, for example, concludes for a "heaven beyond the heavens" in order to locate the ideal—the good, the true, and the beautiful—and interprets the world of experience as a mere reflection of the ideal. Kant divided experience into phenomenal—the world of the natural sciences known through our senses—and the noumenal—the world of values known by reason alone. The Judeo-Christian tradition interprets the moral as an entry by God into the natural world. However, worked out in diverse moral philosophies and theologies, the natural world is in some sense inadequate until connected in some way to the nonnatural or other world of reason or ideal or spirit. Teleological strategies take similar form, but attention is directed to causal structures and to the nature of outcomes that, while variously happiness or pleasure or doing the will of God, also reflect an inattention to the "blooming buzzing confusion" of experience as it is had.

24. Modern social contract theory is characteristically grounded in just such an exercise. The most recent instance is John Rawls's notion of a "veil of ignorance" and an "original position" where all biographical facts are effectively suppressed in order, precisely, to arrive at a morally defensible objective position. To be sure, he provides for some minimal goods that all human beings would acknowledge, but biography and location and interest are explicitly removed. See Rawls's *A Theory of Justice* (Cambridge, Mass.: Belknap Press, 1971).

25. See John Dewey, *Human Nature and Conduct* (New York: Henry Holt, 1922).

CHAPTER 2

Science and Story

INSIGHT AND INQUIRY

Science, law, and psychology are today's "idols of the tribe." But to do ethics, we need a more varied approach to knowledge than we can find in the sciences. Nor can we resign ethics to law or psychology. At the same time, we need all the help we can get. Epistemic pluralism, however, does not call for us to retreat to postmodern anarchy and anti-science, or to reject the proper uses of law and psychology. The sciences tell us a good deal about how and what we can know and, above all, about how we can be assured that our knowledge is dependable. They are both contributory and critical. The law, with its attention to detail and precedent, yields insights that less historical practices fail to achieve. And psychology reminds us of the thickness of motive and feeling that embeds even the most abstract of our activities in our passions.

When we blindly reject the sciences, we are at the mercy of ignorance. When, however, we blindly defer to the sciences—turning science into scientism—we expose our assumptions, even our prejudices. These reflect a hidden curriculum, our traditional, cultural, class, gender, and political values. So we need to distinguish between bias and judgment, particularly because of the modern temptation to reduce truth to opinion and to conclude that all opinions are equally valid. In the so-called hard sciences, the job is done by structured practices in the laboratory and observatory, and by a critical community. The result is a workable notion of what is and what is not so. The distinction between bias and judgment is much more difficult to locate in ethics. But that is not an excuse for surrendering ethics to radical subjectivism. Ethics, after all, is a pervasive project of culture whose presence is variously self-conscious and implicit, individual and communal. And it is a project that is needed and that, in its own way, succeeds. Thus, some kind of moral common sense is at work everywhere, varied as to time and place, to be sure, and yet not anarchic or shapeless. But, as both our successes and our failures tell us, moral common sense is far more mysterious and far less dependable than we think it is. Formal pedagogies and commandments are, finally, only its minor part.[1]

Exposing the assumptions that underlie the sciences is particularly difficult. These assumptions are reinforced by the prestige of the sciences and the success of technology. It is against this background that biomedical ethics can be particularly helpful. The rapidity of its emergence as a new field of inquiry and conduct makes visible what is otherwise hidden. Conflicting lines of development are brought to light. In turn, this provides an index of more general moral phenomena. Like the rest of society, biomedical ethics relies on the sciences and technology, is entangled in law and politics, and at the same time tries to hold on to traditional values. In a voice that sounds very familiar to the rest of us, the clinician complains:

In our pursuit of the scientific aspects of science, the art of medicine has sometimes unwittingly and unjustifiably suffered. . . . The death bed scenes I witness are not particularly dignified. The family is shoved out into the corridor by the physical presence of intravenous stands, suction machines, oxygen tanks and tubes emanating from every natural and several surgically induced orifices. . . . The last words . . . are lost behind an oxygen mask.[2]

Of course, medicine was never a pure art nor an uncluttered relationship between doctor and patient. No matter the romanticism illustrated even in today's "realistic" TV medical dramas, biology, chemistry, and technology have more often than not been its background reality. Religion, status, power, and money have always played a role. However, with today's scientific and technologized medicine and the radical entry of legal, political, and economic considerations into the clinical situation, a novel agenda appears in the examining room. Questions of "access," "equity," and "liability," to take but a few items, shape the language of healing itself and represent in a specific way issues before society and community as well.

But what is revealed is not just a catalog of issues. The sciences are obviously useful for diagnosis and cure. More subtly, they introduce their own structural assumptions into the clinical setting. The disease as problem to be solved replaces the patient as person to be healed. Moral categories like responsibility and guilt continue to signal reference to ethics, politics, or religion. Simultaneously, responsibility and guilt are converted into symptoms. Diagnosis and cure replace atonement and punishment. The sciences also invite cultural and political blindness as their claimed objectivity and universality are inappropriately generalized. To be sure, deliberate blindness—the philosopher may call it usable fiction or heuristic device—makes doing science possible. A hydra-headed image of the sciences as cultural artifacts and as modes of inquiry emerges. The contents, ends, and values of different interests conflict, for example, between knowing and healing. Curiosity—Einstein called it "holy curiosity"—becomes its own reason for being. Lured by it, personal, economic, political, moral, and religious commitments are all too easily masked.

Just when many social institutions like the church and the family surrender their authority, we are becoming ambivalent about the sciences. In recent memory, physics provided the metaphor. Thus, Robert Oppenheimer responded to the successful development of the atomic bomb with Krishna's "I am become death, the shatterer of worlds." Medicine finds its own darkness in the concentration camp experiments of Nazi doctors. And, closer to home, the Tuskegee study of syphilitic African Americans taught us that the search for knowledge can also serve as a cover for racism and the exploitation of the poor and illiterate.[3] Summed up,

In the study, which began in 1932, more than 600 men were recruited by government health workers, who led them to believe they were receiving free medical treatment. Throughout the 40-year study, the men were never told of the experiment and those with syphilis were never told they were infected. They never received any treatment for the disease, even when the use of penicillin became routine in the 1940s. When participants died, researchers offered their families free burials in exchange for the rights to do autopsies so they could gather their final data for the study which [other] researchers say was scientifically flawed from the start.[4]

Despite the Nuremberg Code and the Helsinki Accords, which set ethical standards for human experimentation,[5] moral conflicts continue. For example, in 1997, a study in developing countries on possible interventions in the maternal–infant transmission of HIV (human immunodeficiency virus) was reported. Supported by the NIH (National Institutes of Health) and the CDC (Centers for Disease Control), the study was criticized because existing treatments were not made available to the participants. For proponents, this was simply a fact of life in poor countries as well as a requirement of experimental design. Developing countries could not afford available HIV therapies. Their people were seldom literate enough to grasp, let alone benefit from, access to modern technology.

Indeed, the study was justified because it was searching for treatments that could work under the conditions typical of third-world countries.

But for the critics, the research exposed a "double standard," one for developed countries and another for developing countries. The critics heard echoes of Tuskegee.[6] In defense, the researchers noted that Nuremberg requirements had been satisfied. Participants, after all, were asked for their "informed consent." To the critics, however, this seemed pro forma. Ultimately, the researchers relied on the protocols of scientific inquiry. They wrote, "The most compelling reason to use a placebo-controlled study is that it provides definitive answers to questions about the safety and value of an intervention in the setting in which the study is performed, and these answers are the point of the research,"[7] that is, the needs of actual patients were sacrificed to the needs of potential patients. Reports from more recent efforts in Uganda tell us that the conflict persists. For Ugandan researchers, " 'They [the critics] sometimes talk about this like it's the Tuskegee experiment and we are simple, ignorant dupes,' he [Dr. Peter Mugyeni, the director of Uganda's Joint Clinical Research Center] said . . . 'It's terribly insulting to us and to the Western agencies and individuals who have worked with us.' "[8]

Debates about human experimentation, about informed consent, about conflicts of interest tell us that scientific inquiry cannot be its own moral defense. Further, the compulsion to complete a project without critical reflection on nonclinical as well as clinical consequences can turn science idolatrous. It is noteworthy that the "genome project," the effort to map the human being's genetic structure, includes an allocation—about 5 percent of a multimillion-dollar budget—for the study of its ethical implications. Still, it is just too easy to repress the facts that science is only a collective name for what scientists do and that the ethics of research is filled with ambiguity.

When we turn "science" into a being that "speaks" in an "objective" voice, we ignore the personal, political, institutional, and linguistic frame within which the sciences, like other human activities, take place. Ordinarily, this is not a matter of deliberate dishonesty but of hidden assumptions and attitudes, and even of beneficent motives. For example, we know enough about information-gathering, as in poll-taking, decision-making, and risk-benefit assessment, to realize that the way a question is put shapes the answers we are likely to get. As a description of one research study noted:

[Daniel] Kahneman and [Amos] Tversky's findings emphasize why it is so important to explain genetic information both in terms of gain and loss. Telling clients they have one chance in four of having an affected child conveys one psychological message, saying that they have three chances in four to have a normal baby conveys a different one—even though the statistics are the same. Clients need to be given both constructions of the genetic information.[9]

Encouraged by language and habit, we forget that science is multivalent human activity. In a telling example, Gregory Pence notes the different ways that professional commentators wrote about the case of Elizabeth Bouvia.[10]

These accounts all appeared in scholarly journals which would presumable imply objectivity. However, the two physicians seem to be portraying Elizabeth Bouvia as irresponsible; [George] Annas [a medical ethicist] and Derek Humphrey [the Hemlock Society] seem to portray her as a helpless heroine fighting a cold bureaucracy; and [Paul] Longmore [a disability advocate] apparently sees her as a victim of prejudiced systems and of misguided do-gooder lawyers. Note also that the physicians refer to her as "Bouvia," Humphrey calls her "Elizabeth" and Longmore uses "Elizabeth Bouvia" or "Ms. Bouvia." The physicians say "she got a ride to Riverside [Hospital]," as if she had hitchhiked to some arbitrary location; Humphrey, by contrast, says that her father took her to a place "where she had friends." Longmore emphasizes her desire to be independent; Humphrey emphasizes her physical pain and trauma. Longmore suggests that society is prejudiced against disabled people and thus that Elizabeth Bouvia's disability is not so much her problem as society's problem. Humphrey writes from a point of view "inside" Elizabeth Bouvia; the physicians write from the viewpoint of hospital staff members who must accept patients presenting "management problems."[11]

A pseudo-imperative seizes us: if it can be done, it will be done. Thus, in the debate about cloning, opponents of research prohibition relied on this inevitability and used precisely these words. Moreover, given the whirlwind development of science and technology, keeping up with the event escapes us. As one commentator put it, "The effort to test treatments has never caught up with the large number of procedures, drugs and devices that continue to be created at a fast pace in the health conscious end of the century." And the article adds that it is estimated that "half of all surgical operations and other medical procedures remain without strict scientific evidence of their efficacy and safety."[12] The technological imperative is thus embedded in unavoidable ignorance. New discovery is barely assimilated before the next report appears.

We are increasingly able to reshape the human condition, an invitation to hubris if there ever was one. Death is still our fate, but dying has become a decision and not just an inevitability. At the other end of life, reproduction, too, has become a field for invention. Sperm donation was a center of moral, legal, and religious controversy in the 1950s. By the 1970s, sperm banks had become ordinary. Successful in vitro fertilization—so-called test-tube babies—is less than two decades old. Today, advertisements for fertility clinics compete for attention with those for automobiles and household appliances. The ability to freeze and preserve embryos is even more recent and is as likely to become routine. Genetic research stirs images of immortality and simultaneously of the Franken-

stein monster.[13] Genetic "engineering" promises to eliminate terrifying
diseases but threatens to redesign the species itself. We are caught between the excitement of new solutions to old problems and anxiety at
the emerging legal, social, religious, and moral puzzles that these solutions bring with them.

At the same time, the sciences serve us well. Not least of all, they check
the easy answers of common sense. In a striking example, recent research
on the use of "living wills" and "DNRs" (do not resuscitate orders) illustrates the counterintuitive rewards of inquiry.[14] The SUPPORT study, as
it was called, was a five-year program to improve communication with
terminally ill patients and their families. More than 9,000 patients in five
major hospitals participated. Specially trained nurses served as liaison
between patients, families, and physicians. Contrary to expectation, however, the study revealed that improved communication—which sometimes seems to be everyone's prescription for solving problems—did not
significantly improve the situation: living wills and DNRs were often ignored; "futile" and "heroic" treatments were not minimized; and costs
were not reduced. In short, "We gave people the tools that everyone said
should work, and they didn't."[15]

Scientific procedures are often an uneasy fit with clinical and educational realities. Of course, just about everything we do is caught in life
experiences whose edges are blurred. In clinic and classroom, however,
this messiness is obvious; in the sciences it is suppressed. Moreover,
wherever we look, unspoken values shape the ways fact is identified,
interpreted, and worked with. Accidents of personality and temperament
intrude; realities of geography, time, and resources set arbitrary limits.
Inquiry, however, pauses but does not end. But in clinic and classroom,
the demand for closure introduces urgency to event. For them, the luxury
of Spinoza's sub specie aeternitatis does not exist.

But these, although important, are only surface distinctions. The controlled environments of the sciences trap us in another usable fiction.
We are taught that science is the place where "nonessentials" can be
avoided or, failing that, can be set aside and their effects minimized.
Typically, then, the conclusion of an inquiry begins with the phrase "all
other things being equal. . . ." Of course, things never are equal. Empirical conclusions are only approximations, often very good approximations, to some idealized limit or model. Of course, the design of such
models reflects reality—models are not arbitrary creations—but religious
and secular beliefs, moral and other values, temperament and political
skill play a role in that design which is often and systematically unrecognized. It is revealing, for example, that a military metaphor, as in a "war"
on this or that disease, shapes the way scientific medicine is done and
even the consciousness of its practitioners. Or, as we say, we "mobilize"
the resources of "big" science. Judgments about what is and is not

essential also reflect our interests, our subjectivity. But subjectivity is ruled out by the assumptions of method and eventually is repressed.

It is not surprising that we resort to reductive strategies which promise to evade the uniqueness of the instance. While productive, as the history of the modern sciences demonstrates, these strategies blind us to our doubts. They become not just useful but legislative. The need for simplicity and the struggle for objectivity are themselves preferences that turn out (not always) to be justified by predicted outcomes. As mysterious and nondependable as it is in ethics, a scientific common sense is at work in what Thomas Kuhn calls "normal science." Thus, nature "abhors a vacuum," as we used to say. We'd like to believe that it "acts" in the most direct and efficient way possible. But we can never really know if this is so because we cannot stand outside the world in order to look at it entirely. "Nature," in other words, is a useful "construct." Ockham's Razor is a convenience but not a truth.

Inspired by scientific models, we assume that clinic and classroom should do their work by solving "realistic" problems of healing in the clinic or of learning in the classroom. Reconceived as scientific medicine or as scientific pedagogy, neither clinic nor classroom need worry about problematics, for example, about problems like questions of metatheory, of ontology, or of philosophic anthropology. These abstruse matters are referred elsewhere. Clinic and classroom then need only adapt to their announced ends notions judiciously borrowed from other and less tainted activities. These borrowings are, as it were, chosen from a menu presented from on high and transformed—often uncritically—into instruments for specified purposes. Thus in medical ethics, the attempt to distinguish what is called "biomedicine" from "clinical" experience, to isolate "macro" from "micro" phenomena. The tasks of clinic and classroom are taken to be conceptually simple even if practically difficult. At most, clinic and classroom call for a less exalted kind of theory. This epistemological division of labor, as I have suggested, gives rise, among other things, to the notion that medical ethics is only ethics applied to a particular activity.

Ethics, coming from elsewhere, so to speak, is attached to practice. Hardly self-conscious, ethics is present as common sense. So it is assumed that a given problem is really "technical" or "clinical." Matters of moral value will simply take care of themselves as long as well-intentioned people are involved. But when something goes wrong, the inadequacies of common sense become evident. Unexpected—and usually unwelcome—questions may be raised from alternative perspectives. And these in a pluralistic society and global environment are a fact of life. Typically, we simply proceed to do standard things like blood transfusion in the clinic or saluting the flag in the classroom, until the Jehovah's Witness or the conscientious objector says "no." In a sense, one moral common sense

confronts an equivalent but different common sense. Even more dramatic, of course, is the appearance of novel situations like pregnancy
without fathers or indefinite prolongations of dying. Common sense fails.

To be sure, moral habits are not signs of moral indifference. In practice,
typically, doing ethics cannot be a deliberative activity. Were we required
to pay attention in every instance, we would soon find ourselves morally
and practically paralyzed. Unavoidably, however, the rapid evolution of
biomedical ethics stirs a usable discomfort, and its implications reach
beyond the walls of the clinic. This moral discomfort appears as life-
worlds multiply and as novelty and complexity increase. Of course, we
still echo the past, using incantations like "Do no harm" long after "doing" and "harming" have become problematic. Life, death, autonomy, responsibility, choice, consent have grown more and more puzzling.

It is no accident that biomedical ethics escapes the clinic. But because
of its suddenness, we do not yet understand that what happens within
has meanings, and not just consequences, without. The clinic still attends
to the interpersonal situation. With biomedical ethics, however, its traditional moral content is forced to the question. This opens as a kind of
moral consciousness-raising, as in the biomedical ethics of some twenty
or thirty years ago, and not incidentally as in the early development of
feminism. References to Hippocrates, to traditional Roman Catholic
moral doctrine, and to standard ethical philosophy mark the effort to
transcend the particular. As biomedical ethics develops, however, the
moral assumptions of diverse and diversely located caregivers, patients,
and families are also brought into the open. Generalization and tradition
come under attack. The particular is rediscovered and reconstructed. It
participates in shaping new moral ground. With the increasing interactions between nonmedical and clinical institutions, moreover, biomedical
ethics moves beyond its parochial origins. With this, it exposes moral
activity—the puzzling interplay of the unique and the universal—in a
more dramatic, albeit threatening, way.

The classroom, too, is in motion. The varied ways of moral education
are its index. Thus, moral education is often understood as only another
moment in curricular design. One subject matter, say history or literature,
is replaced by another. Or moral education is interpreted as an instance
of cognitive development, a problem of applied psychology. In a less
secular mood, it may be read as a spiritual or religious problem, or socially and politically as a problem of character education. In short, despite
differences of approach, moral education is perceived as a problem,
which like all problems invites us to look for answers. A certain conventionality attends the project even among those who claim radical creden-
tials. Moral education is seen, too, as subsidiary to noneducational
institutions, to church or state or family, which have education as a derivative obligation. To avoid the mess of religious and secular conflict that

this stirs up, schooling tries to escape by claiming that education is value-neutral. Moral education is only another form of training, an exercise in "values clarification." Schooling then is a servant of noneducational interests, as in a "return to basics" or as in the notion of limiting the task of the schools to skills and techniques. For still others, schooling is really psychology adapted to the roles, relationships, and motivations of teaching and learning. Moral education, on this view, is simply another psychological specialty now twice removed from idea.

In the classroom as in the clinic, moral practices are unavoidably present. But the classroom does not exhibit the self-consciousness of biomedical ethics. Its practices are not in themselves subject to moral inquiry. Instead, they are perceived as matters of conduct, courtesy, professionalism, and administration or as instances of general social relations, that is, their status as *moral* is sublimated. As in the jargon of the teacher, moral education is neutralized as "socialization" and "reinforcement," which entirely evades the criticism and the ambiguity that doing ethics entails. Unlike biomedical ethics, where clinical realities are themselves the substance of inquiry, moral education does not make the classroom its own curriculum. And yet, the classroom is as subject to upheaval these days as the clinic, and often in many of the same ways, such as the introduction of technologies, the encounter with a plurality of languages and cultures, the urgencies of moral conflict. The classroom has become in fact, if not in consciousness, and in a rich but unrealized way, the "experience" that the progressives used to talk about. But we do not pay attention.

Thus, the habit of an intellectual division of labor is exposed as the assumption that certain "generic" fields of inquiry exist which secondary or even lesser fields can appropriate to their uses. Knowing's image is the pyramid or the Platonic "ladder." *True* knowing is radically distanced from doing. To be sure, the identity of these generic fields, of "basics" in another sense, is itself problematic. For some it is theology; for others it is philosophy; for still others it is history; and most recently, it is science. For postmodernists no basics exist at all; there is no "grand narrative." Beneath their absolute skepticism, of course, is the anguish of surrender.

Of course, a hierarchical arrangement of knowledges reflects a particular epistemology and sociology and a particular locus of authority. That is why the progressive's commitments led to the "core curriculum," "learning by doing," and "participatory democracy." And that is why progressivism in schooling is still a center of political conflict. Today, feminist critiques follow a pathway somewhat similar to that of the civil rights movement. For these, the organization of knowledge calls for interactive and egalitarian exchanges between different but entwined inquiries. The circle replaces the pyramid. In a related move, interdisciplinary and transdisciplinary inquiry is driven by the fact that neither knowing nor learning comes to us in disciplinary packages or neatly divided into idea and instrument. Summing it up, we need not surrender to anarchism or to traditionalism in order to locate more pluralistic ways of knowing. To this end, biomedical ethics becomes an agent of epistemological and moral reform.

STORIES

Working in the classroom and the clinic is a rich and mystifying experience. The trouble is that the experience lived through and the ideas we invent to understand it don't fit each other very well. We end up by impoverishing experience or by sacrificing intellect. We set up dual categories like cognition and appreciation, science and art, pure and applied. But these boundaried terms distort what happens. The things they try to name flow into each other whether we will it or not. In other words, we need strategies of interpenetration that do justice to both the need for idea and the richness of detail. With this in mind, I turn to narrative, although I confess my hesitation because of the way postmoderns have turned narrative into dogma. Yet, in clinic and classroom, the connecting moment, the nexus of this act of connection, is the story. With it, generalization and elaboration meet. And that is why thinking with cases can enlighten a moral education which has lost sight of the story.

In the clinical situation, stories are inevitable. To lose sight of them is to lose the patient. The ethicist, claiming to rely on some metaethical basis for the moral coherence of "middle range" concepts like beneficence and autonomy, understands that ideas are finally known and to be known in use. The classroom depends on stories, too. But their integrity as stories is sacrificed and, as it were, we lose the student. Thus, we meet the story with a moral. Concept is not discovered or developed in use but only exemplified. For example, that most austere of modern ethicists, Immanuel Kant, illustrates "pure practical reason" (i.e., ethics) with hard questions like: Is it permissible to lie in order to save a human life? But the deductive move is misleading and the notion of illustration, patronizing. In effect, the student is told that he or she is inadequate to the pure concept, which is really what ethics is all about. The teacher, of course, does not need stories at all except as a tool of communication to the less sophisticated. To be sure, theory and reality are to be bridged by the move from principle to "maxim." But the process starts and ends with the abstract. More attractively, as in the parables of Jesus, principle is conveyed through the story.[16] And yet, the story remains a device, only a pedagogical device.

Austere or elaborated, there is an important difference between cases in the clinic and illustrations in the classroom. In the clinic, the story generates the case and is substratum as well as instrument. Thus, knowledge appears along with and inside of experience. In the background lurk anatomy and biology and chemistry, but these are servants of a way of knowing in practice. For the clinic, they are, as it were, a kind of preknowledge, a not-yet knowledge. To call medicine an "art" is to capture, in part, this epistemology warning us that insight, intuition, and action play an essential role in knowing and not just in learning. Medicine is not simply applied biology any more than biomedical ethics is simply applied ethics.

In the classroom, however, the story vanishes into the illustration that is understood as the instantiation of knowledge gained elsewhere or located elsewhere. Thus, we miss the chance to confront the story and the experience that was its original. Knowledge has, so to speak, an exterior and independent status. This differential geography of the story has consequences. Thus, internship and residency are the central facts of medical education. The case is the vehicle of teaching and learning, as later it will be the vehicle of practice and discovery. On the other hand, "practice teaching" is only a minor component of teacher education, ancillary and not central. Typically, in spite of recurrent complaint, most teacher education programs are not classroom-connected at all. In fact, teachers of teachers are regularly accused of alienation from the classroom. Institutionally revealing is the fact that university-based "laboratory" schools, where knowledge and classroom had direct connection, have all but vanished. Education departments take their place.

I am, of course, tempted to dismiss the criticisms of the classroom as the complaint of critics with an ideological or political agenda. And it is as easy to interpret the effort to elevate pedagogy to theory as a defensive move because teaching provides so little in the way of reward or status. But the relative isolation of practice from theory is not simply a consequence of the sociology and politics of education. More deeply, it reflects a wrong turn in schooling and in moral education, too, the move away from experience and toward abstraction. This is the ironic outcome of ongoing research on the moral education of medical students by Donnie Self at Texas A&M College of Medicine. Classroom- and not clinic-based, it doesn't succeed. Thus, the study, while warning that it is not yet definitive, concludes that it found "no correlation between moral reasoning and the four empathy subscales: perspective taking, empathic concern, fantasy and personal distress."[17]

Of course, the elementary and high school classrooms are designed as an alternative world for students. And the move to protect is justified. But the protective impulse is problematic for moral education. It is assumed that the designed experience of the classroom will ultimately be directly transferable to the fortuitous and ambiguous experience of the world. Illustrations in the classroom are supposed to carry the burden of mediation, to make the connection between the life-worlds of students and real-world complexities. But for that to happen, stories cannot be turned into illustrations, nor can the encounter with real-world complexities be postponed to some unexperienced future. The indifference of students to the alleged import "out there" of what is learned "in here" is revealing. They know that the illustration neither supports nor mediates; it has no roots in the particulars of the event. Students understand the lesson very well. The morality tale gets the conduct it asks for, such as giving correct answers on a quiz. Experience gets a different response, such as behaving in ways that assure survival at home, on the streets, or on the job.

Clearly, any story has its moral structure. It is instructive, for example, that whatever our assessment of Freud, his insights—as much moral as psychological—are rooted in classical legend and theater. Scriptures persist as literature even where faith grows pale. The aesthetically successful novel or drama typically is a moral creation without moralism. In other words, these may be illustrative of the human condition but they are not illustrations. I need not tell a "moral" story in order to tell a moral "story." The classroom, however, is populated with illustrations posing as stories from Aesop's *Fables* to McGuffey's *Readers* to moral dilemmas. Recent examples can be found in the didactic novels of Philosophy for Children.[18] "Character education," using history and biography as its vehicle, seems to take us back to experience.[19] But all too often, converted again into moralism, dimension and voice are lost.

The problem of the "story" is exposed in cognitive development theory. Based on the work of the Swiss psychologist Jean Piaget,[20] it was elaborated as "cognitive moral development" by Lawrence Kohlberg and his colleagues. It has been the subject of continuing critique and amendment, most significantly by Kohlberg's Harvard associate Carol Gilligan. Kohlberg's work begins as scientific inquiry, the effort to discover if, how, and when moral cognition develops in human beings. Although more sophisticated tools have been designed,[21] the experimental instrument is still the moral dilemma. Responses to it are assessed by elaborately worked-out protocols for determining the moral "stages" at which the human "subjects" are to be found.[22]

The initial "test subjects," whose development Kohlberg followed for many years, were all young men. The moral value to be developed and measured was the maturation of a sense of "justice as fairness," an approach to ethics taken from Kohlberg's Harvard colleague John Rawls.[23] Kohlberg's work then was a ready target for feminist criticism, particularly since young women, for the most part, didn't manage to get much past "stages 3 and 4" in Kohlberg's six-stage scheme. His work was also criticized for identifying ethics with distributive justice to the exclusion of alternatives like caring, for its reliance on reasoning to the exclusion of moral passion, and for an individualism without sociability. From the start, Kohlberg acknowledged the limits—the scientific simplifications—that he had deliberately adopted and that he announced explicitly and often. But the announcement was not really heard. Sometimes, it seemed to some of us, it was not even heard by Kohlberg himself. Of course, he had his defenders who, pointing to the creation of "just communities" at a later stage of his work, insisted that he was not dogmatically individualistic and was not indifferent to the affective and political features of moral judgment. More recently, the notion that justice and caring represent exclusive choices has given way to a pluralistic if not eclectic point of view in which both can find their place.[24]

As psychological inquiry, cognitive moral development, whether of the Kohlberg or the Gilligan variety, is well served by the moral dilemma. It allows for the construction of reliable protocols, meaningful measurements, and coherent communication. It is fruitful because it raises manageable questions, invites coherent interpretations, and above all, stirs next-questions—as, ironically, Gilligan's own criticisms of Kohlberg illustrate. However, moral development ideas have not stayed within psychological inquiry as such, but have also been incarnated as moral education, and not incidentally. As Kohlberg wrote:

While dialogue with others scholars was important . . . I felt it necessary to become immersed in the practice of education. . . . Work in the school started with two assumptions of John Dewey's. The first was that one can't develop a theory of bridge building by applying pure research. It can only come out of building bridges. The second was that building a theory of education is a two-way street involving a collaboration between teachers, students, and the educational theorist. . . . The idea of a just community involved dealing with the hidden curriculum of the school or institution, not simply a curriculum of classroom discussion.[25]

Dilemmas are directly transformed into curriculum, and moral stages acquire meaning as classroom expectations and assessments of students and teachers. At that point, a useful tool of scientific research becomes seriously misleading. To see this, it is helpful to take a look at the "dilemma" from three differing perspectives: Kohlberg's experimental model, Gilligan's feminist revisionism, and what might be required for a move from dilemma to case and story. Most familiar, almost to the point of cliché, is "Heinz's dilemma."

In Europe, a woman is near death from a special kind of cancer. There is one drug that the doctors think might save her. It is a form of radium that a druggist in the same town has recently discovered. The drug is expensive to make, but the druggist is charging ten times what the drug cost him to make. He paid $200 for the radium and is charging $2000 for a small dose of the drug. The sick woman's husband, Heinz, goes to everyone he knows to borrow the money, but he can get together only about $1000, which is half of what it costs. He tells the druggist that his wife is dying and asks him to sell the drug cheaper or let him pay later. The druggist says, "No, I discovered the drug and I'm going to make money from it." Heinz is desperate and considers breaking into the man's store to steal the drug for his wife.[26]

A series of questions in the research protocol structures the interviews. Obviously, we are interested in finding out whether or not Heinz should steal the drug. But it is the mode of reasoning that interests the researcher. In other words, the moral content is deliberately thin. Minimalist questions of relationship are asked, such as whether or not Heinz loves his wife; whether or not the judgment would change if she were a stranger. Toward the end of the interview other questions appear, having to do with obeying or not obeying the law, the value of life as against property, and so on, But again it is the reasoning and not the moral content that is important. Of course, embedded in the dilemma and in the questions that follow are moral concepts and principles: "justice as fairness," the universalizability of moral claims, the relative status of law and morality, the obligation to treat everyone equally under equivalent conditions. But it is not difficult to notice that these are procedural questions. The dilemma, in other words, is a focused instrument that deliberately highlights a specific kind of moral thinking in as direct and uncluttered a fashion as possible.

The apparent question, to steal or not to steal, is deceptively simple, just as clinical symptoms like pain or fever are deceptively simple. Of course, both present problems of interpretation, but their underlying intention does not seem to be problematic. In the dilemma, however, moral content is only instrumental to moral capacity, so, as it were, any moral content will do. Clinical content, on the other hand, points back to the specific patient and ahead to differential diagnosis. Symptoms are not interchangeable. The dilemma does a different job. It is a tool for getting at moral reasoning. Clinical symptoms are intended to expose an actual situation. To find out if someone is "thinking like a doctor" is to look at how these particulars are located, understood, worked with. Content does not, cannot, disappear. But in the dilemma, character and event are ultimately nonrelevant. Only principles remain. Then, by setting the replies of the experimental subject against a grid of all prior replies and against the Piagetian assumption that the more abstract and general the reasoning, the more mature the subject, the subject's location on a "stage" scheme is plotted. Periodic follow-up questionnaires are used to measure moral movement or cognitive development. So it is not really possible to say that someone is "thinking like an ethicist" unless ethics can be reduced to a structure of rights and duties, and its performance by any individual—Kant's rational being, for example—having certain generalized characteristics. In an important sense, the subject of the dilemma is unknown and passive; of the clinic, is known and active.

For Gilligan, Heinz's dilemma opens other possibilities. Content cannot be dismissed. Thus, she reports the differences in response between two eleven-year-olds, Jake and Amy.

Jake . . . is clear from the outset that Heinz should steal the drug. . . . Fascinated by the power of logic, this eleven-year old boy locates truth in math, which, he says, is "the only thing that is totally logical." . . . In contrast, Amy's response to the dilemma conveys a very different impression. . . . Asked if Heinz should steal the drug, she replies in a way that seems evasive and unsure. "Well, I don't think so. I think there might be other ways besides stealing it, like if he could borrow the money or make a loan or something . . ." Asked why he should not steal the drug, she considers neither property nor law but rather the effect that theft could have on the relationship between Heinz and his wife. . . . Seeing in the dilemma not a math problem with humans but a narrative of relationships that extends over time. . . . Failing to see the dilemma as a self-contained problem in moral logic, she does not discern the internal structure of its resolution; as she constructs the problem differently herself, Kohlberg's conception completely evades her.[27]

As with any research, the way an inquiry is designed forecasts the kinds of outcomes it will find. Nor is research morally transparent. It is not a neutral process by which this or that hypothesis is to be proved or disproved. Thus, both Kohlberg and Gilligan begin with the notion—explicit in the former, less so in the latter—that in some sense a moral principle or a moral characteristic of some general kind is to be discovered. The dilemma unearths it. It is "justice as fairness" or "caring" or something else. Both Kohlberg and Gilligan explore moral cognition—whether as reason or as intuition—and so both simplify the situation to make that exploration possible. Implicitly, they assign a prior value to moral cognition, and it is only a short step to identifying it as the central value of ethics, if not ethics itself. To be sure, there are genuine discoveries to be made—the elaboration of stages, the shift of relationships, the differing powers of reason. These lead to truth claims, in this instance psychological truth claims. So both Kohlberg and Gilligan proceed in an abstracted way. Morally, there is little at stake. The interest is in an increase of knowledge, which is neither a trivial nor an unworthy goal.

When other interests appear, however, the situation changes, though this is not always evident. The classroom illustration often looks and acts like the dilemma. It is designed, not created, and its aesthetic merit is incidental. Converted from research instrument to illustration, the dilemma's job is to make a point or to pose a choice, as in the fable or the parable. The student is forced to choose between exclusive alternatives.

Mood, temperament, and time are simply ignored. Moral ambiguity vanishes. And this, in itself, conveys an unintended lesson about the nature of the moral situation. As a critic reminds us:

Narrative approaches . . . are arguably those in which the principles are just as subject to reexamination in the light of the particulars of the situation as the other way around. For example, instead of retaining a fixed notion of justice as an impartial principle for distributing benefits and burdens without respect of person, one might allow the history of interactions among bonded siblings looking after a frail elderly parent to point to a rather different understanding of justice when the context is one of intimacy. Justice in this context might be reconceived as apportioning time, energy, and resources differently on different occasions, depending on who needs what, while at the same time ensuring that all members of the family are valued and respected. Here the particulars of the family's history point to a new understanding of a principle, which may, in turn, show up the relevance of other particulars, which may lead us to revise our view of other principles, and so on.[28]

The move from research to pedagogy, signaled by turning dilemma into illustration, is made almost without realizing the radical transformation that has taken place. At the same time, the move to the classroom opens up questions about the research itself and about the researchers themselves. This invites its own story, but nobody tells it. For example, what part does Gilligan's early career as an "associate" of Kohlberg's play in the story of discovery? What part does Kohlberg's status and authority play in the story? What would be heard were the "test subjects" invited to be boys or girls, and not simply male or female respondents of a certain age? Institutional and communal story elements are not addressed. For example, would the story play out differently in a church-sponsored college or in a community college and not in an Ivy League school? Stories, unlike dilemmas and unlike illustrations, are undisciplined and their boundaries are porous.

By contrast, the biomedical ethics "case" is a story before it is a case and remains a story even while it is a case. This is clear enough once we are morally attentive. Indicative are the differing roles of the "attending" and the "consulting" physicians. The former cannot forget the story and be effective; the latter deals with a selected reality, such as the disease to be treated, the surgery to be performed. The consultant's perception is, as it were, somewhere between the attending's and the researcher's. It is problem-centered and moves between "science" and singularity. The attending physician is a storyteller; in conference, for example, the "case" is presented in different ways by attending and consulting physicians. Of course, these days, general practice and internal medicine become specialties. So more and more of us move away from the story. At the same time, the realities of patient and performance break into this move. The story will not disappear.

The case is the locus of medical education that takes place in the midst of the event. In other words, it carries an existential burden that is suppressed in the psychologist's dilemma and the teacher's illustration. So the consultant can be called to attention, can be reminded, by the story. But the illustration lacks a story, so neither teacher nor researcher can be called to attention by experience. To be sure, the case is recorded according to the conventions of medical practice. The chart includes a medical history, clinical indications, diagnostic possibilities, treatments tried and, when necessary, discarded, and so on. It is a clinical diary composed in a specific way, but as such it is an alienated diary and not a narrative. It is set apart from feelings, doubts, hints, temperaments that may be pointed at by means of standard protocols but unexpressed. As it were, the chart is a textbook devoted to a singular event. Like most textbooks, it has functions but neither life nor liveliness. But the story does not go away. The chart is located within a continuing formal and informal conversation. It exists as the notations of an oral tradition also devoted to a singular event. The chart is not the case and the case is not the story and the story is not the event. Beyond the singularity, of course, lurk the past case and the next case. So patterns and reminiscences and forecasts fracture the walls of the case.

The move to biomedical ethics reveals a multitiered narrative structure. With it, the clinical situation is extended. Increasingly, then, it is recognized as far more complicated than traditionally it has been thought to be. The effects of ideological and religious beliefs, of economics, of race, class, and status, of family and family relationships, of cultural heritage, of multiple authorities at the bedside, of prior and predicted difficulties and successes for both patient and caregiver are seen to focus in the instant event. These "nonclinical" aspects have clinical consequences. For example, we learn to distinguish pain as symptom from suffering as experience, a distinction dramatically evident in the experiences surrounding death and dying and the move to pain management, or what is called palliative care.

For biomedical ethics, Heinz's dilemma calls for doing a good deal of aesthetic, moral, psychological, and sociological work. Although it seems to present a medical problem, its content is hardly relevant. The key to the dilemma is its moral *structure*. So just about any relationship that was reducible to an either/or choice within a hierarchy of choices would do, as the other dilemmas developed by Kohlberg et al. demonstrate. By contrast, to locate the event and to tell the story of Heinz's choices would require a certain "thickness." Heinz's choices would have to be explored from more than the single perspective. Many voices would have to be heard, and these would be located in different places and at different moments as time passed and interests shifted.

Like the illustration, the dilemma is truncated, even superficial. It seems that there are only two voices to be heard. In fact, however, we hear only the voice of the researcher who asks, listens, repeats, and interprets the voice of the test subject. And, as the protocols are refined, even the researcher speaks in the third person. Everywhere, character is suppressed. Heinz, his wife, the pharmacist are not present. They are test vehicles matched to test subjects. None of the participants—not in the dilemma, not in the question and response, not in the assessment—has a biography. Once the decision is made to steal or not to steal, they do not have a future either. The passage of time, in other words, is deliberately one-dimensional, reduced to the follow-up interview. The researcher and the subject are the only ones permitted to speak at all, and then only to the moral script shaped by anonymous others. In short, this is a moral inquiry without persons, and this depersonalization is intentional. The assumption is that situation, personality, and passion are only incidental to morality. Scientific inquiry and moral universalism meet.

Without event, urgency is not at issue. The predictable death of the wife does not, apparently, evoke tears or anxiety. The dilemma probes a discrete moment. Unexplored, too, is the political economy of the dilemma. The other politics in the situation—the authority of the researcher who presents the material, asks the questions, and makes the judgments—is likewise ignored. The dependency of the subject as subject is left unexposed. He or she accepts the situation as presented and is responsible for answers already shaped by the setting and the question. Heinz's religion, ideology, and family structure are not germane. The possibility of alternative decisions is deliberately narrowed. "Justice as fairness" focuses on "rights" and "duties," the useful but limiting model of the law, now the moral law, where outcomes are right or wrong, the verdict, guilty or innocent.

In order to qualify for a more robust sense of morality, Heinz's dilemma would be written as a multiple biography and from more than any single perspective. To the voices of Heinz and his questioner would be added the wife, the pharmacist, and not least of all the future patient deprived of the drug if the pharmacist is forced out of business. The test subject would have to be permitted authorship as well, a power that Amy tries unsuccessfully to exercise. And finally, actual stories that might model the dilemma would not be ignored, such as stories of tuberculosis in an earlier day, of AIDS today. In real-world ethics, we meet corporate conduct, individual helplessness, problems of fairness as a social and as an interpersonal matter, cultural and ideological views of property and family. These would inevitably generate other versions of the story. Of course, as this happened, the dilemma as research instrument would vanish. But its utility in the classroom would appear.

Ironically, it is just because cognitive moral development theory is self-conscious—a genuine virtue of the scientific temper that generates it—that it is accessible to criticism as pedagogy. It is misleading for the classroom not because it isolates "justice as fairness" but because it isolates judgment from experience. Gilligan's Amy is constrained by the dilemma, too, despite her efforts to break out. The authority of inquiry finally defeats her—which suggests yet another story, perhaps one of oppression and rebellion. Other forms of moral education are not as revealing. The moral tale and the classroom illustration, like the moral rules and the maxims so beloved of character education, are equally dimensionless and equally empty of actual persons, actual events, and actual urgencies. Because these come to us in the guise of moral common sense and are motivated by felt moral discomforts, their flatness is less apparent. Virtues, as in virtue theory, become unbelievable, too, and not just because they have to be, as Alisdair MacIntyre rightly points out, contextualized in specific societies that assign them both explicit and implicit meaning in a cultural "narrative."[29] They are unbelievable most of all because, as illustrations, they evade the ambiguities of the happening and its story. In short, biomedical ethics generates creativities and inquiries that are absent from the moral education that we try to do.

THE MORAL SITUATION

As I reflect on stories, I have the sense of an endless series of mirror images that fade into the distance because my eyesight grows dim and my energy runs out. I realize that James Joyce's *Ulysses* or Herodotus' *History* is a likely model. For example, I find myself stopping over and over again to explore a question, a possible role, an alternative move of character or mood or plot. And every time I return from this seeming byway to the so-called central line of thought, I see openings for yet other stories. Reflection on reflection also shows that what seems so clear in the beginning is changing, amending, redirecting. I grow anxious, too, since it is hard to keep my moorings under conditions of reflection on reflection. Nor do I explore the possibilities that would open up where they are not dictated by the fact that the situation is framed as a problem. Admitting imagined and actual others into the discussion suggests the probability of responses, imaginations, and reflections that could and would intersect mine. Nor do I think of what might happen were the story recited aloud or danced or sung rather than written down. In other words, the story can be endlessly fruitful but also becomes unmanageable. In the moral situation, I surrender control.

It is just this unmanageability—the way a story takes on a life of its own, the way it stirs possibilities—that makes the story morally rich and aesthetically interesting. So we are inveterate storytellers just because each hearing, each telling is both a reminder and a new experience—the reader-as-author, as Ralph Waldo Emerson alerted us long before deconstruction became the mode of criticism. It is just this unmanageability that makes the story an entry into the moral situation and thereby into moral education: the way it refuses the discipline of time, space, and personality and yet incorporates *a* time, *a* space, *a* personality in any given telling or retelling. It is the story being left free to be itself and not constrained as illustration or fable or parable that enables it to serve epistemologically and pedagogically, and ultimately morally. In that way, the story exhibits experience but, unlike experience, invites experiment without consequences. I can tell a story of villainy without invoking the law court, the prison, or the gallows. I can tell a story of love without the risk of commitment or, less happily, of AIDS or infidelity. In that potentiality, the classroom departs radically and appropriately from the clinic. Protection is preserved.

By contrast, modern approaches to ethics and to moral education are intentionally "thin."[30] They are boundaried conceptually and sealed off psychologically. Paradoxically, this justifies the claim of universality, that is, a boundlessness which derives precisely from this boundaried condition. For the sake of moral objectivity, we deliberately deny moral space to biography, history, community, and culture.[31] Even where motive and intention are attended to, these are generalized over some population having certain nonspecific characteristics. Thus, the reference to the ability to "reason" or the ability to "have interests" or the ability to "know one's interest" or the ability to "feel pain and to suffer." These characteristics—evident in alternatives like deontology and utilitarianism, or in the arguments about the rights of animals or about justice and caring—are selected, even preselected, just because they can come to play a part in the way we perceive a moral account. Other characteristics, like humor or sexiness or tastefulness or obesity or baldness, are simply ignored unless a particular "application" calls them into being. Medicine may find obesity relevant; religion may find humor relevant; romance may find baldness relevant.

Typically, the elements of a moral situation are reduced to cognition, reflection, judgment, decision, and action. Any given ethical theory tends to pick up on one of these, around which the others are then organized. And since in the West, ethics has been the playing field of philosophers and theologians for more than two millennia, it is not surprising that moral *cognitions* take center stage. My response to my way of thinking is illustrative. I keep coming back to the "literature" of the subject, enamored of the *word* because that has been my moral vehicle.

Even where the possibility of moral cognitions is denied, as by emotivists and positivists, it is the *idea* of the sciences as reliable knowledge, much more than the activities of scientists, that shapes the criticism. Emotivists pay little attention to empirical psychologies; positivists pay little attention to empirical sociologies and anthropologies. Action theories are cognitive, too, rooted in judgments and decisions that in turn are derived from rational inquiry and reflection. Nearly absent are the implicit features of the situation that shape the analysis itself. For example, animal rights theorists challenge the moral centrality of reasoning in the name of feeling pain and suffering, and yet the root reference is still cognitive, that is, the concept of rights. Typically, it is left for the historian of philosophy to notice—but only to notice—the Lutheran, Germanic, and academic realities beneath Kant's "pure" and austere ethic. More likely, as in introductory philosophy texts, is a throwaway comment about Kant's habits or about his place in the Enlightenment, which, in turn, is summed up conceptually, that is, without the blood and pain, joy and fear of rebellion. Fearing the accusation of ad hominem argument, little attention is paid to a critical study of the connection between philosophy and biography, history, family life, love, friendship, enmity, anger. Indeed, the vast catalog of human behaviors and experiences is, if dealt with at all, approached in alienated and abstracted fashion. When the connection is taken seriously, it is likely to be dismissed as philosophically irrelevant or as merely the philosophic equivalent of psychobiography.

The philosopher's habit, the "linguistic turn" in philosophy, is forecast in the Socratic impulse to challenge and define and challenge and redefine. To counter its temptations, I turn again to the story. It reminds me that the moral texture of a given action is crucial to an assessment of its moral quality and status. So, for example, a "passion for righteousness" that reveals itself in the intensity of the actor reshapes moral action. The act in itself is already an abstraction. The heat of commitment is invisible, as is the cool rationality of the moral judge. Obedience to duty may rest on a sense of the "right thing to do" or on a felt response to violation. But the act of obedience itself, absent the testimony of the obedient, is left morally unexplained. Moral judgment is voiced differently when delivered by prophet or priest or analytic philosopher. And it is heard differently when contextualized, even dramatized. Thus, compare textbook maxims to Moses descending from Sinai 'mid lightning and thunder with the tablets of the law. Perhaps, it might be said, this is *only* a matter of style or rhetoric. But this begs the question by presuming that style and rhetoric are incidental and do not reshape the message itself. Of course, the likelihood of finding the moral claim convincing is increased by an effective aesthetic, but conviction is a crucial intention of doing ethics and is not simply an add-on to it. Reference to motive and intention is a pallid acknowledgment that the message is not just an abstract directive.

The message completes its meaning and achieves its pedagogical effectiveness precisely because of its aesthetic. As it were, ethics is finally lived and lived through and not simply deliberated upon by "rational beings."

Style is not the only feature of the story that counts. The story embeds morality within personality and history. And so the moral judgment alters with time and place. Consider, for example, a simple but moving instance that was shared with me by one of my students. A young woman left to raise her young son after her husband had died, she wrote about the suicide of her father:

Before my dad died, he wrote me a letter telling me good-bye. . . . He explained to me that he was very depressed and felt all alone. He also said that he loved me more than the world, and for me to one day find it in my heart to forgive him. The letter did make me feel a little better, but I couldn't help feeling mad and confused . . . I didn't understand how a father could leave behind his only child.

With time, I began to understand why my dad did what he did. I think of my dad every day. I think about how he never saw me graduate, he never saw me get married, and he will never see his grandson. . . . It makes me very sad to think about all my dad is missing. . . . Understanding why he killed himself may help me in dealing with his death, but it can never take away the pain. All I can do is hold on to the good memories I have of when I was "daddy's little girl."[32]

Obviously, she judged the act of suicide to be morally wrong and still does. But that does not capture the moral situation in which she found herself as a child nor the moral situation, now different, in which she finds herself today. Of course, we conclude that suicide is morally "wrong" from some religious perspectives. For others, however, it is nonmoral and only "clinical." For still others, it is a relief from suffering and thus morally "right." Yet, to reduce the experience to conclusions, to a definitive collection of judgments, is to miss much of its moral import and to settle for mere relativism. Reading her words, I was concerned, for example, with the moral developments that had shaped this woman's life as a consequence of the experience. Judgment and conclusion foreclose such considerations. Among other things, she worried about how and when she should communicate to her son and about the moral consequences of doing so. She had to deal with forgiveness and acceptance, and not just with judgment. Unless the moral act is a story, that is, is not walled away, considerations of relationships and of pasts and futures are not morally germane. Instead, we make connections by stringing moments together under the umbrella of concept rather than within experience.

My student's struggle is mirrored in the larger debate about physician-assisted suicide. As N. Ann Davis wrote in commenting on the Supreme Court's decision in the Cruzan case:[33]

The view that . . . motivation and intention . . . bear strongly on the moral assessment [of] conduct . . . is widely shared. But there is little agreement on the details.
. . . Many would agree that there are problems both with attempting to arrive at
a definitive determination of an agent's intentions and motivations, and with trying to provide a satisfactory account of how intention and motivation determine
the moral permissibility . . . of our acts.[34]

Shift in position forces moral reevaluation, too. Morality is "situated,"
as feminists claim. Moral perspective and context change when, for example, the doctor becomes the patient or the teacher becomes the student.
Relationships of authority are relevant moral considerations, as are questions of conflict of interest, partiality toward family and friends, issues of
moral objectivity. We see these and like these matters of moral talk
through the lens of our experiences and locations. For example, consider
the comments of the social service director of a long-term care facility
whose mother had serious surgery:

A few weeks before my mother's hospitalization, I visited the daughter of one of
our residents, a woman with end-stage Alzheimer's. She's been lying in bed for
14 years, progressively declining with no evidence of cognition of any kind, barely
responsive at all. The daughter explained how she used to visit more often but
now visits rarely because it is so painful to see her mother in this condition. We
walked into her mother's room and the daughter told her mother she loved her.
Then the daughter began to cry. It was one of the most poignant scenes I've
witnessed. . . . In that moment I promised myself I would "watch out" for this
woman's mother *as if I were her daughter*. Little did I know the time would soon
come when I would in fact, be *the daughter*—loving and hoping.[35]

Personality, passion, and place define the moral situation as ambiguous
and connected, as a story. At the same time, that unmanageability is the
richness of stories; however, it is also their limitation. At some point, an
ending must be declared, but it is a declaration more often than it is a
conclusion. Patterns that lead on to next stories and next questions need
to be discerned, imagined, even if dealing with them is postponed. Failing
that, the moral situation cannot be reached through the story because,
ultimately, it also needs resolution and confesses finitude. Anecdotalism,
jumping arbitrarily from one story to another, will not do. Nor is it possible to evade closure. So the story brings the possibility of a thickness
that ethics needs and at the same time opens up questions of coherence
and practicability. Of course, stories have been used successfully to build
religions, create loyalties, evoke commitments. In the clinical situation,
stories are reshaped as cases, and so as a way of thinking that solves the
problem of thickness and pattern without deserting detail and event. The
puzzle of method and model can be solved.

NOTES

1. For a discussion of the "hidden curriculum," see Howard B. Radest, *Can We Teach Ethics* (New York: Praeger, 1989), chapter 6.

2. Dr. John Farrell, chair of Surgery, University of Miami, addressing a chapter of the American College of Surgeons in 1958. Cited by M. L. Tina Stevens, "What Quinlan Can Tell Kevorkian About the Right to Die," *The Humanist*, Vol. 57, No. 2 (March–April 1997), p. 11.

3. This may sound harsh, and the criticism, anachronistic. After all, a study in 1932 could not have had knowledge of the Nazi doctors' experiments on human subjects nor could it benefit from the Helsinki Declaration on the subject (World Medical Association 1964, revised 1975). In fact, explicit guidelines for human experimentation were developed in the United States in response to events like Tuskegee (see National Commission for the Protection of Human Subjects of Biomedical and Behavioral Research, The Belmont Report [Washington, D.C.: U.S. Government Printing Office, 1978]). Nevertheless, even traditional moral rules like "do no harm" would have cautioned against the experiment, particularly when the effectiveness of penicillin was demonstrated about a decade into the project.

4. Carol Kaesuk Yoon, "Families of Tuskegee Men Feel Emotional Aftereffects," *New York Times*, May 12, 1997.

5. The Nuremberg Code of Ethics in Medical Research was developed after the end of World War II. The Declaration of Helsinki was adopted by the World Medical Association in 1964 and revised at Tokyo in 1975.

6. Marcia Angell, "The Ethics of Clinical Research in the Third World," and Peter Lurie and Sidney M. Wolfe, "Unethical Trials of Interventions to Reduce Perinatal Transmissions of the Human Immunodeficiency Virus in Developing Countries," *New England Journal of Medicine*, Vol. 337, No. 12 (September 18, 1997), pp. 847–849. For further discussion of this theme, see Peter A. Clark, "The Ethics of Placebo-Controlled Trials for Perinatal Transmission of HIV in Developing Countries," and Robert J. Levine, "The 'Best Proven Therapeutic Method' Standard in Clinical Trials in Technologically Developing Countries," *Journal of Clinical Ethics*, Vol. 9, No. 2 (Summer 1988), pp. 156–166 and 167–172.

7. Harold Varmus and David Satcher, "Ethical Complexities of Conducting Research in Developing Countries," *New England Journal of Medicine*, Vol. 337, No. 14 (October 2, 1997), pp. 1003–1005.

8. Michael Specter, "Urgency Tempers Ethics Concerns in Uganda African Trial of AIDS Vaccine," *New York Times*, October 1, 1998.

9. Daniel J. Kevles and Leroy Hood, editors, *The Code of Codes* (Cambridge, Mass.: Harvard University Press, 1992), p. 239. Reference is to Daniel Kahneman and Amos Tversky, "The Framing of Decisions and the Psychology of Choice," *Science*, 211 (1981), pp. 453–458.

10. Elizabeth Bouvia, a twenty-six-year-old California woman suffering from cerebral palsy, was almost totally paralyzed. In 1983, she asked for hospital admission in order to receive pain treatment while starving herself to death. While the lower courts agreed that she had a right to commit suicide, they added that she did not have the right to have others assist her in doing so. Ultimately, the judge

authorized the hospital to feed her against her will and the appeals court let the lower court decision stand.

11. Gregory E. Pence, *Classic Cases in Medical Ethics*, second edition (Boston: McGraw-Hill, 1995), p. 45.

12. Philip J. Hilts, "Medicine Remains as Much Art as Science," *New York Times*, September 21, 1997.

13. A typical news report—one of many—described the discovery:

The cloning was done by Dr. Ian Wilmut, a 52-year-old embryologist at the Roslin Institute in Edinburgh, Scotland. . . .

While other researchers had previously produced genetically identical animals by dividing embryos soon after they had been formed by eggs and sperm, Wilmut is believed to be the first to create a clone using DNA from an adult animal. Until now, scientists believed that once adult cells had differentiated—to become skin or eye cells, for example—their DNA would no longer be usable to form a complete organism.

Wilmut reported that as a source of genetic material, he had used udder, or mammary, cells from a 6-year-old adult sheep. The cells were put into tissue culture and manipulated to make their DNA become quiescent. Then Wilmut removed the nucleus, containing the genes, from an egg cell taken from another ewe. He fused that egg cell with one of the adult udder cells.

When the two cells merged, the genetic material from the adult took up residence in the egg and directed it to grow and divide. Wilmut implanted the developing embryo in a third sheep, who gave birth to a lamb that is a clone of the adult that provided its DNA. The lamb, named Dolly, was born in July and seems normal and healthy, Wilmut said. (Gena Kolata, "With Cloning of a Sheep, Ethical Ground Shifts," *New York Times*, February 24, 1997)

14. "A Controlled Trial to Improve Care for Seriously Ill Hospitalized Patients; The Study to Understand Prognoses and Preferences for Outcomes and Risks of Treatments," *Journal of the American Medical Association*, Vol. 274 (November 22–29, 1995), pp. 1591–1598.

15. Ron Winslow, "Plan to Ease Pain, Cost of Dying Proves Futile, Study Says," *Wall Street Journal*, November 24, 1995, quoting William Knaus, University of Virginia, who headed the study.

16. For a creative and sophisticated modern example of the relationship of story and moral education, see Elizabeth Baird Saenger, *Exploring Ethics Through Children's Literature* (Pacific Grove, Calif.: Critical Thinking Press, 1993), Books 1 and 2.

17. Donnie J. Self et al., "The Relationship of Empathy to Moral Reasoning in First-Year Medical Students," *Cambridge Quarterly of Healthcare Ethics* (1955), No. 4, p. 452.

18. For a brief discussion of philosophy for children, as well as other approaches to moral education, see Radest, *Can We Teach Ethics*, chapter 4.

19. Within the past several years a "character education partnership" has been active in the field. For a recent text, see Thomas Lickona, *Educating for Character* (New York: Bantam, 1991). An example of a text written within a liberal context is Michael Schulman, *The Passionate Mind* (New York: Free Press, 1991).

20. For example, see Jean Piaget, *The Moral Judgment of the Child* (New York: Free Press, 1965).

21. By way of example there is James Rest's Defining Issues Test (DIT). See James R. Rest, *Moral Development: Advances in Research and Theory* (New York: Praeger, 1986).

22. Briefly, Kohlberg identified six stages that may be summed up as follows: stages one and two were egocentric, and understood fairness in terms of individual need; stages three and four were social and conventional, and understood fairness in terms of conformity and lawfulness; stages five and six were principled, and understood fairness in terms of equality and what Kohlberg called "reciprocity," that is, where the identity of the subject was irrelevant other than the fact of his or her status as a rational being (Kant) or a being with legitimate basic interests (Rawls).

23. The notion of "justice as fairness," as Kohlberg used it, was taken over from John Rawls, *A Theory of Justice* (Cambridge, Mass.: Belknap Press, 1971). To Kohlberg's credit, he understood that moral cognition had to have a content to make any sense at all, even if it was only the minimal content he chose.

24. For a discussion of these and other developments, see Lisa Kuhmerker, editor, *The Kohlberg Legacy* (Birmingham, Ala.: R.E.P. Books, 1991).

25. Lawrence Kohlberg, "My Personal Search for Universal Morality," ibid., p. 17.

26. Reprinted in Joseph Reimer, Diana Pritchard Paolitto, and Richard Hersh, editors, *Promoting Moral Growth*, second editions (Prospect Heights, Ill.: Waveland Press, 1990), pp. 54–55.

27. Carol Gilligan, *In a Different Voice* (Cambridge, Mass.: Harvard University Press, 1982), pp. 26–29 passim.

28. Hilde Lindemann Nelson, editor, *Stories and Their Limits* (New York: Routledge, 1997), pp. xii–xiii.

29. Alisdair MacIntyre, *After Virtue* (Notre Dame, Ind.: University of Notre Dame Press, 1981).

30. For a helpful summary of ethics under a modern inspiration, see C. D. Broad, *Five Types of Ethical Theory* (New York: Harcourt Brace, 1930).

31. More recently, "virtue" theory (for example, see MacIntyre, *After Virtue*) and "casuistry" (for example, see Albert R. Jonsen and Stephen Toulmin, *The Abuse of Casuistry* [Berkeley: University of California Press, 1987]) have challenged "modernism" in ethics and attempted a move toward a less analytic method. Feminist theories have, of course, challenged the notion of rationality itself as reflecting a gender-based way of thinking. For example, see Susan M. Wolf, *Feminism and Bioethics: Beyond Reproduction* (New York: Oxford University Press, 1996).

32. E. P., "Death Brings Changes," unpublished memoir, November 1997.

33. Following an automobile accident in January 1983, Nancy Cruzan, a twenty-five-year-old woman, was declared to be in a persistent vegetative state (PVS) and the family asked that she not be kept alive by artificial feeding and hydration. In 1988, the Missouri Supreme Court, overruling the lower court, forbade the disconnection of the feeding tube. On appeal, the U.S. Supreme Court (1990) upheld the Missouri ruling on the grounds that "clear and convincing evidence" of Mrs. Cruzan's wishes was not available, although a "right to die" was acknowledged. However, after the state of Missouri withdrew from the case—its interest in sustaining its statute on withdrawal of treatment having been sustained—a

lower court granted permission for disconnecting the tube. Twelve days later, in December 1990, Nancy Cruzan died. The decision was crucial in establishing the importance of living wills and medical powers of attorney.

34. N. Ann Davis, "The Right to Refuse Treatment," in *Intending Death*, Tom L. Beauchamp, editor (Upper Saddle River, N.J.: Prentice-Hall, 1996), p. 116.

35. Barbara Mitchell, "Somebody's Mother," *Reflections* (Department of Philosophy, Oregon State University), Vol. 4, No. 2 (August 1997), p. 3.

CHAPTER 3

Whose Story Is It?

STORIES AREN'T CASES

When we tell stories, we are on the way to "thinking with cases" but we are not there yet. Stories are seductive. They invite us into a world that seems real enough—we forget it's "only" a story—and yet they are artifacts of imagination and point of view. Beneath the surface, the distinction between fiction and nonfiction is often elusive. And it was just this tempting mixture of appearance and reality that led Plato, despite his traditionalism, to banish poets from the Republic. Stories are dangerous, and not just because they "picture the gods falsely." Stories describe a *what-is* but they pretend to be *what-is*. As such, they substitute one world for another without warning us that they are doing so. Everything we see, read, or hear comes to us without confessing its selectivity, perspective, belief system.[1] As the recurrence of revisionist histories, the revivals of great drama, and the longevity of classical and biblical epics remind us, we tell and retell stories for different ends and from within changing moments. Stories reflect the passage of time and taste, exhibit shifting styles, interests, and values. Typically, however, this partiality is hidden. Stories may serve as escape or excuse, as revelation or obfuscation, but it is not always clear what is escaped and what is revealed. Stories, more often than not, reveal the teller and the told-to as much as they reveal alternate worlds, mirror worlds. The story line is not necessarily the story. Plot can usually be summed up in a paragraph or two, as tens of thousands of high school English students have discovered in cramming

for examinations. Since there are just so many plots to go around, originality is rare. Thus stories seem like each other. Character, conflict, and
style make the difference.

When someone tells the "same" story I've just told, it turns out not to
be the *same* at all. The telling is evoked by the told-to as much as it is
conveyed by the teller. The moment and the mood—indeed, the fact of
repetition itself—shift the story so that retelling is always another telling.
I am puzzled when I hear someone repeat *my* story. It is both recognizable and different. For example, it is a tactic of effective labor mediation
to ask the antagonists to shift places, to retell the story in order to locate
misperception, disagreement, confusion, and, not least of all, to encourage understanding. In the same vein, Lawrence Kohlberg was on target
in calling "moral musical chairs" an instrument for developing moral insight. Nor is it necessarily the "facts" that differ in the retelling. The issue
is seldom one of untruthfulness or error. Untruthfulness and error, after
all, depend upon some baseline "truth." And it is the "truth" that is
elusive.

As with any seduction, what is hidden teases and what is revealed
hides. This adds to the pleasure of stories. Thus, the surprise ending of
an O. Henry story or the denouement of a detective story or the imagination of science fiction. But seduction is problematic when, as in the
clinical situation, we realize that consequences beyond the telling—psychological, moral, political—follow from the story, and vary with its telling. Surgeons tell a surgical story and internists a medical story. We tell
who we are and we hear who we are. Nor is this only a clinical datum.
I recall an incident from my military service at a U.S. Army hospital. Senator Joseph McCarthy was then riding high, and he was holding hearings
of suspected "subversives" at military posts, including our own. I was
discussing the matter with my supervising psychiatrist. The senator's actions seemed to me a violation of civil liberties that called for public
comment, if not protest. I can still hear the psychiatrist's immediate response. "What a terrific opportunity for therapy," he said. I'm sure that
if I had raised the question with the commanding officer, he would have
had a command response. The story calls attention to the puzzling difference between truthfulness and truth, a difference that cannot simply be
dismissed as the difference between subjectivity and objectivity. At any
rate, it is clear enough that the moralist, like the clinician, cannot rely for
judgment on the shifting ground of stories. A move is needed, and that
gets us from story to case. It is a difficult and even dangerous move.

The problematic nature of the story is not simply the result of the
peculiarities of the first person who gets to tell it, the about-to-be patient
who reports his or her discomforts, pains, and feelings. Clearly, he or
she initiates the clinical narrative and so establishes the ground of all

future stories, sets in motion both narrative development and clinical action. But the fact that the story is what it is because of who and when the teller *is*, shadows the reliability of the clinical narrative. A pain *is*; a symptom *means*. For that move from being to meaning, transition from person to patient, is necessary—a shift of place, so to speak. A new transaction take place, a new relationship comes into being, that is, the relationship of doctor and patient. At the same time, the patient's story is the source of clinical diagnosis and clinical error. This double-edged feature is reflected in the effort of the physician to probe, interpret, verify . . . to embed the story in practices. He or she listens beyond the boundaries of this particular story, and yet the story does not go away. Instead, listening enables awareness of how uncertain matters can become. This listening relies on and motivates the institutional demand for standard recording and reporting in order to account for the positional subjectivities of patient and family, and, less overtly, of physician and consultant. Of course, these "standards" are dependent on stories, too. They arise within yet another story, a tradition, the story of the practice community. But its problematics are denied. We do not confess the vagaries of its sources or its intentions. Typically, this practice community story as story is suppressed. We become aware of it only as we attend to history, that is, the history of the creation of the practice community itself. So pretending to exhibit eternal values and unbroken continuities, the medical community is in fact a creature of its moment in time; today's organized medicine is, in fact, a very modern creature.

Standard procedures do more than ensure accuracy and transferability. They are, like other routines, also forms of power and self-protection. As Daniel F. Chambliss notes, "When standard procedure is followed, courage is unnecessary. . . . Sometimes such a case [emergency surgery] will challenge all the staff's resources. . . . To maintain one's composure while under tremendous pressures of time and fatefulness requires all the courage a staff can muster."[2]

But what is missed, particularly when the story is reduced to procedure—a case history, a chart—is that both the teller and the told-to also need to be probed and interpreted. There is no privileged position outside of the event. That is what we learn when an ethics consult faces the difficult case. Thankfully, more often than not, the ordinary moral situation can omit the lesson. If habit did not rule, the patient might never be treated. Yet habit is always under the cloud of distortion. Thus, to call something "ordinary" is already to interpret, but we do not, perhaps cannot, pay attention to what we have done. Like the teller, the told-to has his or her own subjectivity that often goes unrecognized, as if the told-to were merely an observer or recorder, someone who can successfully remain outside of the story. As a doctor wrote:

Student physicians in med school are immersed in a culture in which patients are thought of primarily as biological systems that have illnesses unconnected to their emotional health or their spiritual well-being. One of my most vivid memories of med school is of the Kafkaesque internal medicine conferences in which white coat after white coat would solemnly file into the Faulkner amphitheater. A "presence" would step to the lectern and, without so much as a greeting, deliver a rapid-fire rendition from memory of laboratory values and X-ray studies. The patient was not just anonymous but devoid of any hopes or fears, and never did the physicians express any emotional connection to the person with the disease.[3]

We can catch ourselves in the act of shaping the story to the particularity of the listener that again returns us to the relationship of teller and told-to. Our intentions—to impress, convince, amuse, teach, or what have you—reshape the story. But the listener also has reasons for listening. Response, as it were, becomes part of the story. When there is a mismatch—for instance, I want to amuse, you want to convince; I want to protest, you want to "do" therapy—we miss the point, and the story falls flat. The mismatch can even turn deadly, as in religious warfare over the meaning of a biblical injunction or political warfare over a treaty's history.

Stories fascinate us. But fascination is not sufficient for biomedical ethics or for moral education. Curiosity drives discovery, generates the compulsion to know more, and to find out how it all comes out. Because it is suspect—fascination takes us down blind alleys, tempts us to mere wishfulness—the clinical story needs its efforts at objectivity, impartiality, and authority. These are intended as protections against the story and not just protections of the teller and told-to. As it were, the case becomes an antagonist to the story. However, stimulated by the same experiences that produce the field of biomedical itself—such as the scientific and technological effects on realities like birth and death, the economic conflicts in a universe of finite resources, the challenge to authority in the name of rights and equality, the pluralization of cultures—today's clinical story breaks with tradition. The protections of routine and objectivity aren't working as they once did.

The struggle of story and case suggests a clinical dialectic. For example, the Working Group on Promoting Physician Personal Awareness reported:

Physicians' personal characteristics, their past experiences, values, attitudes, and biases can have important effects on communication with patients. . . . Because medical training and continuing education programs rarely undertake an organized approach to promoting personal awareness, we propose a "curriculum" of 4 core topics for reflection and discussion. The topics are physicians' beliefs and attitudes, physicians' feelings and emotional responses to patient care, challenging clinical situations, and physician self-care.[4]

Luckily, no story is just a story. If it were, it would be, as we say, "merely anecdotal." But a story is part of a literature, and so of an emerging narrative community. Typically, one story leads to another and then another. But, despite efforts at rationalization, what guides the sequence remains unclear. No formal logic predicts which story will flow from another or how it will flow from another. At the same time, there is a thread of meaning that connects them. So we say, "that reminds me . . ." Or else, meaning can be uncovered when stories are interrupted, as in the aside or the commentary. A phrase or word may trigger a memory, although the thing remembered may appear to be utterly disconnected from what went before. So we try to explain the connection and, implicitly, ourselves. Less worthy intentions can be at work, too, like the desire to show off or to make an impression and, in the medical and moral situation, to exhibit authority. Challenged, we explain again, but we hesitate, invent, or hide. As it were, we tell a different story while insisting that it is really the same story.

As the clinical story unfolds, the themes of symptom, diagnosis, and treatment recur. Again, memory plays its part, now institutionalized memory. The story becomes a moment in communal wisdom stretching back over time and conveyed to the future by repetition. The story is becoming a case. Thus,

Despite their lowly status, clinical aphorisms play a role in clinical reasoning, the case-based process that characterizes rationality in clinical medicine. Especially in academic medical centers, an ongoing practical inquiry into the relation of knowledge and action in the care of particular patients takes place daily, almost hourly, on every specialty service. These discussions of individual cases—narrative accounts of medical attention beginning with the patient's presentation of symptoms—model the clinical reasoning that is the goal of medical education. . . . As conversation, these cases constitute much of the profession's communal knowledge and collegiality . . . in the discussion of interesting and troublesome cases, physicians invoke the familiar maxims. "The diagnosis is usually made from the history," they'll say. Or, "Keep in mind Occam's razor." The sayings have the ring of collective wisdom. . . . They are collegial reminders of the weight of accumulated experience and an effective means of closing off discussion.[5]

As biomedical ethics enters the clinical situation—some would say intrudes into it—discussion is hard to close off, authority is in question, and the maxims that guide conduct are as likely to be moral as medical. So clinical conversation comes to include terms like "double effect" and "conflict of interest" and "autonomy." Moral principles like "beneficence" and "nonmaleficence" become shortcuts to judgment. Stories, in other words, are being edited. The mythic doctor–patient relationship, once said to characterize the clinical story, is transformed into an extended set of transactional relationships. In the clinical story being born, the teller and the told-to are pluralized and historicized.

PRIVILEGING THE EVENT

In a time of epistemological innocence, so to speak, it was possible to say unambiguously what the clinical story was about and to know who had the right to tell it. From the doctor–patient relationship, the story was about the knower and the known, and about the symptom, the diagnosis, and the cure. Within the authoritative structure of that story, each referent seemed unproblematic. The patient was the recipient; the physician, the agent; the symptom, the entry; the diagnosis and treatment, the activity. These could, as it were, be lifted out of any similar clinical story and fitted into the "new" clinical story. The story conformed to expectations.[6] Actor and theme and conduct could be understood as parts of a case. The story was still present, still available in the background. The patient could, in a sense, retell it if asked, even protest if misunderstood. Roles and hierarchies, however, were clearly defined. Conventions were observed. Above all, in the traditional narrative, a fact was a fact and what was happening, was really happening. The case was, in other words, a metastory, a story about stories, a story of reliabilities.

Today, of course, the case is technologized. In this modernist rendering—the bedside visit, the checkup, the review of vital signs—the story has difficulty appearing. With telemedicine, the telephone consult, HMO authorizations, and third-party payers, the case swallows the story. At the same time, the case is in danger of losing its hold on reality, of ceasing to be a case at all. A recent report describes the kind of thing that is happening.

It was a routine exchange between nurse and patient, except for one thing: the two were 10 miles apart, communicating over a two-way video hookup with a few medical devices attached. . . . Tele-medicine is helping nurses monitor patients with heart and lung problems, diabetes, serious skin disorders, wounds, anxiety attacks, hemophilia and spinal-cord injuries. . . . But some patients of Kaiser Permanente, the big HMO based in Oakland, California, declined to participate. . . . "A certain amount of what a patient wants is human contact," said William Reed, a senior executive with Olsten Corp., a big home health care company based in Melville, New York. . . . And William England, a tele-medicine project officer in the Federal Health Care Financing Administration, said, "We have reservations about relying on the patient rather than a provider being in the home." But, he added, "If managed care finds that it's a cost effective delivery, we would be interested."[7]

To be sure, no case is ever as neatly a vehicle of community wisdom as tradition would have it. Religious influence, political pressures, and economic considerations are not modern inventions. But it was once possible to act as if these things didn't matter. The myth of the purely medical interest persists. The tonality of the doctor's visit to the bedside, of the patient's anxiety in the hospital or examination room, of the muted fears of the family in the waiting room establish a context where doubt begs for reassurance. Even the frightening diagnosis is strangely comforting. At last it becomes possible to know what is going on and to know what to do about it. The "hopeless" case, after all, leaves many things to be done. The physician tries to relieve pain. The patient and family are freed to admit to sadness, and in the extreme to prepare to mourn. Anxiety is resolved into action. The urgency of control is reinforced. Things, even bad things, become manageable if not soluble. Well hidden, the insecurities of medicine remain. Ignorance is likely. No diagnosis, no prognosis is absolute. Surprise—the unforeseen recovery, the remission—is a possibility. And while this is part of the language of the bedside—"We can't really be sure," and "There's always hope"—doubt is neither communicated nor welcomed. The doctor may want to speak clearly; the patient does not want to hear clearly. Neither escapes the need for self-defense.

Things are changing. Paradoxically, just as medicine is becoming more dependable with the move toward a more sophisticated science and technology, doubt is increasing. Nor is this surprising, for it is the way modern sciences work. For them, the question is the clue and the next question reveals the process of discovery. Probabilities are more effective than certainties; usable predictions emerge statistically. Indeed, doubt itself is institutionalized, surrounded by committees. In medicine, the desirability of a "second" opinion and more; the mobility that makes the search for other medical options likely; the openness to "nontraditional" therapies; the overwhelming availability of tests, technologies, and chemistries. These open the clinical situation to the point where a fact ceases to be an end point. The clinical decision is not dictated but adjudicated. Even death becomes a judgment.[8] Nothing is final until someone says so, and it is the saying as much as the fact that makes it so. But it is not as clear as it once was who the sayer is to be, and with what authority and with what justification. Nor is it clear what counts as a fact. By way of example,

Mr. H. was a 23 year old man admitted through the emergency department with postrespiratory arrest. . . . After three days, neurological evaluations resulted in a determination of brain-death utilizing several diagnostic tests: EEG, Brain Flow Scan, and Physical exam with apnea test. . . . The family . . . would not accept the diagnosis of brain-death. . . . The attending physician was willing to give the family time to adjust/accept the diagnosis. . . . The original neurologist ordered another EEG with the family present. The EEG technologist explained the test and the results in detail. . . . The family continued to deny the brain-death determination. . . . The H. family was unimpressed by the parade of experts.

The director of pastoral care at the hospital remarked about the case:

Is brain dead the same as really dead? Of course not! . . . Brain-death, in my opinion, is simply a futility judgment that has gained widespread acceptance in the
medical community. . . . After all, this brain-dead patient is not a cold stiff corpse
but rather a young, warm body with a chest that rises and falls with every artificial
breath.[9]

The collusion of democracy and science has muddied both case and
story. So the story may overwhelm the case, perhaps in reaction against
the move toward depersonalization that is the loss of the story. At times,
the case vanishes as the patient calls the tune, denying clinical realities,
as when futility is rejected and medical judgment is deemed mere opinion, dispensable opinion. Or else, the case moves from clinic to business
office, board room, or legislature, to other kinds of practice communities.
In turn, these evoke their own stories. So stories multiply and appear in
new kinds of settings. We are left, finally, with the problem of authorship
as the story enters the hurly-burly world of doings and sufferings and
calculatings.

A confusion of stories and cases and contexts is not surprising.
The deconstructionist, as it were, enters the clinic. If he or she is to be
believed, everyone—and no one—is an author. What-is becomes just another fiction, only now it is a fiction that somehow intrudes on experience, perhaps in its more radical rendering is experience. Standing
against this postmodern interplay of illusions are the existential facts that
are, for all their ambiguity, unavoidable obstacles. Prolonged or immediate: death is, birth is, pain is. The kidney or heart or lung or liver does
not do its work. The psychotic patient is in another world. The arm or
leg is broken. There is, in other words, a double truth at work; is-ness
and story share its claims. So it is not possible to deny the existential
fact, but neither is it possible to deny the moment of adjudication. Even
the obvious is less than obvious. For example,

There is no standard clinical definition of "terminal." The word is often loosely
used to refer to any patient with a lethal disease. . . . It should be noted that,
under Medicare and Medicaid eligibility rules, reimbursement for hospice care
requires a diagnosis of a terminal condition with a prognosis of six months or
less to live. This is an administrative rather than a clinical definition of terminal.
We believe that a diagnosis of terminal condition, in contrast to a life-threatening
condition, should be made cautiously. It is perilous to predict precisely how long
a terminal patient will live. More than a few studies have shown that even experienced clinicians are notoriously inaccurate in such predictions.[10]

In the midst of conflict and transformation, the beginning is still the
event. Grant all the complexities of place and position and prejudice, and

the beginning is still the event and the first voice is still the patient's. In other words, the biomedical story does not happen until something else happens, something upon which the story depends for its coming to be. To be sure, the event as told by the patient is an outcome of insight and reasoning, a result of reading the story back, as it were, into its genesis. The event is not nakedly evident but is conveyed in the patient's story and in elaborated clinical narrations. Nevertheless, without the event— however *it* is captured—no story would appear and no story would need to be told.

But all that is still ahead as the story is told and the case evolves. Before these is the event. It is felt and lived by a known someone to whom it is happening before it is conveyed and assessed. And that pragmatic need to convey opens upon the relationship between the aesthetic, the historic, and the clinical. In these modes of conveyance is the opportunity for grasping anew the clinical situation. Obviously, the narration, the case history, the chart, the committee reviews, the recommendations and evaluations are modes of conveyance that move toward abstraction. These tellings, in turn, are dependent in two ways: on the practice community as a community of storytellers and, less evidently, on more primitive intermediate modes of conveyance. The latter persist as reminders of the event: the reported pain, suffering, discomfort, as well as the sights and smells that, encountered in the sick, are so different from those encountered in the not-sick. The waiting room, the hospital corridor, and the patient's room meet the senses before a word is uttered. Something is going wrong. For the told-to, this stirs the hunch, the instinct, the intuition, the educated guess. Without these earliest moves that tie it back to what is going on, the case would, like the classroom's illustration, lack effectiveness as a way of thinking, would be merely abstract and only an exercise. Conveyance begins in response that is felt by the teller and perceived by the told-to. A bodily movement is recognized; a smell, a glazed eye is perceived; a pain is reported. The event carries a tangible language that speaks to the senses before it is measured and calculated. Conveyance includes discomfort—soon a shared discomfort—a feeling that something isn't the way it ought to be. Only later does a category like symptom—medical or moral—come into play, a category that connects story to case and case to other cases.

The event that appears as a unity in the having will soon be transformed, taken apart, translated by story and case. The event also includes my responses to self as other, the internal dialogue in which the event is recognized. In that moment of internality, denials and confessions appear. The event struggles for recognition against my resistance to recognizing it. I don't want to admit I'm sick. I say, "It will pass," or "It's nothing, really." Soon, however, resistance gives way to relieved admission, and with that, control passes to others. The story becomes political as well as physiological. The patient tries for control but soon surrenders. The language of the event is on its way to the language of the practice. Transforming possibilities appear in expressive movements like the reaction to a probing finger or the grunt of pain, and, typically, they appear in some kind of retreat, as in clinical depression or an inability to eat or drink. The body speaks its language, too.

Sometimes, poetry helps us remember the event before it is layered over. Thus, a dying patient is described by his granddaughter:

> He ate sadness
> in that white room,
> with his throat choking when he talked,
> with his hand chained to an infusion, . . .
> unable to escape.[11]

The event is the first utterance of a dialogue, privileging the event as a strategic moment and anchoring all that follows. Yet the event is inadequate, needing the evocations of story, category, and connection in order to "make sense." Failing this, we are helplessly lost in responses. At the same time, the need to "make sense" threatens the loss of the event in the category.

Sometimes, to be sure, all we can do is respond, standing by helplessly and letting event be event. The dialogue can go nowhere. This failure of dialogue signals that we do not know how or where to proceed and, in many instances, if and why to proceed. Thus, the modern puzzle of "medical futility" that accompanies technological sophistication and economic scarcity, and that is a confession we do not want to make. Indeed, "futility" reveals the ambiguity of stories just because it is both self-evident and elusive. I "know" when the situation is futile, yet cannot provide a usable definition. So I recall an ethics committee searching for futility "guidelines." The discussion ended with the agreement that the judgments of futility could be made only in the actual case.[12] Futility, we realized, is laden biographically, culturally, religiously, morally, economically, and psychologically. These transform the "self-evident" physiological judgment of futility, forcing medical decision to account for what seems arbitrary from within the clinical situation. Like so much else in biomedicine, futility turns out not to be a purely medical notion. For example,

Last year, attorneys for Fairfax Hospital asked me to be an expert witness on medical ethics for the Baby K. Case. The infant girl, who has anencephaly, was born on October 13, 1992. Anencephaly is a congenital lack of cerebral cortex and almost always leads to death shortly after birth. The standard of care in pediatrics is comfort care only and allowing the infant to die as no treatment exists to replace the cerebral cortex.

Prior to caesarean delivery, her mother Mrs. H., demanded full treatment . . . based on her religious views. She believes that God will heal Baby K. . . . The dispute, which is complex, is about the moral weight of parental autonomy and religious liberty when conflicting with physicians' recommendations based on standard of care. . . . If anencephaly is not the ultimate type of futility case, then the word "futility" is meaningless and physicians have no authority to refuse any demand for treatment. . . . The bottom line for me is that in any ethical view that tries to balance respect for persons with fairness in using the community's resources, everything has limits, even a mother's love and faith in God.[13]

Futility may even be an aesthetic category. It tells us that sometimes we can only be witnesses, perhaps commentators, like the chorus in classical Greek tragedy. Helpless, we are yet drawn in. We are no longer merely strangers. Another dialogue opens, the dialogue of letting go. A religious sensibility thus intersects clinical and moral sensibilities. We encounter the themes of fate and surrender. We learn that the story ends but does not finish. Acceptance replaces closure. Thus biomedical ethics amends the clinical story. The drama of victory and defeat, the "war against disease," that shaped an earlier story allowed us to desert the patient when "nothing more can be done." It was left for family, nurse, and chaplain to remain behind. But today the physician will know that he or she is expected to remain, too. Preparation for death and dying becomes an explicit feature of the practice community. As Howard Brody remarked, "My patients, above all else, want me to be there for them through the course of the illness. . . . The problem is . . . you get to the few exceptional cases . . . and you've genuinely run out of other options. . . . Can I then abandon the patient because I have to say, 'No, medicine doesn't do this [assisted suicide] anymore? . . . Or, do I say, 'Is it appropriate for me to go the last mile that the patient's asking me to go with him?' "[14]

We can, of course, be very busy and still have little to do. A student of mine, a nurse, remembered her first assignment:

Room 3, Bed 2: Seventeen-year-old boy, C3–4 fracture, paralyzed, on the ventilator, arrives. Football practice injury. His family, school and community are devastated. He is the star player. Kenny only lived a month or so. I remember thinking he was lucky.

A seventy-year-old C5 fracture—from a tornado. Not another one. On a ventilator. He lives about six months. I'm glad this is finally over.

Room 4, Bed 2: Seventeen-year-old—motor vehicle accident. C3–4 fracture, paralyzed, on a ventilator. We had a lot of opportunities to let this boy die, but we didn't.[15]

With hopelessness confessed, we learn humility and frustration. Even the futile story makes novel connections, as when the doctor learns to remain at the bedside. The conversation continues, although the event's initiation is vanishing into fatality.

Still, we try to deny the event. We escape to the case and don't hear the story. Oedipus-like, we blind ourselves. Oedipus-like, we pay the penalty. The event, left behind, returns, a surprised act of memory. We are forced by event to connect, perhaps trying to tame it by renaming it as emergency or as diagnosis. Once named—the magic of naming—other stories and actions are enabled. But—ambiguity again—blindness is enabled, too. The event is so terrifying that we can tolerate it only by losing it in language, by hiding its character. In that, we reveal we are radically unprepared for the return of the story. And we have set ourselves up for unpreparedness. Thus, a doctor confesses:

I had always felt inexpert when a patient was near death. I knew I was not alone: the gallows humor evinced comments like "the patient is circling the drain," or "about to transfer to Central Office," reflected the clumsy way all of us in the hospital dealt with impending death. Give me a patient with massive gastric bleeding or ventricular fibrillation and I am a model of efficiency and purpose. Put me at a deathbed, a slow dying, and purpose is what I lack. I, who till then have been supportive, involved, can find myself mute, making my visits briefer, putting on an aura of great enterprise—false enterprise. I finger my printed patient list, study the lab results on the chart which at this point have no meaning. For someone dealing so often with death, my ignorance felt shameful.[16]

Or, as a nurse put it:

We have become
those old crusty nurses
we used to pity and avoid.[17]

Stories are not just expressive and responsive. There is a demanding pragmatism in them. They transform the fortuitous into the deliberate. Of course, recognition of an event signals readiness to see, hear, smell, and above all, attend. Memory's eye is trained to see connections. For this, we need models that, like adage and maxim, find event and evoke response. But models have a way of turning mechanistic, impersonal, distant just because they are successful. Successful models reveal that stories become a story which is so well known that it need not be told at all, only signaled. So the story is ritualized, reenacted. The setting is the practice community. In it are located the wisdoms of the calling, its culture, so to speak. But the community also evolves. Thus, it provides both the institutional memory for stories and accretes new stories, although slowly. Organized as and around cases, the practice community is a wisdom literature accessible to its initiates. It conserves, transmits, legitimates. As Alisdair MacIntyre puts it:

By a "practice" I am going to mean any coherent and complex form of socially established cooperative activity through which goods internal to that form of activity are realized in the course of trying to achieve those standards of excellence which are appropriate to, and partially definitive of, that form of activity, with the result that human powers to achieve excellence and human conceptions of the ends and good involved are systematically extended. . . . A practice involves standards of excellence and obedience to rules as well as to the achievement of goods. To enter into a practice is to accept the authority of its standards.[18]

But let things change radically, and the culture loses its moorings. The reenactment empties of content, becomes pro forma. So refinding the continuum of event and response, of story and case, becomes a critical instrument for modeling and re-modeling. Older ways pass into emptiness. The struggle to amend, reconstruct, and replace is waged, now a struggle between orthodoxy and its subversion.

CASE AGAINST STORY

When we privilege the event, we commit ourselves to acts of attentiveness and memory, in particular to recognizing that something is happening to someone in a certain way at a particular time and place. To privilege the event, then, is to understand that it is, in the first instance, its own reality. It is original, that is, it is my event. No matter that similar things seem to have happened to others, no matter that memory reminds us of like happenings; to the patient, the event is in and for itself. It has a first-person reference—it is happening to me and I am happening to it. It has a particular profile. To be sure, this originality invites distortion. After all, things are happening to others while they are happening to me. Things are happening to those who are asked to help and to those who respond or fail to. The edges of the event are blurred and the population of the event grows. But the event encapsulates me, produces a radical isolation of the self. Typically, then, as patient I build walls and resist connections. Of course, I ask for help, for relief. Yet the concern of the other, personal or professional, is both accepted and turned away. An outer civility nods with gratitude at words and acts of sympathy. But these expressions are superficial. Deep down, I do not believe that the other can really care, because the other cannot really know my pain. Within me, the event is imperious. My world narrows to me, and the acts of the others which enter that world are referred back to me. I am, in a sense, again the infant for whom world and self are identical.

This loneliness tells us that the clinical event is always frightening. In one way or another, the clinical event says that something is going wrong with me and that something is threatening me, that something is changing me against my will. The examining room, the hospital, the clinic reinforce this sense of threat, if by nothing else than by their radical otherness—whiteness, sterility, mysterious instruments, anatomical charts. These places are, after all, not freely chosen. I enter involuntarily, as it were. In such a setting, the seeming triviality is not trivial to me; it is trivial only to the other. I complain where no complaint seems justified. The anxiety of "what ifs" is present. Behind even the most routine of procedures—such as the annual checkup, the tonsillectomy, cosmetic surgery—is the unspoken fear of disability and death. In turn, this fear is encouraged by my helplessness. So the event and its story carry mood and tonality. But these, paradoxically, become hideaways, too, so that the clinical ends—relief, cure—may be defeated by the refusals which defend me against anxiety. At the extreme, this is institutionalized as the "noncompliant patient" the diabetic who does not follow a diet, the pregnant woman who drinks, the patient who "forgets" his or her medications. But, in a way, all of us are noncompliant. The story is suppressed, as if the event were not happening, or else it is compulsively repeated, as if incantation would cause it to vanish. Resistance, then, is the barrier to the event.

Breaking into the story becomes necessary. But this is not easy. So shock is required, the shock that allows the story to reveal the event. The shock is yet another physiological fact—a sudden failure of mind or body where helplessness is completed. Even the emergency like excessive bleeding or stroke will need a return to the story, and through it to the event. The emergency medical team will respond to the symptom, but this is a temporizing action, a way of holding the situation steady. As is said, the goal is to "stabilize" the patient. But, sooner or later, the patient, or surrogate, will have to find ways to participate to make action beyond the moment possible.

At the same time, the pragmatics of the clinical situation do not allow indefinite postponements. Scarcity of time and resources, on one side, and imperatives of diagnosis and treatment, on the other, carry an urgency of response. So it is not accidental that practices are designed to break into denial, to force the message that things are not ordinary and that matters cannot wait. Reminiscent of nothing so much as entry into military basic training—which has a similar intention—clothing is removed and a special costume—the embarrassing and revealing hospital gown—takes its place. Intimacies vanish—physical, psychological. Machinery is attached to the body so that breathing, eating, drinking, and blood circulation become symbiotic functions. Time itself is reordered and rescheduled. Food and drink are transformed into diet and dosage.

Excretion is measured and recorded. Indeed, the ordinary choices of living, each and one by one, are replaced. To be sure, this shock strategy walks a risky line between encouraging infantilism and waking to reality.

At the same time, it is assumed that the physician, the nurse, the attendant are somehow apart from the anxiety of the patient. The practice community constructs a reality that delivers the message. Its costume and language are designed to shape that reality and to keep it hidden from those not admitted into membership. Authority, and so the power to decide, is signaled by the white coat, the ever-present stethoscope, the ability to enter the patient's spaces without permission. No doubt this activity is partly accounted for by clinical necessities like rapidity of communication and response. And part is accounted for by a grant of authority like the license to invade the body with knives and the mind with chemicals. And part of this activity is accounted for by yet other necessities, like management and control of more than one patient at a time under conditions that always threaten to break loose. In short, the routines of the practice community have their reasons.

But there are also reasons that are not unambiguously good. Hospital routines, for example, may owe their existence to conveniences that have little, if anything, to do with care or function, and much to do with protecting the practice community. Often, routines assist the patient toward a childhood already forecast by his or her retreat to ego. But then, children are more easily controlled than adults. Record-keeping will, these days, represent defenses against lawsuits rather than clinical needs. Or an accidental tradition may simply dictate that things be done because "that's the way we've always done it." Behind it all, the good and the not so good, two kinds of things happen. The patient is turned into an object; the physician and nurse are turned into an authority. The relationship becomes manipulative and political. The same messages that break into anxiety or insulate the caregiver from chaos become modes of distancing, and thus modes of protection on all sides. As patient, I cede power over myself; I am relieved of responsibility. As caregiver, I take power; I am competent to responsibility. This exchange of powers may be formalized as "informed consent," but situation and anxiety more often than not empty consent of content. Thus, the event and the story are translated into the abstract language of the case. The caregiver goes through the motions because rapid and automatic conduct reflects the needs of the clinical situation. But routine also serves to reinforce the distinction between object and authority. In the outcome, the patient welcomes passivity and the authority of the other becomes decisive.[19]

The clinical situation is ambiguous, its meaning ambivalent, its genesis obscured, and its outcome in doubt. It is not surprising, then, to find practices that drive toward the security of clarity. But reality demands hesitation. Yet another anxiety is present, now the anxiety of authority. As caregiver, I must be assured and reassuring, not only for the patient's sake but also for my own. For example, a psychiatrist writes:

A truer cause of care providers' negative feelings toward these patients may be that care providers cannot identify with patients whose physical symptoms are affected by their minds. . . . Further, if they have not identified this possibility with themselves, they may find it exceedingly threatening that persons' emotions *can* cause physical symptoms . . . I recall, as an example, care providers who suspected that a patient had psychogenic blindness. They walked with him arm-in-arm, guiding him directly into the path of a chair. They presumed that if his blindness was truly psychogenic, on an unconscious level he would "see" the chair and avoid it. . . . I recall painfully, my responding in this manner to a patient who was physically healthy but, for psychological reasons, began to fall. When she began to fall, I froze. I did not immediately respond by attempting to catch her. Rather, at that instant, I thought: "She is falling *intentionally* to seek special attention."[20]

Denial and separation make tolerable the things I actually and legitimately do to another and the risks I take for another. Consider the events of a single hour in the hospital room, the invasions and probings that are typical and normative. In fact, failure to invade is failure to do one's duty. Consider how this must reflect back into the being of the nurse or doctor who both recognizes and at the same time dares not recognize a fellow human being. The insulation of the patient is paralleled by the insulation of the caregiver. They may reach toward one another but cannot, perhaps cannot afford to, meet.

Anxiety cannot help but accompany ambiguity. This is as true of the patient as of the physician and nurse. Nothing more clearly reveals this than the language we use. As Arthur Caplan writes:

The language cops would certainly be appalled to see what doctors and nurses do to the language in the privacy of the workplace. But while the grammar may be flawed and the terminology opaque to the outside, the medical slang tossed around in the hospital trenches shows just how uneasy doctors and nurses feel about the value of what they do in our emergency rooms and intensive care units and their doubts about what it does to the patients who receive it.

It may offend some ears to hear that dirtballs and technopatients are common terms among healers who work in these settings. But the language reveals the values crisis that simmers just beneath the surface in these places as health care professionals vent their anger and ambivalence.

No one wants to think of Mom or Dad being flogged by medical technology, but the reality is that there does come a time as the doctors and nurses know when "aggressive care" becomes more aggressive than caring.[21]

The formal and informal language of the practice community can be heard as insensitivity. Of course, language facilitates the ability to move quickly and effectively. But it also is an insider code that announces who does and who does not belong. Authority, after all, has historically captured language in order to exercise control. But more deeply, language is an instrument for managing the anxiety of patient and caregiver alike. Pain and death are inescapable and yet must be escaped. I recall a nurse who presented the case of an ALS patient (amyotrophic lateral sclerosis, or Lou Gehrig's disease) to our ethics committee.[22] There is no cure. A patient can survive for many months, all the while deteriorating and suffering before finally dying. The doctors had, by and large, deserted. The nurses continued their efforts to postpone death, responding to the family's wishes and resenting the doctor's retreat. Everyone regretted that "extraordinary measures" had been taken when comfort care would have served. But now, it was too late to change the way things had to be done. I was struck by her description of the frustrations and angers of the nurses and by the tone of commitment and despair in which she reported. She would catch herself as she spoke, retreat to the language of the case, break out again into the language of the story. It was clear enough that person and practice, as it were, struggled with one another. At the same time, language enabled practice to survive prudence and feeling.

Gallows humor appears in the informal language of the practice community. I can recall the tricks we played on each other in the hospital where I served during my brief military career: the false reading of an X-ray that panicked the novice physician, the apocryphal stories recited in sure-to-be-overheard tones about medical students and interns and corpses. Humor, as usual, enables me to distance myself from you, emphasizes our differences, confirms my superiority. It is another device, another control and protection.

Physicians' shoptalk is not so much boring as it is filled with tales that would strike outsiders as tragic and gruesome. . . . Let one personal experience clarify the point. No sooner did I join a medical school faculty than I met with the chairman and chief of service of various clinical departments . . . to explore what interest each department might have in social medicine. . . . Much of these first conversations turned on "interesting cases," which typically involved descriptions of devastating illnesses. . . . At first I thought these stories were an initiation ritual—was a historian trained to do archival work up to the stuff of medicine? But I slowly learned that this was not a rite of passage but a sharing of anecdotes and gossip; they assumed that because I was part of the faculty, I too would be fascinated by shoptalk.[23]

In many ways, then, language, humor, and routine separate nurse and doctor from the dangerous things that must go on in the clinical situation. As laughter, incantation, or automaticization reveals, the extraordinary must be transformed into the ordinary. Without intending it, then, the practice community isolates caregiver and patient. For the former, however, the extraordinary must become ordinary as a matter of survival; for the latter, the event is extraordinary in its being. Language and routine conspire toward forgetfulness. The case, as it were, defeats the story. At the same time, the event and the story will not go away. The story, then, defeats the case. As with the nurse who reported the ALS case, a double message is inevitable.

CASE AND STORY

The patient, struggling to keep his or her story, resists becoming a case. The practice community, on the other hand, needs the case in order to do its work and in order to be a practice. It is, to be sure, an unequal struggle. The power of the practice and the helplessness of the patient conspire against the story. But, declaring victory for one or the other, we lose the clinical situation. That is clear enough once we recognize that it is moral, cultural, and political as well as psychophysiological. Histories, values, and communities are at work in shaping the medical "indicators," and they, in turn, are reshaped by those indicators. If nothing else, this elaborated sensitivity to the clinical situation is an outcome of the renewed attention to biomedical ethics. As Mark Kuczewski sums up what he calls a "consensus on method":

Much of the ethicist's skill consists of an ability to transcend the limits of the readily available perspectives from which to construct the narrative.

The perspectives of the health care providers and the perspective that can be gleaned from a chart review often characterize the patient in terms of the limited setting, time frame, and orientation of the hospital. These perspectives conceal much that is of great importance in understanding the moral issues at hand. The knack is to reconstruct the case such that the problems and conflicts . . . form a coherent story. This is usually a process of weaving together a number of different narratives: the patient's, the family's, the various health care providers', the institution's.[24]

Transforming the battle of story and case into dialectic, letting story and case grow each other, is the task. For this, it is not sufficient to privilege the event only as an initiating moment, as if, having done its work, it can safely be put aside. Nor is it sufficient to rely on a story of stories, the case as instance of communal wisdom. So the language of the subject and the language of the practice community meet. But it is an uneasy meeting. Claim and counterclaim become even more vigorous when it is understood that the protections of the practice are threatened by the story and the safety of ego is threatened by the case. But the story cannot vanish and the case cannot be evaded. Illustrating this fact is an oral history on the early days of the AIDS epidemic:

Dr. Leonard Calabreese was one of those who spoke publicly to try to calm people's fears. He recalled a town meeting in a rural area of Ohio on whether a girl with AIDS should be allowed to attend school:

This was like out of some Fellini movie; it was like this angry crowd out there. And I stood up there, and I'm sure I was looked at as this—I probably had hair back then—this long-haired, big-city guy, out there to calm the masses; like "Oh, there's nothing to worry about." And I learned very early on that first of all, 80 percent of people range from being highly compassionate and totally open-minded and uninformed. And 20 percent of people range from being frankly bigoted to mildly bigoted. . . .

And that was a tremendous experience. Angry people! And people saying things that I never even could make up. And then by the end of the night, having the 80 percent of people take over the meeting—because it got mad at the 20 percent that were angry—and finally having a small child get up, like a junior high kid, saying: "I don't understand what you adults are all arguing about because we know how you get AIDS. We know how you don't. And she's just a little girl. She's crippled."[25]

The dialectic of story and case reconstructs our understanding of the clinical situation, acknowledging its originality and its commonality. Of course, this does not always succeed, particularly since the politics of the practice community is powerfully reinforced by the institutions that sustain it, such as medical school certification, licensing, and credentialing.

As a practical matter, it is often possible to act as if the event can be put aside and to treat the case as if it had no story. Unambiguous symptoms, diagnoses, and treatments are presumed to present themselves as unproblematic. Of course the complexities of the clinical situation have not disappeared. Values, interests, and culture remain. But they do not come to the surface. In other words, problems are solved but problematics do not appear. As the common wisdom has it, "If it isn't broke, don't fix it." Unfortunately, however, it is seldom clear whether success flows from the clinical situation as such—it is in fact unproblematic—or whether it flows from the pragmatics, habits, and politics of the practice. Indeed, everything conspires to evade the question.

For better or worse, bioethics disturbs this idyllic situation. So the practice community tries to tame it. For example, it is a commonplace these days to incorporate autonomy and informed consent into the language of the practice community. Typically, patient decision-making is presumed, although it is not unusual for the patient to yield this power to the physician. "Do what you think best" and "What would you do in my place?" are characteristic expressions at the bedside. These are, however, signs of surrender as often as they are assertions of trust. The communication signaled by autonomy and informed consent is subverted. Thus, the physician is uncomfortable with the demands imposed by what are taken to be intrusions into the clinical situation. It is not so much that these are misunderstood or intentionally shortchanged. Rather, the excuse of busyness, together with a presumed medical common sense, justify moral inattention. Moreover, the physician—unlike the nurse—is often inarticulate, unprepared for a discourse that marries story and case. As a survey in Seattle and Minneapolis of 182 families with chronically ill or disabled children reported, "One third of unsupportive experiences were with the very people whose support was needed most: health care professionals, mainly doctors. . . . Other recent studies, as well as interviews with several doctors and patients. . . . show [that] doctors still have a hard time breaking bad news, especially when the patient is a child." The article continued:

"We get very little training in dealing with these issues," said Dr. Robert W. Blum, a pediatrician at the University of Minnesota School of Medicine. . . . "As is true of people in general, we often don't know what to say."
A national survey of 230 primary care doctors released this month by Louis Harris & Associates supported Blum's view, with 61 percent of them saying that the current medical education curriculum did not adequately train them to communicate effectively with patients. . . . Although medical schools students and residents get more training in talking with patients and families than they did a decade ago, doctors say it is often just an elective one-day workshop.[26]

Indeed, the adoption of bioethical references by the practice community almost ensures that they will, more often than not, become routine and so thus pathways to forgetfulness. Thus, the signing of a "consent form" becomes an admissions procedure. But coming, as it does, in the midst of the anxiety of hospital admission and along with seemingly endless forms and documents, it gets the same pro forma treatment as other routine information. Later, consent to specific tests, to surgery, and to other treatments will be discussed, often by a very busy physician, anesthetist, or resident, under conditions where refusal of consent is almost unthinkable. With managed care, ironically, consent does become a salient feature of the clinical situation, but now for economic and legal reasons. At the same time and for the same reasons, the lack of ongoing connection between physician and patient makes the consent discussion itself ambiguous and abstract. After all, discussion of urgent matters like life and death—and for the patient this is the pervasive background of the clinical situation—relies not just on what is said but also on implicit messages. It accompanies words with the cues and interpretations that arise from actual relationships. The intention of informed consent, however, is lost in the new sociology of medicine. "Living wills" and "medical powers of attorney," if acknowledged at all, tend to get similar treatment.[27]

Case and story have difficulty coming together. But what was once the common sense of the matter—the doctor knows, the patient obeys—is under challenge. Clearly, this is likely for nonclinical reasons. Public policies like tax-supported access to medical care and new institutional arrangements like HMOs make it legally, economically, and politically necessary to account for patient choices. Change appears for clinical reasons as well. The possibility of technically prolonging dying, for example, introduces choice to patient and family in ways scarcely imagined a short time ago. Similarly, genetic information and techniques like in vitro fertilization open questions that the physician alone cannot answer. Not least of all, the pluralization of American society raises issues of participation unknown when the clinical situation presumed that an unacknowledged middle-class and white cultural norm was applicable to all.[28]

As different voices gain legitimacy in society, their speakers gain visibility in the clinical situation. Thus the shift in research protocols that once simply took for granted that results of studies of men could, as it were, be applied to the treatment of women. Similarly, and more radically, the diversity of American society now forces acknowledgment that clinical judgment and decision-making are not univocal, are not simply facts of medical biology and specieswide characteristics. For example, in a study to determine "the differences in attitudes of elderly subjects from different ethnic groups toward disclosure of the diagnosis and prognosis of a terminal illness . . ."

The researchers found: "Korean American and Mexican American subjects were more likely to hold a family-centered model of medical decision-making rather than the patient autonomy model favored by most of the African American and European American subjects."[29]

And, in a study on the Navajo Indian reservation in northeast Arizona:

Informants explained that patients and providers should think and speak in a positive way . . . 86% of those questioned considered advance care planning a dangerous violation of traditional Navajo values. These finds are consistent with *hozho*, the most important concept in traditional Navajo culture, which combines concepts of beauty, goodness, order, harmony, and everything that is positive or ideal. Discussing negative information conflicts with the Navajo concept of *hozho* and was viewed as potentially harmful by these Navajo informants.[30]

The clinical situation is interrupted by moral, gender, and cultural issues. With this interruption, case and story cannot avoid the dialectical relationship. The tradition of authority that set these against each other is passing. Thinking with cases gains an enriched content.

NOTES

1. For a discussion of this theme, see Richard Rorty, *Philosophy and the Mirror of Nature* (Princeton, NJ: Princeton University Press, 1992).

2. Daniel F. Chambliss, *Beyond Caring* (Chicago: University of Chicago Press, 1996), p. 51.

3. Alan Bonsteel, "Behind the White Coat," *The Humanist*, Vol. 57, No. 2 (March/April 1997), pp. 15–16.

4. Dennis H. Novack et al., "Calibrating the Physician: Personal Awareness and Effective Patient Care," *Journal of the American Medical Association*, Vol. 278 (1997), pp. 502–509, *Abstracts*, August 13, 1997.

5. Kathryn Montgomery Hunter, "Aphorisms, Maxims, and Old Saws," in *Stories and Their Limits*, Hilde Lindemann Nelson, editor (New York: Routledge, 1997), p. 216.

6. The case presentation, still taught in medical schools, includes patient's chief complaint(s), history of the present illness, medical history, family and social history. In these busy days, this rough topical outline is often accompanied by a patient self-administered checklist as well as by other standard forms intended to ensure accuracy and completeness.

7. Milt Freudenheim, "Medical Care by Telephone: Bedside Manner from Afar?" *New York Times*, February 24, 1997.

8. With the development of transplant and other technologies, and the need for a more rigorous allocation of finite resources, it became particularly important to agree upon a definition of death that was both functional and determinate. From this emerged the notion of "brain death." See "Report of the Ad Hoc Committee of the Harvard Medical School to Examine the Definition of Brain Death, a Definition of Irreversible Coma," *Journal of the American Medical Association*, Vol. 205 (1968), pp. 337–340; President's Commission for the Study of Ethical Problems in Medicine and Biomedical and Behavioral Research, *Defining Death* (Washington, D.C.: U.S. Government Printing Office, 1981). Once again, however, developments outrun definitions, so the issue is under review. See Robert D. Truog, "Is It Time to Abandon Brain Death?" *Hastings Center Report*, Vol. 27, No. 1 (1997), pp. 29–37.

9. "Case Presentation: Brain-Death and the Optimistic Family," *Community Ethics*, Vol. 4, No. 1, 1997.

10. Albert R. Jonsen, Mark Siegler, and William J. Winslade, *Clinical Ethics*, fourth edition (New York: McGraw-Hill, 1998), p. 24.

11. Masayo Kubota, "Grandpa," *The Lancet*, Vol. 350, No. 9085 (October 18, 1997).

12. The inability to arrive at a definitive policy on "futility" is typical. Thus, the Council on Ethical and Judicial Affairs of the American Medical Association urges "health care institutions . . . to adopt a policy on medical futility" but concludes, as we did, that it must follow a "due process" approach. The "Houston Protocol" on medical futility—*Journal of the American Medical Association*, Vol. 276, No.

7 (August 21, 1996), pp. 571–574—similarly concludes for a set of procedures rather than a substantive statement.

13. John C. Fletcher, "Reflections of an Expert Witness in the Baby K. Case," *Bioethics Matters*, Vol. 3, No. 2 (April 1994), p. 8. In another instance:

The case involved a 72-year-old woman in the Massachusetts General Hospital who had multiple medical problems, was comatose and brain-damaged, and was being kept alive on life-support systems. The daughter insisted that doctors continue to keep the woman alive, as this had been her mother's wish. The doctors refused to honor the request because they claimed that the treatment was futile. They removed the woman from the ventilator, and she died shortly afterward. (Kenneth Praeger, "When Medical Treatment is Futile," *Wall Street Journal*, June 29, 1995)

The doctors were sued and a jury found them not guilty of negligence. "It was the first time that a court had exonerated doctors who were sued because of failure to provide treatment that a patient wanted."

14. Howard Brody, "Choosing Death," *The Health Quarterly* (WGBH, Boston), transcript #204 (March 23, 1993), p. 6.

15. Lori Otterstrom, "Trauma Season Begins," unpublished essay, March 1996.

16. Abraham Verghese, *My Own Country* (New York: Vintage Books, 1994), p. 364. I recall a conversation with the executive director of our local hospice. She called my attention to the fact that medical education curricula rarely include the subject of "death and dying." In the past year, however, the American Medical Association announced the development of programs to remedy this defect.

17. Sandy Smith, "Burnt-out Offerings," in *Between the Heartbeats: Poetry and Prose by Nurses*, Cortney Davis and Judy Schaeffer, editors (Iowa City: University of Iowa Press, 1995), p. 185.

18. Alisdair MacIntyre, *After Virtue* (Notre Dame, Ind.: University of Notre Dame Press, 1981), pp. 175, 177.

19. For an empirical study of this process of objectification, see Chambliss, *Beyond Caring*.

20. Edmund G. Howe, "Deceiving Patients for Their Own Good," *Journal of Clinical Ethics*, Vol. 8, No. 3 (Fall 1997), p. 212.

21. Arthur Caplan, *Moral Matters* (New York: John Wiley, 1995), p. 40.

22. A discussion of some of the ethical issues raised in dealing with ALS can be found in David Goldblatt and Jane Greenlaw, "Starting and Stopping the Ventilator for Patients with Amyotrophic Lateral Sclerosis," *Neurological Clinics*, Vol. 7, No. 4 (November 1989), pp. 789–806.

23. David J. Rothman, *Strangers at the Bedside* (New York: Basic Books, 1991), p. 135.

24. Mark Kuczewski, "Bioethics Consensus on Method," in *Stories and Their Limits*, Hilde Lindemann Nelson, editor (New York: Routledge, 1997), p. 137.

25. Malcolm Browne, "For Doctors, Years of Grief and Daring," *New York Times*, December 23, 1997. Excerpts are from eighty interviews in Columbia University's oral history program.

26. Susan Gilbert, "Forget About Bedside Manners: Some Doctors Have No Manners at All," *New York Times*, December 23, 1997.

27. See "A Controlled Trial to Improve Care for Seriously Ill Hospitalized Patients; The Study to Understand Prognoses and Preferences for Outcomes and

Risks of Treatment (SUPPORT)," *Journal of the American Medical Association*, Vol. 274 (1995), pp. 1591–1598; *JAMA Abstracts*, November 22–29, 1995.

28. For example, a study by Thomas E. Finucane and Joseph A. Carrese of the Department of Medicine, The Johns Hopkins University School of Medicine, noted:

Whether a patient's race should be routinely included in the presentation [of a case] and if so where, is not well established. Standard references for medical school clinical diagnosis courses make different recommendations. One text notes that "identifying data, such as age, race, or ethnic origin, birthplace and occupation serve [*sic*] not only to establish who the patient is, but also to give you some tentative suggestions as to what kind of person you are talking to and even what the likely problems might be." Another, while including race among identifying data, notes less enthusiastically that "race is of some importance in diagnosis; sickle-cell anemia occurs almost exclusively in blacks" A third excludes race from the identifying information, suggesting that it be reported at the beginning of the physical examination.

And the report concludes that "racial bias in case presentations is not limited to a single institution. . . . Case presentation is generally taught during the second year of medical school and practiced extensively during the third and fourth years. It is thus a skill largely acquired prior to residency training. Sixteen medical schools are represented by the house officers in this study." ("Racial Bias in Presentation of Cases," *Journal of General Internal Medicine*, Vol. 5 [March–April 1990], pp. 120–121)

29. Citations from *American Medical Association News*, September 13, 1995, reporting research by Leslie J. Blackhall, Department of Medicine, Pacific Center for Health Policy and Ethics, University of Southern California.

30. Joseph A. Carrese and Lorna Rhodes, "Western Bioethics on the Navajo Reservation—Benefit or Harm," *Journal of the American Medical Association*, Vol. 274 (1995), pp. 826–829.

CHAPTER 4

White Coats and Business Suits

CONTEXT AND EVENT

It is a mistake to treat case and story as if they exist only in their own universe. But it is tempting to do so. The patient reduces world to ego, centering experience on body and self. Pain, fear, and anxiety drive this isolationist move. The patient not only *is* dependent but becomes *a* dependent, and welcomes it. Institutionally, we encourage the patient toward this constricted self, as can be observed in the admissions office, examining room, or hospital room. The typical hospital visit is brief. Conversation, such as it is, is conventional and desultory. This is reinforced by the instruction to keep things pleasant (i.e., don't intrude). Institutional routines become a way of life for the patient. Sickness, thus acknowledged, ends in retreat from the world and disconnection from others. Consequently, recovery and recuperation are as much a return to the world as a biomedical outcome.

The clinician is also tempted toward isolation, the loss of the story on one side and the reduction of the world to the practice community on the other. Of course, context persists. But, like the patient, the clinician resists context as intruder. The clinical situation becomes a closed-away world.

The move from story to case serves to break into isolation. Located in the practice community, the case connects as well to other practice communities, that is, appears at the intersections of law, business, religion, and so on. The case attaches to other cases, becomes a genre. Together, practice communities constitute a genre, too, distinguished by a meta-language, a language of professional code and status, of procedures for achieving status, and of rites of passage. At the same time, stories appear within a field of stories, and so constitute yet another genre, exhibiting characteristic styles of construction and communication. Again the case connects. With that, the genres meet. The clinical situation is thus both of itself and by others. And we need the case to reach shared meanings. These take us outside the clinical situation and outside the practice community.

The clinical event is in motion, so it is difficult to know which world events are relevant to it and which are indeed intrusions. The case then tries to reject the world as puzzlement. Yet it cannot have meanings without taking account of it. So while the patient tries to read the world through ego, the caregiver tries to read the world through practice. Ultimately, the clinical event is found in a moving web of relationships. Thus, management, control, and coherence are in jeopardy. Hierarchy and habit become a defense as much as a privilege.

By way of illustration, consider how demography has shifted the context of the clinical situation. As infant morality rates decline, more children are around than ever before. More of the old are around, too. An increase in birthrate joins with improvements in hygiene, diet, housing, work life, chemistry, and technology to extend longevity. Biomedicine plays its role in generating this demography and at the same time is altered by its demands. New medical specialties appear, such as geriatrics and genetic counseling, and older specialties change, as in prenatal and neonatal care. Care for the dying becomes an extended process with its own disciplines and requirements. Given the numbers of people now living, demand increases for goods that are inevitably scarce. Under such a condition, it is no surprise that markets dominate because they privilege haves over have-nots. Nor is it surprising that the practice community is seen to produce a consumer good. As never before, conflicting priorities end in an unavoidable economics and politics.

At the same time, expectations do not stop at national or regional borders. Cultural and political considerations come to play a larger role as practices respond to the politics of demand. Large numbers and global realities shift attention to macrocosmic issues. Standards of treatment and of experiment are embodied in global codes. New forms of exploitation appear, too, as in the dumping of unsafe drugs in third-world countries. Mobility and communication announce possibilities and threats, and so in turn force reconstruction of the clinical situation. Like the rest of society, it becomes multilingual and multicultural, often in spite of itself. Newly amended sociobiological disciplines like ecology and evolutionary psychology join new medical specialties and subspecialties.

Of course, these developments would not be problematic were it not for the globalization of democratic values. The Enlightenment project produced a changed sense of who counts and for how much. Egalitarian expectations appear in sub-Saharan Africa, in Latin America, and in Asia as much as they appear in Europe and North America. With the intersection of democratic values and demographic patterns, the world event enters the local event and, inevitably, the clinical situation. It lives in an impacted world.

While global standards evolve,[1] regional and local customs complicate their content. Thus, declarations of rights are embodied in treaties and statutes where compromises and silences are inevitable. Rights of privacy and self-determination, however, are limited by traditions. Cultural pluralism is thus an ambivalent mix of global homogeneity and communal heterogeneity. Typical of both is the Convention on Human Rights and Medicine that was adopted by the Council of Europe in 1997. Among other things, it provides for equitable access to health care, informed consent in both treatment and experiment, confidentiality, privacy of genetic information, fairness in organ transplantation. So global standards reflect Western biomedical ethics and its concerns. But these echo in different ways in non-Western societies. Biomedical discourse is globalized, too, as in the World Health Organization and the World Medical Association.

The language of rights exhibits the universalism, rationalism, and individualism of its eighteenth-century sources. Its reality, however, ranges from pious reference to institutional performance. A "patient's bill of rights," posted in every American hospital, exhibits that reality. But America is not alone, although it might be understood as a pilot project in the evolution of biomedical ethics. Terms of art adopted by the practice community move beyond national boundaries. Autonomy—the term owes its existence to Kantian moral thought—reflects its roots in democratic individualism. Claims of autonomy—as in self-determination—are, however, heard everywhere. Typical derivations like a "reasonable person" standard reflect the attribution of rationality to all human beings. And rationality, in turn, is understood as the ability to know and to act in one's own interest.

The presence of democratic values and expectations in the clinical situation is, no doubt, also a consequence of the social and cultural challenges to authority that reached a climax in the 1960s. "Participatory democracy," which was their slogan, now appears in the inclusiveness of the ethics consultation and more generally in the presence and legitimacy of a multitude of voices at the bedside. Diversity, which once upon a time was masked by middle-class and professional assumptions, is now celebrated as a natural extension of the democratic impulse. Thus, judgment and decision occur in the presence of a collective only some of whose members were once permitted to be present. Paradoxically, however, authority is shifted away from physician, family, and community, and vested in near-absolute terms in the patient.

To be sure, context may create new standards and expectations, even new intentions, while conduct resists change. For example, in a review of how physicians and institutions handle death and dying, a report of the doctor–patient relationship exhibits both changed consciousness and persistent habit.

Isaacs also never talked about death with his regular doctor . . . [who] said that he never learned about preparing patients for death either in medical school or training on the wards. "It's just not ingrained as part of our history and practice," he said. . . . [Beth Israel] is one of the first hospitals in the state to create an ethics committee to explore these difficult matters. . . . But even here the reality of how patients and doctors talk about death intrudes daily on decisions about care. . . . "As a practicing physician you'd think I'd have learned," he said. "But I'm still lazy on the subject." . . . In Isaacs' case, [the doctor] acknowledged that he "absolutely should have" talked with him about proxies and "end of life" care options, but did not. "Even if I couldn't talk with him," [he] conceded, "I should have with his wife and daughter."[2]

With the civil rights movement, the "war on poverty," and the rise of feminism, we have become much more aware of how class and caste shape the way people are treated. For example, dialysis first became available as a treatment for kidney disease at Swedish Hospital in Seattle. With machinery scarce and costs high, the treatment could not be made available to everyone who needed it; later, federal legislation would make it available to all who needed it. Rather than leave the decision to the marketplace or the physician, a committee consisting mostly of laypeople was named to assure just distribution. National attention was drawn to the committee by the media. "*Life* assigned its first woman reporter, Shana Alexander, to cover the story of the committee [November 1962] . . . It was Alexander who coined the term *God Committee* . . . She also described in detail the committee's criteria, which would come to be called the *social worth standard*."[3] These criteria were later described by two sociologists:

[T]he specific, often unarticulated, indicators that were used reflected the middle-class American value system shared by the selection panel. A person "worthy" of having his life saved . . . was one judged to have qualities such as decency and responsibility. Any history of social deviance, such as a prison record, any suggestion that a person's married life was not intact and scandal-free, were strong contraindications to selection. The preferred candidate was a person who has demonstrated achievement through hard work and success at his job, who went to church, joined groups, and was actively involved in community affairs.[4]

No longer the "melting pot," we celebrate the distinct cultural identities of blacks, Latinos, Native Americans, women, elderly, gays, and so on. These identities enter the clinical situation. For example, we realize that AIDS patients or unwed mothers are seen through the lens of class. I recall a discussion with a group of blacks in a small southern town. Older participants remembered when the local hospital admitted "Negroes" through a separate entrance and treated them in separate facilities. It was clear that the memory still encouraged a certain skepticism—and not just among the old—about the good intentions of the hospital and its caregivers.

Context is also evident in our ambivalence about gays. Sexual orientation is supposed to be a "neutral" clinical factor in research and treatment. However, as an article on genetic research put it:

The culture in which scientists live and work influences both the questions they ask and the hypotheses they imagine and explore. . . . Attention to these contextual details shows that research into sexual orientation is different from research into most other physical/behavioral variations. Since sexual orientation is the focus of intense private and public interest, relevant inquiry cannot be studied independently of societal investment. It is naive to suggest that individual researchers might suddenly find themselves in the position of neutral inquirers. . . . We are seeking to highlight that the very motivation for seeking the "origin" of homosexuality has its source within social frameworks that are pervasively homophobic.[5]

Perhaps nothing is more striking than the changing relationships of clinic and law. Accusations of negligence and malpractice are typical, although their frequency and cost have been exaggerated. Specialties like obstetrics are particularly vulnerable, and practice responds as often to legal as to medical considerations. "Defensive" medicine—such as excessive laboratory testing—is the result of actual or perceived legal threat. Ethical issues are interpreted as matters of law. Judgments about confidentiality, abortion, surrogate motherhood, physician-assisted suicide depart the clinic for the courthouse.

Yet it is no secret that behavior goes on pretty much as before. For example, following the Quinlan and Cruzan cases, the courts upheld the right of patients to refuse life-sustaining treatment. Advance directives and living wills were embodied in federal and state statute.

In short, there is now a body of literature, policy, law, and regulation that presents a generally agreed upon set of basic principles as well as procedural recommendations for incorporating those principles into clinical practice. However, there has been very little research to determine whether clinicians know about these recommendations, agree with them, or find them useful. . . . To explore these questions, we conducted a survey at five hospitals. . . . The results of our survey reveal an important gap between the views of practicing clinicians and the pre-vailing guidelines.[6]

Practice communities are conservative, often for good reasons. Safety and risk are at war, and suffering and survival are at issue. Nor is change necessarily benevolent. But context will not be denied and, ultimately, reconstructs the nature and role of the clinical actors. As David Rothman puts it:

In the post–World War II period, a social process that had been under way for some time reaches its culmination: the doctor turns into a stranger, and the hospital becomes a strange institution. . . . The familiarity that had once characterized the doctor–patient relationship gave way to distance. . . . By the same token, the links that had tied doctors to their communities . . . were replaced by professional isolation and exclusivity. Finally, the bonds of neighborhood and ethnicity that had once made a hospital a familiar place for its patients were practically severed, giving to the institution an alien and frightening atmosphere.[7]

Case and story still carry traditional meanings. But with the accelerated impact of context, case and story carry other meanings as well. Not least of all, they are forced to account for complicated collectivities that become, as it were, actors in the story and agents in the case.

THE EXPANDING AGENDA

It sometimes seems as if it is impossible to keep up with developments, let alone with what they mean. For thinking with cases, this ever-expanding content becomes an obstacle and an opportunity. Events accelerate. The result is often mysterious and so provokes curiosity. Sampling some of the things now typical of the biomedical scene is illustrative. Equally illustrative is the fact that these samples will be changing even as this text is read.

The first thing that strikes the mind's eye is tempo. I can recall the founding of the Hastings Center some twenty-five years ago to deal with what we now call biomedical ethics. Back then, the field had no name. The Center's bimonthly journal stood alone in a discipline that had yet to be defined. Today, organizations and journals proliferate, conferences and workshops are ubiquitous, graduate degrees are offered, and formal appointments as "ethicists" and "ethics consultants" are made, especially at teaching hospitals and larger urban hospitals. We are, as it were, in the midst of what Thomas Kuhn called a "paradigm shift." Policy, institution, and practice take on new shapes even as "normal" medical ethics continues.

For centuries, medical ethics reflected the concerns of a practice community that was localized in the doctor–patient relationship. Typical were traditional codes of professional conduct. "Do no harm," confidentiality, and professional duty were taken to be morally sufficient. Such codes paid as much attention to the relationships between the members of the practice community and, not least of all, to the obligations they owed each other. Of course, things changed—but slowly and comfortably. This tempo became more rapid, however, with the introduction of methods of treatment that were technically and scientifically sophisticated, and with social, political, and legal developments that moved patient autonomy to the moral center. At first, these changes showed up at the edges: in military medicine, in biological experiment, in international law, in national research policy. Inherently unstable, a double reality of conservative practice and crisis-driven innovation could not long continue. Popular expectations, the mythic powers attributed to the sciences and technology, and the politics of individualistic democracy broke down the walls between routine and surprise.

The shift in interest from physics to biology, the Darwinian shift, had its impact, too. Of course, medical and biological innovation had begun to radicalize change in the late seventeenth and eighteenth centuries. Sterile technique, knowledge of anatomy and of the causes of disease, inoculation, attention to public hygiene and diet changed the way medicine did its work. Economic needs like preserving the wine industry in France and the survival of cattle in Germany led to what at first appeared only as technical fixes like pasteurization. But neither science nor technique was boundaried. What worked in one place might work elsewhere and everywhere. The Luddite impulse surrendered to the technological imperative. Consequently,

Technology holds sway over medicine and its public because of its self-perpetuating character and its enhancement of power, as well as its capacity to induce wonder, root us in the immediate, remove ambiguity and increase certainty. Since this is not well understood, it is hardly surprising that technology, by itself inert and useless . . . should be blamed for the troubles it brings. The real culprits, however, are the doctors who use it, the public that loves it, and the narrow knowledge on which it is based . . . the spectrum of pathophysiological and anatomical criteria for disease and normality, now largely defined and perpetuated by the technology.[8]

At first, invention was assimilated into practice slowly. By contrast, within the last five decades or so, a radical shift toward scientific medicine has become dramatically visible. It can, without too much historic distortion, be dated from World War II and the Korean War. Medicine, perceived as attending to the cure of disease and not the care of patients, became a narrower art. Comfort and reassurance—the fabled "bedside manner"—were displaced by treatment and, moreover, treatment that was effective. At the same time, political, legal, and moral innovations responded to events that at first seemed far from the clinical situation. Nuremberg (1947) and Helsinki (1964, 1975) legitimated informed consent for potential experimental subjects and started us on the way to its generalization over the range of choices as such. Medicare (1965) and, somewhat later, Medicaid, announced new rights in a time when the expansion of rights was the rallying point of social reform. With the civil rights movements and a growing feminist movement, the debate about abortion was climaxed by *Roe v. Wade* (1973). New players were introduced into the clinical situation.

The sciences were changing biomedical realities. James Watson and Francis Crick described DNA's double helix in 1953. By 1993, the Human Genome project, aiming to draw a map of the human being's forty-six chromosomes, was under way. Some were predicting that "genetic exams will give the doctor a much more precise tool to assess risks and give advice. There will be personalized schemes for a new kind of preventive medicine."[9] The forty years between double helix and the genome saw the identification of genetic diseases, the disciplines of genetic counseling and of genetic engineering. As early as the 1960s, a prenatal screening test was developed for identifying phenylketonuria in fetuses—a genetic disease that can cause retardation, which can be prevented by a special diet if started at birth. Today both scientific journals and popular media almost daily announce genetic discoveries that predict the likely occurrence of this or that human sickness: Tay–Sachs disease or sickle-cell anemia or breast cancer. Screening for Down syndrome was developed in the 1970s, and for cystic fibrosis in the early 1990s. With screening came problems of choice where choices had never existed before. Issues of confidentiality took on new shape (e.g., genetic information might be used to deny medical or life insurance, and thus put jobs at risk). Where screening revealed the probability of a disease like Huntington's, for which no treatment existed, the question of whether to screen or not to screen, and the problem of disclosure—by doctor to patient and by patient to blood relatives—posed a tragic dilemma.

Cloning suddenly, or so it seemed, moved from pulp fiction to biological fact. Scientists at the George Washington University Hospital announced the cloning of the initial stages of a human embryo in 1993, and in 1997, Ian Wilmut announced that he had cloned a sheep from the mammary cell of a ewe. In 1998, there was the announcement—no doubt highly speculative—of the intention to establish privately funded human cloning experiments despite the call by the National Bioethics Advisory Commission for a moratorium. More recently still (November 1998), scientists at the University of Wisconsin and at Johns Hopkins announced the cultivation of embryonic stem cells, the primitive, non-

differentiated cells that later develop into specific organs. This announcement was followed about a week later with the news of successful efforts
to create an embryonic cell that was part human and part cow.[10]

The first heart transplant was performed by Christian Barnard in South
Africa in 1967.

[T]he six-month survival rate was only 22 percent. . . . More than 100 centers
around the world were performing heart transplants the year after Barnard pioneered the procedure. By the mid-1970's, there was only one, at Stanford University. . . . It was the development in the early 1980's of the immunosuppressant
drug cyclosporine that reinvigorated the entire field of organ transplantation. . . .
Eight of 10 heart transplant recipients now survive at least one year. The 10-year
survival rate is about 60 percent. . . . Today some 2,200 heart transplants are done
nationwide each year but an estimated 45,000 Americans annually could benefit
from the procedure. . . . The average cost . . . is $148,000, but with the added
expense of an extended hospital stay . . . and the $30,000-a-year cost of medica-
tions, the total package can easily come to a half-million dollars.[11]

Transplantation of kidneys, lungs, livers became a normal part of practice.
At the same time, organ shortages forced hard choices and increased
medical costs.

AIDS opened up the dark side of the clinical situation. Helplessness
was made all the more frustrating by the assumption that for every disease there had to be a cure. In June 1981, the Centers for Disease Control
had identified three cases of what was initially called "gay-related immune
disorder." By July, 108 cases had been reported. That fall, cases had been
found in babies of drug-addicted mothers and in hemophiliacs. No longer
a "gay" disease, it was renamed "acquired immunodeficiency syndrome."
By 1990, 60,000 Americans had died from the disease, and by 1994, about
400,000 cases of AIDS had been diagnosed. In Africa, AIDS had reached
epidemic proportions, with infection rates ranging between 10 and 25
percent.[12]

When the disease was identified with gays and drug users, it was easy
to ignore or, according to some less-than-charitable clerics, to see it as
God's punishment for evildoing. But it soon was evident that HIV and
AIDS afflicted heterosexuals, children, and patients exposed to the disease as a result of blood transfusion. A massive campaign to devote resources to research and care was successful, in no small measure because
of the activity of movie and sports personalities, as well as because of the
radical political action of AIDS victims themselves.[13] The vulnerability of
the clinical situation to modern public relations techniques was dramatically exposed. At the same time, the disease was fatal, and although drugs
that delayed or ameliorated symptoms became available, cure remained
elusive.

By 1996, with the development of an AIDS "cocktail" and the effectiveness of protease inhibitors, HIV infection could be controlled for many but not all patients. As one of them remarked, "It no longer signifies death. It merely signifies illness." Yet the AIDS experience is not erased from memory. As Andrew Sullivan wrote:

When I would tell my straight friends, or my work colleagues or my family about these things, it wasn't that they didn't sympathize. They tried hard enough. It was just that they sensed that the experience was slowly and profoundly alienating me from them. . . . The awareness of the deaths of one's peers and the sadness evoked and the pain you are forced to witness . . . all this was slowly building a kind of solidarity that eventually eliminated my straight friends from the most meaningful part of my life. There comes a point at which the experience goes so deep that it becomes almost futile to communicate it.[14]

With AIDS, the biomedical agenda reaches to our most intimate feelings and fears. This becomes evident, too, when we take a look at what is happening to birth and death. Parenthood always has its problems, but it was conceptually and biologically unproblematic. And then sperm banks and artificial insemination became feasible, and the first "test-tube" baby was born in England in 1978. Infertile couples now had hope where none had existed before. At the same time, surrogate motherhood opened the question of how motherhood was to be assigned and by whom. We came to speak of "birth" mothers and, by implication, of other kinds of mothers. The use of sperm (and later of egg) donors made the meaning of parenthood itself ambiguous, with attendant moral, legal, and emotional puzzlements. With in vitro fertilization came the greater likelihood of multiple births,[15] and of excess embryos and the problem of what to do with them, as well as of abandoned deposits in sperm banks.

Recently, embryo research has shown fetal tissue to be useful in discovering the causes of developmental anomalies, understanding fertilization, and easing the symptoms of Parkinson's disease. At the same time, resistance to the use of the embryo has emerged, due in no small measure to the social and religious divisions evident in the abortion controversy. An Embryo Research Panel was appointed in 1993 to make policy recommendations to the National Institutes of Health. As George Khushf remarked:

Some of the possibilities associated with embryo research involve a radical challenge to traditional ways of human procreation. Included among these possibilities are cloning; having a genetic parent who is dead before the child is conceived (use of oocytes from cadavers); having a parent who has never been born (use of oocytes from an aborted fetus); cross-species fertilization; cross-species gestation; the creation of a chimera through the combination of a human embryo with one from another species; the birth of an identical twin several years apart (or even the use of a twin as the gestation mother of her sibling); or extrauterine or abdominal pregnancy (perhaps allowing for male gestational mothers). Some of these may not be scientifically possible. However, even if they were, the Panel concluded that they were too problematic socially. Unfortunately, little reason was given for why it is important to protect such traditional approaches to procreation. In fact, the recommendations are somewhat ironic, since they are framed in the context of an acceptance of artificially assisted reproduction, which has been itself viewed as a fundamental challenge to such traditional methods. . . . Why wouldn't the Panel's arguments be extended to in vitro fertilization as well?[16]

The new technologies have also made possible the survival of fetuses that once could not have survived. "Viability" when *Roe v. Wade* was decided (1973) was about twenty-eight weeks. Now it is around twenty-three to twenty-four weeks. I recall visiting a newborn intensive care unit (NICU). The infants, many small enough to be held in the palm of the hand, lived in their incubators, attached to tubes and gauges, technological equivalents of the mother's womb. The parents sat there sadly, hopefully, observing their babies at a distance.

Mother and fetus are caught not only in an overpowering technology but also in the workings of the law.[17] For example:

In California, a woman was advised by her obstetrician to stay off her feet, not engage in sexual activities, and avoid street drugs. . . . When she did not follow this advice and gave birth to a baby with brain-damage who soon died, the mother was charged under a criminal statute with failing to provide support, a law intended to force men to provide for women they have made pregnant. In the District of Columbia, a court ordered a woman dying of cancer to undergo a caesarean section, against her wishes and those of her husband and parents, in order to try to save the life of a 25-week fetus, even though testimony states that the operation would shorten the mother's life. The caesarean section was performed. . . . She died and so did the nonviable fetus. An appeals court later said that the original judge acted improperly.[18]

In South Carolina, a woman addicted to cocaine was found guilty of criminal neglect because her baby was born with cocaine metabolites in its system. The decision, later upheld by the Supreme Court of South Carolina, turned on the notion that a viable fetus is a person, and hence that the state's child abuse statute applied.[19] Similar cases have been reported in Illinois, Wyoming, and New York, although South Carolina is unique thus far in identifying a viable fetus as a child.

If the beginnings of life are reshaped, so, too, is the end of life. We prolong dying, sometimes almost indefinitely, it seems. Consequently, a new set of choices appears. Patients may refuse treatment or decide that it be withdrawn. Advance directives and living wills are protected by federal statute. At the same time, dying is surrounded by an overwhelming technology. For example, in a bedside visit prior to an ethics committee

consult, I saw an eighty-year old woman paralyzed by stroke, unable to
communicate or to eat or drink or breathe on her own. She was kept
alive by the machinery. For one of her children, this merely "prolonged
the inevitable." For another, the "vital signs," no matter how dependent
on technology, meant that her mother was still alive and that "while
there's life, there's hope." For the physician the case was hopeless. Eventually, a court had to decide the issue and allow the woman to die.

Ambiguity surrounds the dying process as family members argue the
alternatives or as caregivers experience the conflict between "battling
death" and letting die. Suicide and euthanasia have been debated in many
cultures and over many centuries.[20] Yet, less than twenty-five years after
Quinlan, we accept ideas like refusing treatment, refusing nourishment,
and DNR orders. These, it is held, let "nature" take its course. We try to
distinguish these from euthanasia and physician-assisted suicide (PAS),
which are said to invite us to "play God." And our attitudes and distinctions are psychologically and culturally understandable. But the debate
takes a difficult turn as PAS becomes an issue of public policy. Already
one state, Oregon, has twice approved a referendum authorizing PAS.[21]
Other states—California, Washington, and Michigan—have turned it
down. And while the Supreme Court did not find a "right" to die in the
Constitution, neither did it forbid PAS. Instead, and in recognition of the
inconclusive nature of the current debate, it referred the matter to state
legislatures, in effect inviting continuing public debate and policy "experimentation."[22]

Story and case have features that language, statute, and policy do not
and cannot capture. Yet terms that seem clear enough, like "quality of
life" and "death with dignity," have entered public discourse. For example, in reflecting on living wills and advance directives, it is clear that the
decisions made when in good health are not necessarily the decisions
that will be made when older and ill. Brief moments of survival may be
significant to a dying individual or to his or her family. Earlier, such moments might have been dismissed as trivial. Nor is terminal illness—itself
problematic—the only place for quality-of-life discussion. An Alzheimer's
patient who may have years of living ahead does not enjoy the quality of
life he or she enjoyed before the onset of the disease. Yet living on cannot
be assumed to be without value. Nor is "death with dignity" a self-
defining term. Dignity may be equated with autonomy for some, while
for others it may be derived from values like endurance, the virtues of
suffering, the will of God, or what have you.

Illustrating the ambiguities of death and dying is the case of Donald
Cowart, known as "Dax." In 1973, he was burned over 67 percent of his
body in a propane gas explosion. When the emergency medical techni-
cians arrived, he asked for a gun with which to shoot himself. In severe
and continuing pain, he was in the hospital for 232 days. Repeatedly he

tried to refuse treatment. Each time his request was overridden. His mother wanted everything to be done, and it was her judgment that was accepted by the physicians although Dax's competence was not in question. Dax survived, blind, disfigured, and with only partial use of his hands. As the result of a settlement with the gas company, Dax became a millionaire, graduated from law school, and married. He was and is a campaigner for patient autonomy. In a 1997 interview, he said:

During many years of speaking engagements, I have maintained with confidence that I believe myself to be much happier than most other people around me despite my disabilities. This usually leads many to conclude that my physicians were right and I was wrong concerning my wish to die. My response has always been that even though I am glad to be alive . . . my physicians were still wrong because, despite my current benefits associated with being alive, the price I had to pay in terms of pain and suffering in order to be alive today was simply too great. They were also wrong because they had no right to interfere with my autonomy. . . . I still believe that I should have been allowed to have acted at my own peril.[23]

But puzzles of death and dying are not found only in landmark cases or dramatic stories. They are part of the ordinary experience of ordinary people. In all likelihood, they have witnessed the prolonged dying of a family member or a friend. Haunting them is the image of dying among strangers, connected to a machinery that postpones but cannot cure. Separated from home and family, and emotionally if not actually abandoned by caregivers who know the situation is hopeless, people die alone and often in pain. In response, and in an effort to displace or at least radically minimize PAS, pain management and comfort care have developed rapidly. Pioneered by the hospice movement, "palliation" is a "new" medical specialty, and older clinical attitudes that paid little attention to pain and suffering are slowly, very slowly, being eroded.

Meanwhile, the costs of dying are prohibitive, often impoverishing the patient and his or her family, and a burden on already strained social resources. Indeed, as one provocative commentator wrote recently, there may even be a "duty to die."

The costs—and these are not merely monetary—of prolonging our lives when we are no longer able to care for ourselves are often staggering. If further medical advances wipe out many of today's "killer diseases"—cancers, heart attacks, strokes, ALS, AIDS, and the rest—then one day most of us will survive long enough to be demented or debilitated. . . . A fairly common duty to die might turn out to be only the dark side of our life-prolonging medicine and the uses we choose to make of it.

Let me be clear. I certainly believe that there is a duty to refuse life-prolonging medical treatment and also a duty to complete advance directives refusing life-prolonging treatment. But a duty to die can go well beyond that. . . . Many older people report that their one remaining goal in life is not to be a burden to their loved ones . . . Often, it would be wrong to do just what we want or just what is best for ourselves; we should choose in light of what is best for all concerned.[24]

The expanding agenda reveals an emerging conflict of case and story with culture and society. It takes us, then, to what is happening to the space in which the clinical situation finds itself.

COMMITTEES AND CORPORATIONS

Case and story are eclipsed by collective realities that radically alter their geography and politics. The clinical situation remains central for the patient, the doctor, and the nurse. But rationalization comes to dominate the clinical situation. At times, as with the notion of a community's "standard of care," this works to the advantage of the patient, if in no other way than by introducing ignored or suppressed alternatives. More often than not, however, statistical, technical, and market values shape treatment decisions. Choice is transferred from person to bureaucracy. Despite such developments, rationalization can be a useful reconstruction of the practice community itself. It can be beneficial for the patient and instructive for the caregiver. For example:

Evidence-based medicine trains doctors to search medical journals and databases for tests and treatments that have helped large groups of patients. Then they apply the information to their own patients, under the statistical assurance that what holds for groups is likely to be valid for individuals. This strategy is sweeping medicine in the United States, Canada and Britain, widely hailed as the crucial long-sought link between research and practice—a kind of intellectual golden spike that will allow the results of the best medical research to run smoothly forward into the hospitals and doctors' offices where medical decisions are actually made. But critics say it may compromise important parts of the art of medicine, in which doctors consider each patient's unique quirks, habits and preferences.[25]

In many ways, the practice community is enriched. Technology makes this possible and manageable. Similarly, with the increase in medical costs, organizational structures are being adapted to make medicine more efficient. Borrowing from business and manufacturing, and reflecting the democratic impulse, traditional hierarchies are being eroded. Drawing on management reforms like "quality circles" and "total quality management" (TQM), more and more "stakeholders" enter the clinical situation. The notion of a caregiving "team" has become a cliché of practice. It remains true, however, that the physician has the last word. But that word is less likely to be uttered with the absolutism it once enjoyed. It is challenged in ways once unthinkable and by people once expected to be silent and obey.

Reconstructing the clinical situation in a participatory environment is also a response to the inadequacy of individualized actions. As the SUPPORT study confirmed, the attempt to exercise patient autonomy through living wills, advance directives, and DNR orders failed more often than not because its assumptions did not challenge the habits of the practice community. Rationalization, then, confronts tradition. It may be read as a dual move. It includes "stakeholders" in the clinical situation, that is, the borders of the practice community grow vague. And it expands the authority not just of patients but also of communities.

The practice community is surrounded by specialized committees that often include administrators, lawyers, economists, clergy, social workers, theologians, and philosophers. As with so much else, this development was rapid and often bewildering. For example, in the 1960s two physicians, Henry Beecher and Henry Pappworth, published studies showing that a number of experiments on human subjects reported in refereed scientific journals had failed to get informed consent.[26] News of the Tuskegee experiments broke in 1972. While less outrageous, the studies showed that the violation of patient rights was not limited to Nazi doctors in Nazi Germany, nor was it ended by the Nuremberg code. In response, the National Institutes of Health mandated that all institutions receiving federal funds for experiments involving human subjects establish institutional review boards (IRBs) whose approval is necessary before research can proceed. Since federal funds are just about everywhere, IRBs are found in local hospitals as well as in research centers.

Following the Quinlan decision in 1976, hospital-based ethics committees began to appear. Typically, they make recommendations, review cases and policies, and mediate disputes. By 1995, the Joint Commission on Accreditation of Healthcare Organizations required hospitals to provide for ethics review. And, as managed care and market-based medicine evolve, organizational ethics review is on the way, too.[27] As a physician said to me, "The real ethical problems these days aren't about individual cases so much as about what's happening to hospitals and medical practices, and about what's happening to access for people who can't get medical insurance." To be sure, the practice community always had to pay attention to nonclinical communities like the clergy. Now the range of participation and the items that may be reviewed continue to expand. The closed-away world of the practice community opens. Often this works to the benefit of practitioner and patient alike. Of course, it complicates life, increases costs, and takes time.

The participating communities include some new and troubling members. With increased costs and technologized medicine, the hospital of yesterday—community-sponsored and community-based—is today more likely to be a unit of a regional or national corporation, often a for-profit corporation. It is not unusual for hospitals to purchase medical practices and to employ physicians directly. Alternatively, group practices are incorporated and often employ management companies to provide administrative services. As one study reported, "Between 1983 and 1994 the proportion of patient care physicians practicing as employees rose from 24.2% to 42.3%, the proportion self-employed in solo practices fell from 40.5% to 29.3% and the proportion self-employed in group practices fell from 35.3% to 28.4%"[28] Inexorably, organizational homogeneity is replacing institutional variety.

It is not unusual for hospitals to offer market incentives to encourage physicians to refer patients. As one investigative report summed up the matter:

Hospitals, of course, have long recruited doctors with generous enticements—like signing bonuses, consulting contracts and outright purchases of their practices. For Columbia [Columbia-HCA, the largest for-profit hospital corporation in the country], able to bring vast wealth to the courting game, these deals have been instrumental in the drive to dominate medical marketplaces.

But, because their financial returns are tied directly to those of their hospitals, the doctor-investors are stepping into different and, to many health care experts, troubling territory. . . . In recent months, Columbia's financial relationships with its doctors have come under heightened legal scrutiny. The federal agency that runs Medicare is examining whether Columbia doctor-investors are violating a federal conflict-of-interest law.[29]

Health insurance has expanded rapidly from the days of the not-for-profit Blue Cross and Blue Shield programs. Typically, it is more and more likely to be offered by for-profit companies, and even the "Blues" are deserting their nonprofit status. For a long time, these "third-party" payers hid the costs of treatment and hospital stays from patients. They simply raised rates and paid the bills. Together, then, insurance companies, hospitals, caregivers, and patients created a culture of financial indifference. With Medicare and Medicaid, however, standard diagnostic categories (DRGs) and standard payments set limits, and in turn these limits were universalized. Ultimately, this payment pattern evolved into a process of distant and bureaucratic approval. But these controls didn't do the job. A new form of organization, "managed care," was invented—health maintenance organizations (HMO), preferred provider organizations (PPO) and so on. These are well on the way to replacing traditional relationships of doctor and patient and the traditional single practitioner. By 1998, it was estimated that some 150 million people were subscribers to some form of managed care. So corporate entities, "artificial professionals," came to be included in the clinical situation and increasingly to dominate it. Corporate agents—clerks, CPAs, business managers, and nurse and physician administrators—operated within nonclinical constraints. The market, as it were, redefined the clinic.

Technology and sociology, and not only economy, characterized these new corporate participants. Thus,

Within HMOs a new elite rose to power: doctors and statisticians who could wield computer-generated data in the battle for greater medical efficiency. These experts could pinpoint a medical issue—such as how long to hospitalize a heart attack patient or how best to care for asthmatic children—and then pick apart the problem with a computer-aided analysis of how 100,000 or more such patients were being treated. . . . With that information in hand, HMO overseers could goad doctors to improve their scores. Some physicians fought this data brigade. . . . But in the world of managed care, people who relied on "In my experience . . ." seldom won an argument. Those holdout doctors were trumped again and again by the stern response: "According to our data . . ."[30]

Managed care brought with it new and puzzling issues of biomedical ethics. Conflicts of interest were institutional and no longer personal. Maximizing profits competed with the needs of patients. Statistically based clinical judgments could not account for the existential qualities of story and case. With that, care and treatment were limited not so much by available knowledge as by resource allocation. This rationing might be acceptable, even if regrettable, if democratically arrived at. Instead, it became, even more than in the past, a function of affordability. Corporate strategies aimed at "cherry-picking," that is, enrolling people who were less likely to need medical services, such as the young and the healthy. Those with expensive needs and few resources were resigned to a shrinking number of not-for-profit or tax-supported community hospitals, or else left to fend for themselves. Confessing this shift of values, President Clinton appointed an Advisory Commission on Consumer Protection and Quality in the Health Care Industry to draft a "bill of rights."[31] Few commentators remarked on the assumption that medical care was a consumer good.

The inclusion of corporate agents in the clinical situation had effects on the other participants as well. For example:

[Dr. Robert] Berenson recounts the change in attitude he underwent in caring for an elderly woman with a rare form of cancer when he was paid under risk-sharing arrangements. She represented an economic loss, and he "ended up resenting the seemingly unending medical needs of the patient and the continuing demands . . . [of her] distraught family." The problem was not the patient's requests or performing the work. But under the risk-sharing system, very sick patients devastated his accounts. Risk sharing makes "patients who come in often for care from me . . . or who want a referral for specialty care begin to look like abusers."[32]

John H. McArthur, dean of the Harvard Business School, and Francis D. Moore, of Brigham and Woman's Hospital, wrote: "The current trend toward the invasion of commerce into medical care, an arena formerly under the exclusive purview of physicians is an epic clash of culture between commercial and professional traditions in the United States."[33]

The reallocation of powers in the clinical situation finds a membership at war with itself. It becomes a very troubled place as the narrative of case and story is overpowered by the voice of the "artificial professional."

VOCATION VERSUS TRADE

The patient is often the beneficiary of today's more effective medicine. But at a price. He or she becomes an object of manipulation by the members of practice communities, many of whom are invisible and have little appreciation of the clinical relationship. Of course, the patient was a dependent and the doctor–patient relationship was paternalistic. But paternalism grows impersonal and bureaucratic. Symbolically, the house call, which softened paternalism, has all but vanished—and with it the ability of the physician, the patient, and the family to know each other. For instance, "Despite the growth in other home health care services, the number of house calls by physicians has declined dramatically during this century. . . . A very small percentage (0.88 percent) of elderly Medicare patients, mainly those who are very sick and near the end of life, receive house calls from physicians."[34] In part, this is due to the use of technologies that make the office visit more effective. And with specialization, the patient usually is referred to one or several physicians who, in turn, probably know little more of the patient than symptom, diagnosis, and treatment. As one doctor summed it up:

At one time in health care, we valued the doctor–patient relationship as paramount. As doctors become more specialized, they gained more and more intellectual satisfaction from the disease rather than from health or, in some situations, even from the patient. That shifts the focus away from the humanism of the profession. Even some internists look on a patient's problem as a "disease," much the way some surgeons look on a patient as a "procedure." This pernicious tendency abstracts medicine and depersonalizes the patient.[35]

The larger part of the move from home to office, however, is due to a changing economy and limited resources. House calls take time, and time is not only precious but expensive. As one troubled doctor said to me, "There's no 'DRG' for talking with a patient."

Traditionally, the patient was someone to be cured and cared for. So the expanded clinical population, in particular its corporate members, seems at first only to build on what went before. But absent traditional relationships—usually ongoing and local—that is not really true. Whatever its faults, practice was a relationship of persons and not of anonymous voices. Choices, at the very least the choice of physician—and latterly, with informed consent, the choices of patients—were central facts of the clinical experience. But choice is narrowed and transferred—for instance, the choice of insurer precludes many other choices, and that choice is likely to be made by the employer rather than the patient.

Stranger speaks to stranger in a world where decisions are more and more often made on statistical and commercial criteria. The roles and responsibilities of both caregiver and patient are reshaped to someone else's tune. Hospital admissions are delayed; hospital stays are brief; specialist care is restricted; costly therapies are challenged. Hospital staffs come to include minimally trained people who do the so-called routines—taking temperatures, reading blood pressures, checking liquids—and who work for low wages. But they are not ready to catch the nuance of symptom that may hide in the routine and signal a serious condition. The patient's story, always difficult to tell, and the patient's voice, always difficult to hear, are thus likely to be lost. And this happens just when the expanding agenda increases existential anxiety.

But nothing is more revealing of the shifting reality of the clinical situation than what is happening to the caregivers themselves. An editorial in the *New England Journal of Medicine* warned:

If our professionalism is endangered now, it can only suffer more when health care dollars shrink further. Both the federal government and the states are seeking to reduce the enormous amounts they spend on health care. Much of the remaining funding for health insurance comes from employers, who no longer pay whatever premiums are required of them by insurance companies but instead shop around for the best financial deal. Many employers, emboldened by their recent successes in negotiating lower rates with managed-care companies, are continuing to demand further price reductions from insurers. In turn, the insurers solicit and win deep discounts from doctors.[36]

Caregivers must respond to the expanding agenda. At the same time, they must find their way in a different kind of practice that constructs a different kind of institution with a different kind of politics and economics. For this, the practice community did not prepare its members. And because so much of the future is set by the past—by communal mores, by apprenticeship, and by thinking with cases—the mood is one of resistance and frustration. Newly redefined roles appear. The "family" physician becomes the "gatekeeper" with obligations to the patient on one side and to the corporation on the other.[37] Given differing interests—the interest of the patient in the best available care and of the corporation in controlling costs—conflicts are more than likely. These are resolved by a system of benefits to and punishments of the physician. He or she is rewarded with bonuses when annual allocations—fixed per-patient allowances (capitation)—are not fully expended. He or she may be dropped—fired—when these allocations are exceeded by more than a predetermined percentage.

Nurses and not just physicians take on new roles. For example, nurse-practitioners, registered nurses who have advanced degrees and have passed state or national certification examinations, have ordinarily worked in primary care directly under a physician's supervision. Now there is likelihood of the independent nurse-practitioner, and this move toward professional recognition is certainly overdue.[38] But motives are mixed. Thus,

"There is a movement under way," said David Snow, a senior vice president of Oxford Health Plans . . . which added four Manhattan nurse practitioners to its roster in what he called "an experiment in independence." He added, "We view the evolution of nurse practitioners as something that consumers are asking for." The movement so far is a nascent one, driven by a combination of consumer demand, a vigorous campaign by the nurses to expand their role, and the advent of managed care with its emphasis on cost control.[39]

Traditional practice always had to deal with economic costs and rewards. Today, tradition surrenders to entrepreneurial and managerial values that reflect the growing domination of the commercialized features of the clinical situation. At the same time, the professional as employee— a new status for most physicians—and the power enjoyed by corporate organizations has led to what one headline writer called "Doctors Are Thinking the Unthinkable: Unionization." While involving only a relatively small number, reports as of 1997—from Arizona, Florida, Massachusetts, Nevada, New Jersey, New Mexico, New York, and Washington—tell of numerous efforts by doctors and by nurses to unionize and to affiliate with organized labor.

Patient advocacy was always a responsibility of the caregiver. The physician and nurse might at times be silent adversaries or might join against unreasonable family demands. Perhaps the hospital itself was the enemy.[40] Today, however, the adversary is more likely to be the insurance company, the HMO, the hospital holding company, the government. Power has shifted, and advocacy becomes a struggle between clinical effectiveness and professional survival. Indeed, patients and their families are advised to be their own advocates, although it is difficult to see how they can be competent to take on the task. Apart from the natural inequality of the clinical situation and the structural inequality between collective and individual, when illness happens, patient and family are focused on treatment and not on competitive bidding. That we encourage nonprofessional advocacy further confirms the shift to medicine as a consumer good.

The expanding agenda has other consequences for caregivers. For example, nurses and doctors have, no doubt, been affected by the AIDs crisis in many ways. Especially in the beginning, the obligation to treat confronted anxiety about fatal infection. But AIDS also challenged the identity of the physician and nurse at the point where professional and person intersected. One study reported, "Although physicians who were not heterosexual appeared to identify more strongly with their [AIDS] patients and assisted patients in committing suicide to a greater extent than their heterosexual colleagues, sexual orientation was only one of the four factors that were associated with assisting a patient with AIDS to commit suicide."[41]

Genetic screening generates its own puzzles.

Can we explain the purpose of the particular test? Do we know the nature of the disorder that's in question? . . . What are the benefits? . . . What are the risks? . . . Can we give a client any forewarning about some of the decisions likely to follow after the text results come in? . . . Are we aware of supportive counseling recourses? . . . Will there be disclosure to family members? . . . What about third-party payers? What about insurance? . . . Do we tell a woman who's having testing for one thing that it's likely we might find out about nonpaternity?[42]

Physician-assisted suicide (PAS) further reveals the ambiguities of obligation. While medical associations oppose PAS, 56 percent of doctors in a Michigan survey supported allowing doctors to help a patient commit suicide and 60 percent of Oregon doctors approved of PAS. In a study of cancer specialists, 57 percent had been asked for help in committing suicide and 13.5 percent had written a lethal prescription.[43] Similarly, nursing associations oppose PAS and euthanasia. Yet, in a controversial survey of 852 intensive care nurses, "141 (17 percent) reported that they had received requests from patients or family members to perform euthanasia or assist in suicide; 129 (16 percent of those for whom data was available) reported that they had engaged in such practices; and an additional 35 (4 percent) reported that they had hastened a patient's death by only pretending to provide life-sustaining treatment ordered by physicians."[44] Finally, PAS stirs conflict within the person of the professional. Timothy Quill reported:

Many people have asked me, "Aren't your patients scared of you after writing this [Quill's report of his assistance to his dying patient, Diane]? Aren't they frightened of you because you're talking about death here?" The answer to that was absolutely not. What was most striking about my own patients' response to this was that everybody came in with a story, a story they had never told me before about something they had witnessed in a family member or a friend. My office hours took forever, and it was very emotionally draining because these stories were stories that make your hair stand on end. They were stories of really severe suffering. The witnessing of such severe suffering is one of the most powerful experiences that drives us today.[45]

The expanding agenda, the interaction of various practice communities, and the altered space within which the clinical situation happens, raise questions about the meaning of the healing professions and threatens their survival as professions.

A certain mystique still surrounds the physician. This is understandable, for surely no other profession sanctions behaviors that involve bodily invasion and that touch so closely on existential concerns about birth, survival, and death. At the same time, the doctor must build a practice or, as is more likely in today's environment, sign into a corporate practice. Typically, he or she needs to repay the debts incurred by medical education and to earn a living. This mixed set of demands—to be a bringer of life and death and to be a successful tradesperson—is clearly not new. Myth, however, tended to hide the fact so that everyone knew it and everyone denied it. Thus,

[T]he Hippocratic corpus is marked by a deep and unresolved tension between obligations to the patient and the protection of self interest. Physicians in those days made their living as itinerants, with their reputations preceding them as they approached the next town on their travels. Obviously, it would redound to one's economic calamity if one gained a reputation for having very high mortality rates—it still does, in fact. Thus, the Hippocratic writers . . . enjoin against aggressive management of life-taking disease as part of an agenda of protecting the physician's self-interest.[46]

To be sure, demystification is the modern habit. The shift of decision-making to the patient should not be exaggerated but is nevertheless a fact. The controls exercised by administrators and by corporate agents strip away the near absolute authority physicians once had. Yet the mystique does not entirely vanish. The portrayal today of the doctors as human beings—making mistakes, getting tired, having love affairs, being in debt—is typical of the media. At the same time, doctors—unlike lawyers, engineers, teachers, social workers, and priests—are also portrayed as effective and powerful, and as willing to make sacrifices of time, energy, and wealth because of the demands of duty.

Popular imagery reflects social realities. Thus, whatever the vicissitudes of the expanding agenda and the clinical situation's changing space, it remains true that medicine is still viewed primarily as a calling and not merely as a job. The practice community still preserves a sense of fiduciary responsibility. As a guidebook for medical students put it:

Defined as faithfulness to duties and obligations, fidelity is inherent in the physician–patient relationship. However, this faithfulness carries more than the conventional weight of obligation because of the special nature of the relationship: a vulnerable person, ill or with troubling symptoms, comes to the health professional with anticipation and hope generated from experience with and a general understanding of the role of that professional. The patient anticipates that the physician will be knowledgeable, trustworthy, and competent in medical judgment and practice and she hopes for solution of the problem(s). Her problem may be minor or life threatening, sometimes the difference unknown by her, and she must depend on the physician's faithfulness to interpret and to provide competent service. The implications of illness, real or potential, require a different commitment from those of usual commerce and social activity.[47]

While this description reflects the self-image of the physician—and of the nurse as well—it is confronted by a reality that subverts it. Calling is embedded in the sacred. Even when secularized as a profession, it is identified by the fact that criteria of knowledge and training, and rites of admission, are set by the members of the practice community for themselves. Older members are obligated to induct newer members. Not least of all, admission is measured by moral as well as skill criteria. A certain altruism is presumed, symbolized by the priestly features of the profession and reflected in the notion that the caregiver cannot legitimately turn away the person in need. Even the risk of illness and death—as in epidemics—or the frustration of trying to treat the resistant and unpleasant patient, cannot justify the professional's abdication. Finally, the role transcends secularity. The professional is connected to a world beyond the giving and getting of daily life. The professional is set apart.

Of course this is an idealized view, but it is still operative in language and conduct. Against it, as Edmund Pellegrino, writes, "all professions are increasingly being regarded as services, even as public utilities. . . . Professions . . . will acquire dignity and standing in the future, not so much from the tasks they perform, but from the intimacy of the connection between those tasks and the social life of which the profession is a part. . . . The collectivity will increasingly be expected to take responsibility for how well or poorly the profession carries out the purposes for which it is supported by society."[48]

The patient's story and the caregiver's case are caught in a conflicted environment. If the emerging shape of the clinical situation is unclear, its direction is not. Along with the inclusiveness of the democratic impulse, the sophistication of scientific medicine, and the notion of a more widely shared authority, the clinical situation is also the home of one of the more problematic features of the wider society, the inappropriate universalization of market values. This tells us that the problems of "whose story is it" and what "learning with cases" means, now become even more difficult to grasp.

NOTES

1. See the Universal Declaration of Human Rights proclaimed by the U.N. General Assembly on December 10, 1948. Obviously, a declaration does not of itself provide for performance. Nevertheless, the Declaration sets a standard and announces a direction. Like Pandora's box, once opened, for good or ill, it cannot be closed again and put away.

2. Esther B. Fein, "Failure to Discuss Dying Adds to Pain of Patients and Family," *New York Times*, March 5, 1997.

3. Gregory E. Pence, *Classic Cases in Medical Ethics*, second edition (Boston: McGraw-Hill, 1995), p. 298.

4. Renee Fox and Judith Swazey, *The Courage to Fail: A Social View of Organ Transplants and Dialysis*, second edition (Chicago: University of Chicago Press, 1978), p. 232.

5. Udo Schuklenk, Edward Stein, Jacinta Kerin, and William Byne, "The Ethics of Genetic Research on Sexual Orientation," *Hastings Center Report*, Vol. 27, No. 4 (July–August 1997), p. 9.

6. Mildred Z. Solomon et al., "Decisions Near the End of Life: Professional Views on Life-Sustaining Treatments," *American Journal of Public Health*, Vol. 83, No. 1 (January 1993), p. 15.

7. David J. Rothman, *Strangers at the Bedside* (New York: Basic Books, 1991), pp. 108–109.

8. Eric J. Cassell, "The Sorcerer's Broom: Medicine's Rampant Technology," *Hastings Center Report*, Vol. 23, No. 6 (November–December 1993), p. 39.

9. Dennis Breo, "Altered Fates: An Interview with Francis Collins," *Journal of the American Medical Association*, Vol. 209, No. 15 (August 21, 1993), p. 2021.

10. Nicholas Wade, "Scientists Cultivate Cells at Root of Human Life," *New York Times*, November 6, 1998, and "Human Cells Revert to Embryo State, Scientists Assert," *New York Times*, November 12, 1998.

11. Charles Siebert, "Carol Palumbo Waits for Her Heart," *New York Time Magazine*, April 13, 1997, p. 41.

12. Donald G. McNeil, Jr., "AIDS Stalking Africa's Struggling Economies," *New York Times*, November 15, 1998.

13. For the story of AIDS, of public neglect, and of the campaign to overcome it, see Randy Shilts, *And the Band Played On* (New York: St. Martin's Press, 1987).

14. Andrew Sullivan, "When Plagues End," *New York Times Magazine*, November 10, 1996, p. 57.

15. In 1995, which is the last year, at this writing, for which U.S. figures are available, there were 365 sets of quadruplets and 57 sets of quintuplets, sextuplets, and more.

16. George Khushf, "Embryo Research: The Ethical Geography of the Debate," *Journal of Medicine and Philosophy*, Vol. 22, No. 5 (October 1997), p. 510.

17. For a useful discussion of the implications of this issue, see Deborah Horn-stra, "A Realistic Approach to Maternal–Fetal Conflict," *Hasting Center Report*, Vol. 28, No. 5 (September–October 1998), pp. 7–12.

18. Terry M. Perlin, *Clinical Medical Ethics: Cases in Practice* (Boston: Little, Brown, 1992), p. 71.

19. *Whitner v. State of South Carolina*, July 15, 1996, 1996 *Westlaw* 393164.

20. For a brief review, see Ezekiel Emanuel, "The History of Euthanasia Debates in the United States and Britain," *Annals of Internal Medicine*, Vol. 121, No. 10 (November 15, 1994), pp. 793–802.

21. The Oregon "Death With Dignity" Act was approved by 51 percent to 49 percent in a referendum in 1994 and, after legislative intervention was approved, by a 60 percent to 40 percent vote in 1997. It provides that terminally ill adult patients can obtain a physician's prescription for lethal drugs when the physician predicts the patient's death within six months. Among the safeguards are a fifteen-day waiting period, the need for two oral and one written request, a second medical opinion, and counseling for patients with judgment impaired by depression.

22. The Supreme Court announced its decision on June 26, 1997, in *Glucksburg v. Washington* that no fundamental liberty was violated by state statutes forbidding physician-assisted suicide, and in *Quill v. Vacco* (New York), that such statutes did not violate the equal protection clause of the Constitution. It held that there was a legitimate distinction between physician-assisted suicide and the withdrawal/withholding of treatment.

23. Glenn McGee, "Dear Dax . . . ," *Penn Bioethics*, Vol. 2, No. 4 (Summer 1997), p. 4.

24. John Hardwig, "Is There a Duty to Die?" *Hastings Center Report*, Vol. 27, No. 2 (March–April 1997), pp. 35, 36.

25. Abigail Zuker, "Evidence-Based Doctoring May Help Weed Out Dubious Therapies," *New York Times*, December 16, 1997.

26. Henry Beecher reviewed 22 experiments in "Ethics and Clinical Research," *New England Journal of Medicine*, Vol. 274 (1966), pp. 1354–1360; Henry Pappworth reviewed some 500 experiments in *Human Guinea Pigs* (Boston: Beacon Press, 1968).

27. See Joint Commission on the Accreditation of Health Care Organizations, *Ethical Issues and Patient Rights* (Oakbrook Terrace, Ill.: The Commission, 1998), chapter 3.

28. Philip R. Kletke, David W. Emmons, and Kurt D. Gillis, "Current Trends in Physicians' Practice Arrangements, from Owners to Employees," *Journal of the American Medical Association*, Vol. 276 (August 21, 1996), pp. 555–560.

29. "For Biggest Hospital Operator, a Debate over Ties That Bind," *New York Times*, April 6, 1997.

30. George Anders, *Health Against Wealth* (Boston: Houghton Mifflin, 1996), p. 37.

31. Appointed in March 1997, the commission delivered its sixty-four-page report to the president in December. Republican opposition was immediate, as was the opposition of corporate providers and the Business Round Table. See "Bill of Right for Patients Sent to Clinton," *Medical News and Perspectives* (American Medical Association), January 7, 1998.

32. Marc A. Rodwin, *Medicine, Money, and Morals* (New York: Oxford University Press, 1993), p. 144.

33. "New Health Care Model Needed to Balance Economics vs. Professionalism in Medicine," *Science News Update* (American Medical Association), March 26, 1997.

34. Gregg S. Meyer and Robert V. Gibbons, "House Calls to the Elderly—a Vanishing Practice Among Physicians," *New England Journal of Medicine*, Vol. 337, No. 25 (December 18, 1997), pp. 1815–1820.

35. Michael D. Wertheimer, "Surgery," in Leonard Aster, editor, *Life After Medical School* (New York: W. W. Norton, 1996), p. 145.

36. Jerome P. Kassirer, "Our Endangered Integrity—It Can Only Get Worse," *New England Journal of Medicine*, Vol. 336, No. 23 (June 5, 1997), pp. 1666–1667.

37. For a discussion of the strengths and problems of the "gatekeeper" under the British system, see Robert Baker, "Professional Integrity and Global Budgeting: A Study of Physician Gatekeeping in the British National Health Service," *Professional Ethics*, Vol. 2, No. 1–2 (Spring/Summer 1993), pp. 3–34.

38. See Suzanne Gordon, *Life Support* (Boston: Little, Brown, 1997), pp. 100–101:

Physicians have long fought to keep NPs (nurse practitioners) from being reimbursed by private insurers. . . . And physicians have opposed moves to give NPs caring for patients the ability to prescribe medication for those patients. State government can choose to give prescriptive authority to NPs. The fact that some do and some don't has to do with the power of the physicians' lobby in a particular state—not with nurse practitioners' qualifications. NPs working in areas with a limited supply of physicians or in areas unattractive to physicians have apparently been deemed more capable of prescribing medications.

39. Milt Freudenheim, "Nurses Working Without Doctors May Start New Trend," *New York Times*, September 30, 1997.

40. For a position statement reflecting the traditional problem of advocacy, see "The Role of the Critical Care Nurse as Patient Advocate," press release, American Association of Critical Care Nurses, 1989.

41. Lee R. Slome et al., "Physician-Assisted Suicide and Patient with Human Immunodeficiency Viral Disease," *New England Journal of Medicine*, Vol. 336, No. 6 (February 6, 1997), p. 420.

42. Colleen Scanlon, "Management of Genetic Information: Professional and Ethical Challenges in Nursing," *Critical Care Nurse*, Vol. 16, No. 5 (October 1996), p. 101.

43. These reports are summed up in Elisabeth Rosenthal, "When a Healer Is Asked, 'Help Me Die,' " *New York Times*, March 13, 1997.

44. David A. Asch, "The Role of Critical Care Nurses in Euthanasia and Assisted Suicide," *New England Journal of Medicine*, Vol. 334 (May 23, 1996), pp. 1374–1379.

45. Timothy Quill, "Physician Assisted Suicide: Progress or Peril," in Kenneth R. Whittemore and James A. Johnson, editors, *Dying in America: Choices at the End of Life* (Charleston: Medical University of South Carolina, 1995).

46. Laurence B. McCullough, "John Gregory (1724–1773) and the Invention of Professional Relationships in Medicine," *Journal of Clinical Ethics*, Vol. 8, No. 1 (Spring 1997), p. 12.

47. Dan C. English, *Bioethics: A Clinical Guide for Medical Students* (New York: W. W. Norton, 1994), p. 26.

48. Edmund D. Pellegrino, "Toward an Expanded Medical Ethics: The Hippocratic Ethic Revisited," in Robert M. Veatch, editor, *Cross Cultural Perspectives in Medical Ethics: Readings* (Boston: Jones and Bartlett, 1989), pp. 34–35.

CHAPTER 5

Making Moral Sense

STORIES AREN'T GOOD ENOUGH

To make moral sense in the clinical situation, we rely on traditional moral resources. The clinical situation, even under its new and puzzling conditions, still needs to be reinterpreted from within moral history. But this doesn't quite do the job. The search for usable moral ideas continues.

Thinking with cases is the clue, but it is not clear exactly how that thinking takes place. The case is not just another name for the story. As we have seen, the story is layered by time and character, by teller and told-to, by style and mood. It is the way in which experience is opened up to self and to others. Thus, I tell myself a story as a prelude to retelling it. This begins when I find myself a person-in-need. The story then stands between my being a person and my becoming a patient. It conveys my presence and invites retellings in order to arrive at shared meanings. I do not simply dwell in some original story. To be sure, the event remains a permanent subtext. The original story is its reminder and, at the same time, becomes the center of other stories. So whatever else happens, it is imperative that the story not be trivialized, forgotten, or displaced. It is the invitation for someone to make story into case.

Differently structured, the case is both narrative and agenda. It is shaped by ideas and values, and by an intended outcome. These connect the case to other cases, to practices, and to background sciences like biology and chemistry. Thus the case recasts the story, moving it from the particular to the generalizable. The case is addressed not just to any listener—as in telling of pain or discomfort or fear to a family member or friend—but to a member of the particular practice community. This membership is signaled by training, title, costume, and language. It is also individuated, signaled by proper names, relationship histories, and personal style—the fabled "bedside manner," for instance. The case, in other words, adds a different particularity, the professional relationship, but that particularity is, paradoxically, both singular and general.

The case faces in several directions at once. It is unique as the story is unique, but it also transcends the story, becoming an event in the history of the practice community. The case selects from the constellation of actions typical of that community. Failing that, it announces the need for novel actions that then become candidates for entry into the constellation of actions. Through the case, biomedical experiment emerges from and returns to the practice community. But, unlike a good deal of science, where intellectual curiosity may be a sufficient reason, the experiment is completed only with that return. The evolving constellation of actions is guided by the *pragmata* of care and cure. By contrast, the religious story or the love story also tells of a person-in-need. But the responses need not fit within a practice community. The story does not become a case. The lover's love remains particular. The mystic is typically an outsider, often an annoyance to prophet and priest alike. The religious story may simply evoke appreciation or contemplation but not, except in an extended sense, doings-to and doings-for.

The case already embeds elaborated connections, for example, to traditions, philosophies, treatment choices, standards, personalities, hopes. So the case already has a history and makes a forecast. Thinking with cases relies on these connections, and these connections are quite concrete. They are made through prior cases, an instructed intuition. Unlike the presentness of the story, which, as it were, freezes time or brackets lived-through time, the case looks backward and forward. The present cannot be its only dimension.

Idea, value, and intention are reorganized within the case, which now illuminates the story for the sake of the clinical situation. Hence the part cases play, as in teaching rounds or in the master–apprentice relationship. Consequently, successful intuitions serve as tests for novices—more primitively, ordeals—in qualification for membership. At the same time, the abstractions of a scientized medicine can obscure the case. Like the story, the case can be lost. It can be trapped by a protection-motivated interpretation of the "standard of practice," as in a defense against accusations of negligence.[1] The standard, then, is both aspiration and limitation. It is ultimately conservative, so novelty generates discomfort and disorientation. This tells us that something—a technique, an idea—or someone—a nurse-practitioner, a lawyer, a patient—is being paid attention to outside of the ordinary boundaries of recognition. Biomedical ethics is just such a telling. It calls attention to the moral import of structural, scientific, and technical novelty, and to challenges to membership and its prerogatives.

This opening-up is illustrated by the discourse surrounding physician-assisted suicide. For example, in "The Slow Code—Should Anyone Rush to Its Defense?" Gail Gazelle writes, "Slow codes, also known as partial, show, light blue, or Hollywood codes, are cardiopulmonary resuscitative efforts that involve a deliberate decision not to attempt aggressively to bring a patient back to life. . . . No data exists [*sic*] on slow codes, but they are not uncommon."[2] Further, a survey by the Center for Ethics in Health Care

contacted 3,944 eligible physicians in 1995. A total of 2,761 or 70 percent responded. According to the respondents, 60 percent of Oregon physicians believe physician-assisted suicide is ethical and should be legal in some cases, 46 percent might be willing to prescribe a lethal dose of medication if it were legal to do so, and 7 percent have complied with requests for physician-assisted suicide.[3]

Acknowledging a clouded situation, the Supreme Court's recent opinions on the subject (June 1997) recognized that the public process was still in motion. Thus,

the court's tone was measured and sober, in contrast to the sharp language that sometimes pervades the court's constitutional debates . . . [Chief Justice] Rehnquist noted that "throughout the nation, Americans are engaged in earnest and profound debate about the morality, legality and practicality of physician-assisted suicide." He said the court's approach "permits this debate to continue, as it should in a democratic society."[4]

Cultural diversity also calls for reconstructed legitimacies. For example, in a study of the influence of ethnicity on end-of-life decisions, the authors note:

Given a scenario of a terminal illness, Hispanics were more likely than non-Hispanics to choose each of the following life-sustaining measures: cardiopulmonary resuscitation, intubation, administration of antibiotics, feeding tube placement, intravenous nutrition, and hospitalization. Hispanics were more likely to answer "yes" to questions about wishing to have the life-sustaining measures of intravenous nutrition or a feeding tube.[5]

Technologies open the question of legitimation, too. Thus, in "The Era of the Patient," the author remarks:

Many of these novel problems were created by a group of innovative technologies that rescued patients from life-threatening physiological failures of vital organs. . . .

The first of these technologies was the artificial respirator, introduced in the mid 1950s. . . . While the technology removed many from the brink, some never got much beyond it and were consigned to lingering—still alive, but no longer aware of surroundings or people and destined never to get better. Trying problems emerged. How to decide whether life supports should be maintained? What ethical standard to apply to this question? And by whom? Family? Physicians? Clergy? Courts? Legislatures? The present or past statements of the patient?[6]

The relationships between practice communities shift. For example, "a staff of non-medical experts with knowledge of management, economics, and business . . . gradually has donned the mantle of administrative leadership. . . . [This] has produced a growing rivalry between professional and administrative personnel, intensified by differences not only in their training but in their values as well."[7] So the case carries ideas, values, and intentions that are not medical at all. This is not entirely novel. Religion once demanded its due; the laws that once criminalized insanity forced the practice community to give way to nonmedical authority. But the present situation is, if not unique, surely dramatic. The case thus occupies a contested ground between care and power.

To think with cases is to exhibit the practice community. The case is not merely form but transformation of story, of tradition. With that transformation, the epistemological usefulness of the case becomes understandable. But, given today's dis-orientation, the case is also problematic and not just a problem. It remains the vehicle for the skills of cure while it struggles to account for a bewildering array of outsider communities, institutions, and persons.

The case may be saved by the story, which is why keeping hold of the story, sometimes in spite of the case, is urgent. But this has its own dangers. It is all too easy to be lured by the anecdote, which *is* but cannot *represent* or *validate*. Being is its virtue. The story captures experience in its singularity but is easily reduced to gossip, to mere anecdotalism. In defense, we are tempted to collect stories into boxes with generic names like "allegory," "love story," and so on. Thus, we reduce story to typicality, turn story into a pseudo case. It is all too easy, perhaps unwittingly, to replace singularity with category, to indulge ourselves in an implicit Platonism.

At the same time that the story warns us against merely sorting things out, it alerts us to stories yet to come. These connect us to the perceptions, memories, and perspectives of family, friend, and caregiver through a particular person-become-patient. There will soon be many stories. This opens up a thick and complicated way of doing ethics, telling us that ethics is embedded in havings and doings and livings-through. The diversity of life-worlds at the bedside makes the point.[8]

Sooner or later, the case appears. The problem, then, is to sustain the ethical richness of the story while engaging the case. That entails a critical sensibility, an aesthetic sensibility. The tension between story and case is not simply a problem of intellect, that is, not simply an epistemological problem. The case also invokes the power of status and "secret" knowledge. This is evident enough in the struggle between marketplace and practice community or when new populations like the elderly, women, and minorities find their voices. The attitudes of the African-American community are illustrative.

A recent message on one of the e-mail bulletin boards sent by a college student read, "I believe that the AIDS virus was developed in government labs for the purpose of controlling black folks." In September, 1990, *Essence*, an African American magazine . . . had as a lead article "AIDS: Is It Genocide?" In 1991, the *New York Times* quoted Clarence Page, African American columnist and Pulitzer prize winner: "You could call conspiracy theories about AIDS and drugs fringe ideas, but they seem to have a large following among the black intelligentsia. . . . [And] you find it at all levels."[9]

Reaching back to the "participatory" ethos of the 1960s, terms like "empowerment" and challenges to "paternalism" enter the vocabulary of the practice community.[10]

Biomedical ethics connects with "the great moral traditions with principles and rules and with the new emphasis on moral psychology."[11] But both positivism and the postmodern mood in ethics call into question the meaning and reliability of ethical ideas. And events escape intelligence. Moral sense remains elusive. At the same time, the case cannot be put on hold until clarity appears.

COMMON SENSE

The practice community has its narrative, its institutional memory, which makes available meanings, interpretations, and protections to its members. These create a normative atmosphere for its members and separates them from outsiders. Thus, the transmission of meanings between older and younger members typically involves a ritualized transfer marked by title, costume, language, and ceremony. The communal aura, when disrupted, becomes visible, as in the notion of "*informed* consent." At that point, the practice community resorts to seeming rules but really to its power. And that is justified because the stakes in the clinical situation—life and death—ensure that the practice community will enjoy a certain insulation from other practice communities even when this protection is challenged.

Like the priesthood of earlier times, the practice community still has privileged status. Its wisdom, however, is both affirmed and subverted.

It is not surprising, then, that resistance and frustration are joined to the typical confidence of the community to produce a psychologically painful and philosophically ambiguous situation. The separation of member and outsider becomes ambiguous, too, particularly as the outsider asserts rights not just against but within the community. Doubt about status, legitimacy, and prerogative appears. Anger and impatience are likely. Complaints about interference and the "noncompliant" patient become symptomatic.

I recall another discussion of "futility." A couple of cases were described that called for palliative care. As is typical in such situations, however, family members reiterated the familiar "Do everything for mother."[12] While the caregivers agreed on the pointlessness of treatment, they complained angrily that "autonomy" and the "law" left them helpless to act on their best judgment. As they put it, they had to "go through the motions," resuscitating one patient or dialyzing the other. This, they noted, was "useless" for the patients, exhausting for the caregivers, and demoralizing to everyone.

A tone of resentment pervaded the discussion. "Ethics" and "law" became the enemy and, by extension, the patient and the family became the enemy, too. Outsiders—"ignorant outsiders" was the unspoken phrase—could overcome the practice community's wisdom. It seemed, too, that the nonclinical members of the committee were included among the outsiders and even as enemies. These members were by and large silent. When they did speak up, it was to reinforce the caregivers' views. Efforts to shift perspective, to grasp what the family was saying, to explore alternative interpretations of the situation were ineffective. These efforts were reduced to a dismissive *"They* can't give up hoping for miracles." The story, in other words, surrendered to the case. Suggestions to shift perspective were acknowledged in an abstract way—this was, after all, an ethics committee—but were viscerally ignored. Of course, the outcome satisfied no one.

A good way to grasp the porousness of the community's boundaries is to take a look at what is happening to a characteristic motto: "Do no harm." It is based on the Oath of Hippocrates:

I will neither give a deadly drug to anybody if asked for it, nor will I make a suggestion to this effect. Similarly, I will not give a woman an abortive remedy. . . . Whatever houses I may visit, I will come for the benefit of the sick, remaining free of all intentional injustice, of all mischief.[13]

But context makes the difference. "Abortive remedy" meets *Roe v. Wade*, and the "houses I may visit" are replaced by the office of the practitioner, who is visited by the patient. In a different tone, the Prayer of Maimonides reads, "Thou hast chosen me to watch over the health of Thy creatures. . . .

Inspire me with love for my art. . . . Do not allow thirst for profit, ambition for renown and admiration, to interfere with my profession."[14] Brought up to date, as in the Oath of Geneva (1948), the tradition reflects the experience of world war and holocaust. Thus, "I will not permit considerations of religion, nationality, race, party politics or social standing to intervene between my duty and my patient. . . . I will not use my medical knowledge contrary to the laws of humanity."[15] And under ideological inspiration, the Oath of Soviet Physicians (1971) begins, "[I swear] to dedicate all my knowledge and all my strength to the care and improvement of human health . . . and to work conscientiously wherever the interests of society will require it."[16]

The tradition, in other words, is really quite diverse, although this is masked by the community narrative. For example,

The historic sources point to a moral tradition in Western medicine which properly can be called "Hippocratic." . . . it cuts across cultural and national boundaries. The most concise and widely held expression of the Hippocratic tradition is the Hippocratic Oath. Taken at graduation, it signifies entry into a moral community. . . . In reciting the oath . . . graduates declare their allegiance to an ancient, honorable, and durable tradition, the survival of which is important for the welfare of the sick and of society.[17]

The tradition claims to speak to eternal values. It is this that supports members of the practice community facing risk and error.[18] And it is this that defends against the invasions of others. The differing sanctions—the family guild of Hippocrates, the sacred community of Maimonides, the laws of humanity of Geneva, and the good of society of the Soviet—are effectively ignored. Oaths are reduced to *the* "oath," which becomes a "folk" wisdom said to transcend boundaries of space and time and belief. Indeed, it is just this ontological status of the practice community's wisdom that justifies the member's conduct to him/herself, to the other members, and to the outsider. Challenges, then, are felt not just as personal and professional differences but as affronts to the universe itself, as it were.

"Do no harm," seems like a sacred invocation. But, in a demythologized age, that will not do. Given its form, we treat it as a moral commandment. At that point, however, the self-evidence of the "rule" disappears and tradition meets another threat to its stability, moral inquiry. The terms "do" and "harm" are not unequivocal. The subject of the command— who it is that is doing—denotes a various population. So-called nontraditional medicine admits others to the practice but not to the practice community. Nurse-practitioners and midwives challenge membership status and privilege. Team practice pluralizes the subject and opens the question of duty's distribution. Consumerism confounds the question of agency; that is, doing involves intention, judgment, decision, and action, and these are no longer owned solely by the practice community's members.

"Harm" is not self-explanatory, either. Needlessly causing pain, suffering, frustration, injury violates the oath; prevention of such an act is a duty. But harm's reference changes. To be sure, pneumonia was indeed the "old man's friend," so even the fight against death had its limits. But a changing sense of what counts as harm is emerging. Echoes of "do no harm" are heard on both sides of the debate about physician-assisted suicide. For some, to keep alive under certain conditions is to do harm; for others, to assist in death is per se to do harm. We even hear the notion of "wrongful life" applied to the birth of seriously damaged infants. Letting "nature take its course" may be seen as a "benefit" or a "harm."

What might be called managed deaths, as distinct from suicides, are now the norm in the United States, doctors say. The American Hospital Association says that about 70 percent of the deaths in hospitals happen after a decision has been made to withhold treatment. . . . Doctors say they often discharge patients from a hospital with the implicit understanding that they are sending them home to die, with a morphine drip for pain or without the ministrations of what they would call overzealous doctors at a hospital who might start antibiotics to quell a fever or drugs to stabilize a fluttering heart.[19]

The law also drives this shift in the practice community. "[H]ospitals, lawyers, and right-to-die advocates say there is a new wave of lawsuits seeking to hold hospitals, nursing homes and doctors liable for ignoring living wills and other advance directives. . . . Increasingly, lawyers are arguing that treatment against a patient's will is a form of battery. . . . This is a new area of law and the legal theories are still developing."[20] With the development of hospice care and pain management, harm is reinterpreted as a distinction between "aggressive" and "passive" care. And then, there is the talk of a "duty to die."

While he was governor of Colorado, Richard Lamm became, for a time, a troubling national presence, not as a result of his politics but because of the challenge he issued to the citizenry in every state. "At an autumnal age," he said, "it is a moral responsibility to make room for the young. As leaves fall from the trees in the fall, so old people have a duty to die."[21]

Faced with ambiguity, the practice community retreats to a generalized sense of duty. But it is not clear where the object of duty is located—duty to whom: the patient, the family, the third-party payer, the society. Similarly, other values are challenged. Once upon a time, the "sanctity of life" was taken as self-evident. Today, "there is not always consistency within and among traditions. For example, while many religious persons espouse a doctrine of sanctity of life . . . few practice that view consistently. Almost all holders of that view can, when pressed, think of instances when causing a death is not the worst possible outcome."[22] The notion of "dignity" becomes ambiguous, too, as in the argument over "death with dignity." Similarly, the "virtues" of suffering yield to pain management.

Ambiguity forces acknowledgment of the connection between the practice community and cultural, social, and religious values found in the other communities around it. This reveals that the practice community is less independent and less isolated—and so less protected—than it claims to be. As Edmund Pellegino put it,

What is at issue is the credibility and authority of the moral covenants that are at the heart of the [Hippocratic] oath, i.e. the promises to act primarily for the benefit and not for the harm of patients, to protect their confidences, to refrain from performing abortion and euthanasia and from having sexual relations with patients or their families, and to lead a life of moral integrity. Do these precepts retain their moral validity? Should they be revised to conform to contemporary mores? How free are physicians, society, and the profession to reinterpret and revise them?[23]

The common sense of the practice community still serves, but less and less effectively. We may approve or not, but the import of this development cannot be denied.

RULES

The virtue of community wisdom is located in the security it provides to its members and to outsiders as well. This virtue is exigent. The practice community, after all, is authorized to act against the moral habits of society—to invade body and mind, to prescribe drugs, to inflict pain for the sake of cure. Both members and outsiders need reassurance: the doer, in order to ground the doing in transcending sanctions; the done-to in order to accept the doing in good faith. In the clinical situation, doubt is typically repressed; a "useful fiction," if you will, appears. Exposure of that fiction as a fiction comes as a shock, is felt as a threat, and evokes a denial. The patient, more often than not, still says "You know best," and the physician still agrees. But the "normal" relationship becomes even more fragile in the situation of pace and intrusion. So the emerging challenges to community wisdom are a mixed blessing. Of course, participation, consultation, the liberty to choose or not to choose, and truth-telling are values to be honored in a democratic society. They override the practice community's values. But this does not come about without its cost.

Once the "useful fiction" is exposed—that is, members of the practice community do not always know what's best—it is impossible to restore it. To be sure, efforts to deny that it is a fiction continue. Thus nostalgia for the "doctor–patient" relationship is still found in the talk of public life and practice community, despite the fact that experience has already been radically altered. But guild authority, the role of "organized medicine" as public advocate and partisan lobbyist, is not only a mask for self interest. It derives legitimacy from the tasks that the "useful fiction" once performed, tasks that served both member and outsider. In its place, a more realistic language and practice respond to the demythologizing of the practice community. Communal culture and sacred covenant are on the way to secular contract. Explicit rules take the place of implicit habits. The shift is signaled by the rapid emergence of biomedical ethics itself as a way of absorbing the process of revaluation into the practice community. That, of course, does not happen easily. More often than not, the assimilation of biomedical ethics into the practice community is "only" symbolic, and later on may well turn out to be another "useful fiction."

To be sure, symbolic usage may mask interests alien to the narrative of the practice community, as when market values are transmuted into "more effective ways of doing medicine" or rationing of resources is transmuted into "objectivity" and "fair access." Fictions, however, also serve as heuristic devices, as with the "infinitesimals" of calculus, as with the "fictional person" in corporate law, and as with the "self-evident truths" of the founding fathers. After all, it is the *particular* symbol used that in its very particularity announces one kind of perception rather than another. So the fact that it is biomedical ethics which often carries much of the burden of demythologizing the practice community is in itself instructive. Biomedical ethics calls attention to persons, values, and obligations external to the practice community. It redirects attention although it does not dictate outcomes.

The practice community reflects what is going on everywhere else. As Paul Tillich put it, the "foundations are shaking." Ironically, a certain ordinariness begins to reshape the practice community even as its task remains extraordinary. Doctors, we say in a mood of discovery, are "also human," but the *discovery* is sad and frightening. Another tension arises between historic mission and social existence, a tension reflected among members of the practice community who experience disorientation and even dismay. Typically, older members of the profession remark, "If I were thinking about going to med school today, I don't think I would do it," and "I wouldn't become a doctor if I'd known then what I know now." More than a few report that they'd rather their children not follow in their footsteps.

The practice community loses its presumed independence and traditional sanction. "Do no harm" invites the patient's subjectivity. Since I know what's best for me and since I make decisions about myself, then what I say is all that counts. For the rest, it is up to you—the members of the practice community—to satisfy my desires. That, of course, is the import of the shift to patient as consumer. The practice community becomes another collection of merchants. Fortunately, neither an unrecoverable fiction nor a marketplace medicine exhausts the alternatives. Consistent with modernism, the possibility of an elaborated collection of rules and rights exists. These can serve as mediating moments that ultimately could allow for a reconstruction of the community. Considered as ends, however, rules and rights subvert the value of communal habit, the ability to respond quickly and securely in situations where reflection and inquiry can be destructive.[24]

Moral ideas emerge when we face actual problems. Often, this is taken to mean that arriving at moral ideas is the token of completion, that is, the philosopher's illusion that ideas are points of ultimacy. Even so, sympathetic an account of the relationship of ethics and experience as the following leaves the impression that story and case only initiate the moral process.

Our demarcation of moral phenomena is a significant *starting point* for "doing ethics." It recognizes that morality is an ongoing human enterprise that long predates the attempts of any philosopher to understand it. It also means that the philosopher's systematic and explicit account of morality will be *grounded* in the ordinary practice of morality. . . . In that sense, the philosopher "discovers" (or perhaps "uncovers") morality rather than invents it. . . . [This] insures that our account of morality will ring true to the human experience of morality. There will be no problem of "principles" or "axioms" so abstract or so general that their *application* to real problems turns out to be impossible.[25]

In such accounts, experience does not play a nontrivial role. But the desired outcome is still the principle, axiom, or rule, only now it is the usable or realistic principle. The return to experience is only an "application." With that, the notion of thinking with cases is lost. Biomedical ethics becomes an instance of standard empirical methods. Its unique features are in its substance, not in its way of thinking.

The possibility of cloning human beings is a striking example of the relationships of ethics, experience, and rule. Cloning can be assimilated within standard moral categories. This is particularly evident where these categories have a religious basis. Thus, the Vatican "is highly unlikely to give its stamp of approval to the cloning of humans. Roman Catholic teaching . . . rejects reproductive technology that replaces sexual intercourse."[26] A Lutheran scholar notes, "The possibility of human cloning is striking in one sense only because it breaks the connection [between marriage and begetting children] so emphatically."[27] Jewish commentators, by and large, see no principled but much practical difficulty. Several Buddhist respondents to a recent inquiry "seemed to treat human cloning as a *koan*, a perplexity posed to Zen students as a way of eliciting personal insight. . . . If anything about human cloning intrigued respondents, it was the question of whose *karma* the clone would inherit."[28]

Scientifically minded commentators follow a similar path. Typically, they opt for "free inquiry," although the standard categories—"normal" science and "normal" ethics—remain unchallenged. The National Bioethics Advisory Commission calls for a politically prudent (i.e., secular) five-year moratorium on efforts to clone human beings.[29] By contrast, Joseph Fletcher, more daring than the rest, put the matter in the context of evolution: "Man is a maker and the more rationally contrived and deliberate anything is, the more human it is. . . . [Therefore] laboratory reproduction is radically human compared to conception by ordinary heterosexual intercourse."[30]

The traditionalist sees cloning as an extension of human fertility by immoral means, and the modernist sees it as an instance of liberation. But both treat the issue as a replay of moral discourse and only another exercise of moral reasoning. The content of standard theological or moral discourse is enriched, but the terms are not changed. A conservative temper eases the absorption of novel events into the practice community. It provides for a transition that, while not seamless, is nevertheless more acceptable than an explicit break with past symbolic life.

Ethics, however, is not simply an artifact of reason but a personal, cultural, and historical activity. In this context, the response to news of cloning, the intuition that something utterly different was taking place cannot be dismissed as uninformed popular reaction or media "hype." I think back to a series on medical ethics for hospital staff. To our surprise, attendance at a discussion of cloning was more than three times the normal, and the discussion unusually vigorous. Nor was this peculiar to us. Thus,

The leader of the sheep cloning team, Ian Wilmut, Ph.D., of the Roslin Institute near Edinburgh came to the National Institutes of Health [NIH] in Bethesda, Md., to talk about the work 3 weeks after the research report was published in *Nature* (1997; 385: 810–813). He also spoke in Baltimore, Md., at a meeting sponsored by the Cambridge Healthtech Institute and at the US Department of Agriculture research center in Beltsville, Md. In 45 minutes, he quietly summarized before a packed auditorium at the NIH the 10 years of painstaking scientific work involved in nuclear transfer.[31]

References to the Frankenstein "monster" and to "playing God" were heard from public and professional groups. More adventurously, the new possibilities of reproduction open questions of choice and judgment, not least of all about the structure of family and generational relationships. The notion of intentionally reshaping character and destiny, already implicit in modern genetics, raises anew possibilities and dangers that range from eliminating deadly disease to encouraging a new eugenics movement. But most puzzling of all in its unpredictability, the species itself is opened up to intention. A report of a recent conference of molecular biologists and molecular geneticists noted,

Members of the public and even many scientists are unaware of how close science is to germline engineering, said Dr. Michael Rose, who studies the genetics of aging at the University of California at Irvine. . . . Germline genetic engineering "really touches the essence of who we are, what it means to be human," said Dr. Gregory Stock, a conference organizer and director of the Science, Technology and Society program at UCLA's Center for the Study of Evolution and the Origin of Life. "We are talking about intervening in the flow of genetic information from one generation to the next. We are talking about the relationship of human beings to their genetic heritage."[32]

Our haste in arriving at conclusions that fit within normality suggests a moral anxiety which itself calls for exploration. Failing that, we alienate doing ethics from other kinds of doing. We opt for an ethics that claims to be universal, timeless, and thin—another useful fiction, perhaps.

In looking at the substance of biomedical ethics, we recognize the inchoate process of doing ethics embedded in the notion of thinking with cases, of thinking with and not just about particularities. Cloning, like AIDS, PAS, and all the rest, raises questions of meaning and practice, questions of relationship, of doing good and avoiding harm. These questions are simultaneously individual, social, cultural, psychological, theological, and moral. The central actor in the ethical story, the human being, is caught in a process of redefinition and, with that, a challenge to his or her values and ends. That suggests the inadequacy of reducing the questions raised by human cloning to the merely practical—such as the danger of harm to the embryo and fetus, the unpredictability of outcomes as the cloned individual grows up, the puzzles of property law. It suggests, too, that the popular reaction touches upon something genuine but inarticulate in experience. And it suggests that "normal" ethics misses the point. A conservative strategy is only a holding action.

The clinical situation, understandably, needs reliable habits of practice and reliable rules of case management. These serve to reduce a potentially paralyzing ambiguity to a tolerable range of choices and actions. Absorbing cloning within the "normal" certainly typifies the response to dilemmas of practice and policy. But experience resists category. Policy and practice in biomedical ethics, at least, inevitably turn personal. So cloning is also the opportunity for the infertile couple to have a child of their own or for the family whose child has died to contemplate the possibilities of rebirth. Some, of course, would call the choice unwise, as it may be, and others would call rebirth an illusion, as it may be. But that discussion, calling attention to cases, is precisely where rule and habit surrender to the needs of moral reconstruction.

At the same time, the personal more often than not turns us toward public policy. Thus, the history of abortion since *Roe v. Wade*. Illustrative, too, is the notion of "informed consent," which is today a "foundational concept" of medical ethics. To paraphrase Immanuel Kant, whose notion of moral autonomy underlies it, consent without information is empty; information without consent is pointless. Yet,

The origins of informed consent in medicine are somewhat murky. . . . The requirement of simple consent to medical treatment was well established in the United States before World War II, and the Nuremberg trials of Nazi physicians made this a requirement of international law. But the elaboration of the requirement of consent to medical treatment and its transformation into informed consent according to Jay Katz, one of the leading authorities on informed consent, "surfaced, seemingly out of nowhere." . . . The entire informed consent paragraph [in the first informed consent case, California, 1957] was adopted verbatim, and without attribution, from the *amicus curiae* brief submitted by the American College of Surgeons. It is an ironic twist of history that informed consent was dreamed up by lawyers in the employ of physicians.[33]

As Katz remarked in that article, "twenty-six years was too brief a time 'to bring about significant changes in a 2000-year-old-tradition of silence.' "[34] In a later essay, he added, "the all too sweeping traditional view of patients has misled doctors into believing that medicine's opposition to informed consent is largely based on patients' incompetence rather than on an apprehension, however dimly perceived, that disclosure would bring into view much about the practice of medicine that physicians seek to hide from themselves and their patients."[35]

"Informed consent" is now a commonplace in the language of practice, but it is by no means uncontroversial. For example,

The doctor has lied ever since Hippocrates, and in most of the world, truth-telling is still considered bad medicine. Dr. Jimmie Holland, chief of psychiatry at Sloan-Kettering, recently surveyed oncologists in 22 countries. She says, "In much of Europe, South America, most of Asia—they consider it unethical to tell. They say, 'America is so brutal, you make it so difficult for the patient, and we are kind and gentle.' " But just yesterday, America was identically kind and gentle. . . . In 1961, in a study published by *The Journal of the American Medical Association*, 9 out of 10 doctors said they generally concealed a cancer diagnosis from their patients.

But by 1977, the ratio had been reversed. More than 9 out of 10 said they usually told the truth.[36]

This rapid change in the practice community was marked by the comments of the President's Commission on the Study of Ethical Problems in Medicine and Biomedical Behavioral Research. It noted, "There is very little empirical evidence to indicate whether and in what ways information can be harmful. Not only is there no evidence of significant negative psychological consequences of receiving information, but on the contrary some strong evidence that disclosure is beneficial." The commission noted studies showing that preoperative counseling reduced anxiety and that providing information was useful in "burn treatment, in stress experienced by blood donors, in childbirth, and in sigmoidoscopic examinations."[37]

Informed consent calls for a nondefined patient literacy and binds the caregiver to the desires and judgments of that patient. It announces a duty—to inform, to secure consent—and seems to assume that the duty is self-evident. Efforts to accommodate the requirement—for instance, by specifying the kinds of information that are obligatory, the kinds of consent that count as consent—leave in the physician's hands the decision as to what does and does not constitute relevant information. The temptation to simplify, restrict, and select may, no doubt, be resisted in good faith, but evidently the practice community retains the power to decide. Thus,

Medical criteria and standards have been formulated by the various specialty groups. . . . They are consistent in their position that any intervention derives its justification from the scientific evidence that it provides a diagnostic or therapeutic benefit. . . . Support for the professional determination of standards is also found at a broader social level. In its landmark opinion in *Brophy* v. *New England Sinai Hospital*, the Massachusetts Supreme Court, upholding the right of Paul Brophy to be free of unwanted, life-sustaining medical treatment, ruled that individual physicians could not be required to remove or clamp Brophy's feeding tube if it would be "contrary to their view of their ethical duty toward the patients." . . . The Supreme Judicial Court also ruled that a hospital and its staff "should not be compelled. . . . [to act] contrary to [their] moral and ethical principles, when such principles are recognized and accepted within a significant segment of the medical profession and the hospital community."[38]

"Informed consent" surely has symbolic value. It announces that the practice community cannot retain its insulation and that the outsider must assume responsibilities once reserved to the community's members. Yet the distinction between clinical judgment and curative goals defeats responsibility. Like the more generic distinction between means and ends, judgment and goal may be analytically separable, but in the case they melt into one another.

With terms like withholding treatment, withdrawing treatment, double effect, palliation, and surrogacy, a new language points up the emergent features of end-of-life decisions. Yet, like informed consent, they pose a puzzle. For example, since Quinlan, decisions to withhold or withdraw treatment have become moral and legal patient rights. On most analyses, withholding and withdrawing are morally equivalent. Both call for patient consent, both "let nature take its course," both rely on a common medical diagnosis and prognosis, and both have the same outcome. But as I review the literature and listen to what physicians and nurses say, withholding treatment is less likely to be problematic than withdrawing treatment. At work is a psychological difference between these actions. Withdrawing treatment is felt to involve complicity in "killing," while withholding treatment is simply to "stand aside." The logic of moral argument does not ordinarily change that feeling. The distinction, which seems to contradict moral rationality, cannot be dismissed or trivialized as *merely* psychological. Both story and case remind us that feelings and histories are legitimately present in the moral situation.

Acknowledging the confusions of withholding and withdrawing treatment in terminally ill patients, a standard clinical text suggests,

In place of these distinctions [ommissions/commission, active/passive, withholding/withdrawing, ordinary/extraordinary], the principle of "proportionality" has recently been endorsed by many ethicists. This principle states that a medical treatment is ethically mandatory to the extent that it is likely to confer greater benefits than burdens upon the patient. . . . In recent times, the original meaning of this distinction, which originated in Roman Catholic moral theology, has been obscured. Today, it seems to refer to the elaborateness, rarity, or investigational nature of a procedure. Originally, it designated the relation or proportion between the expected benefits of treatment and the burdens and disadvantages thereof.[39]

This shift to a rule of "proportionality" relies on the seeming clarity of a utilitarian calculus. But it really replaces one kind of problem with another, that is, whether the results of a cost/benefit analysis and an assessment of consequences can be morally determinative. Certainly, deontologists would disagree. But the rule succeeds precisely because metaethical questions are kept out of the discussion. It pays attention to the feelings that make withdrawing treatment seem more onerous than withholding treatment. By forcing reflection on the particulars, it recalls both caregiver and patient to story and case, to what constitutes a benefit and a harm in the actual event.

The rule of "double effect" has also entered the lexicon of the practice community. Like proportionality, it is taken from Roman Catholic moral theology. The rule was developed in the Middle Ages in order to work out a morally acceptable position where avoiding all harmful actions was not possible. More recently, it has been used to resolve abortion dilemmas when forced to choose between the survival of the mother or of the fetus, or the likely death of both. Double effect, according to Catholic doctrine, states that

the permissibility of the action depends largely on whether the bad effect is intended or merely foreseen and permitted to happen. In addition, it must also be the case that,

1. The act itself is not intrinsically wrong.

2. The good effect is produced directly by the action and not by the bad effect.

3. The good effect is sufficiently desirable to compensate for allowing the bad effect.[40]

Thus, administering massive doses of pain medication is allowable even when it is known that such doses, in themselves not "intrinsically wrong," will eventuate in the death of the patient. Double effect works a fine— and problematic—distinction between intention and foresight. To be sure, the notion of intrinsic moral values builds on an essentialist ethical theory—that some actions are always and by nature wrong, and others always and by nature are right. It allows us to deny the role of the pain medication itself as a cause of death. Intention becomes the moral criterion. Lacking the "intention" to kill, the caregiver is not a moral agent. He has, as it were, "clean hands" and a "clear conscience."

The puzzles of intention, however, cannot be ignored. For the believer, it is verified by an all-knowing deity who finally examines our conscience. So a false intention—say, to cause death but deny it under the cover of double effect—would be revealed, if not on Earth, then in eternity. As a secular instrument, however, double effect relies on the "word" of the caregiver. It presumes good faith and moral character. In a sense, then, it returns judgment to the traditional habits of authority and ultimately legitimates the calling. Yet it is precisely the erosion of legitimacy, of trust and authority, that generates an interest in explicit rules like double effect.

Double effect becomes even more problematic when it makes another fine distinction, the distinction between moral intention and psychological motivation. Intention invokes the will to act on a motivation or a desire. "Motivation in itself might be good or bad . . . but it does not constitute intention until the will is fixed on the object."[41] The caregiver must have a clear and explicit purpose in order to reassure others that his or her state of mind is as reported. Again, the issue is one of trust.

And not least of all, trust in oneself. Self-deception is an ever-present possibility.

In the clinical situation, unambiguous and uncluttered purposes, especially where pain and dying are involved, are unlikely to be available. After the fact, analysis may expose such purposes, but by then a failed or unclouded purpose is no longer relevant. Double effect, in other words, really serves as a form of reason-giving that sustains the caregiver in a difficult if not impossible situation. In practice, it also has unintended consequences. As several commentators have noted, "the rule has reinforced absolute societal and professional prohibitions against directly and intentionally causing death. . . . Concern about violating the rule's absolute prohibition against intentionally causing death may account for the reluctance of some physicians to honor their patients' requests to withdraw life-sustaining therapy."[42]

RIGHTS AND PRINCIPLES

When contract replaces covenant, rules provide a way station between habits of practice and some other destination. Less and less able to draw upon traditions of authority and trust, rules must rely on secular explanations. Given the move toward democratization, the rules must be translatable into generally understood language and rest on generally accepted secular justifications. It is no longer acceptable to retreat to mysterious formulations—clinical, theological, or philosophic—although such formulations persist. Now, however, these formulations deliver mixed messages, are as likely to be both functional abbreviations—such as DNR (do not resuscitate), EEG (electroencephalogram), and CPR (cardiopulmonary resuscitation)—and incantations. The member of the practice community needs to be able to say to the outsider why a given rule is adopted, what sustains it, and how it is supported by the evidence. These explanations and justifications are drawn by the practice community from other communities—for instance, biomedical sciences for verification, philosophy for moral vocabulary, religion for sanction—and, not least of all, from the general culture.

It is not surprising that the practice community turns to the notion of rights as support for rules. Central to this turn is the notion of autonomy, which is both a moral principle and a background theme of culture, and which is loosely equated with liberty. Thus, autonomy sustains the notion of informed consent, the right to refuse treatment, and so on. A right to confidentiality is asserted based in a more general notion of a right to privacy. " 'The right is paramount and nonnegotiable,' says a Boston psychiatrist. . . . '[It] guarantees that health information is protected and no longer a value-added option,' [Denise M.] Nagel stated, adding, 'Any company that ignores the need for medical record privacy in their health plan will be at a serious competitive disadvantage.' "[43]

Rights are responses to violation. In other words, if there were no actual wrong, there would be no reason to invoke a right. Further, if there were no conflict over rights, there would be no reason to invoke principles that allow us to sort out the conflict. In this process of rules, right, and principles, we are led back to some presumed ground of moral reality. This is what lends credibility to the notion that a right is discovered to have been there all along, and not invented. A right, unlike a rule, may be "self-evident," or else connected to some transcending reality like nature or human nature or God's provenance. In turn, a claim of some kind, such as of integrity or of tradition, is now explicitly formulated as the exercise of a right. Moreover, as a legacy of the Enlightenment project, the weight of a rights claim invites efforts to convert just about any preference into a right. Weaker terms like *entitlement*, which carries the notion of request, or *expectation*, which carries the notion of hope, will not do. As corporate players enter the clinical situation, rights to equality and choice, dignity rights, evolve. And the continuing "discovery" of new rights has become almost epidemic, as in a right to die and its complement, a right to live; a right to choose; a right to know; a right to care; a right to have children; a right to abortion; and so on. So-called "positive" or opportunity rights, like rights to care and attention, and not just rights to be let alone, appear in great number.

The increase of rights "talk" parallels the ability of modern scientific medicine genuinely to effect cures. In other words, when real benefits are available, then a right to those benefits becomes a relevant expectation. The fear of harm is similarly enlarged to include greater concern about risks and violations. Claims for, as with access to health care or to new technologies, and claims against, as with negligence or wrongful life, lead to the assertion of a generalized right to "best available" care. However, in articulating rights, moral discourse tends toward legalistic discourse, that is, to a language of duties, violations, and punishments. So it is not surprising that the courts become a point of last resort for the moral dilemma. It is not just that we are a litigious society, although we certainly are, but that ethical talk since the Enlightenment's focus on the "social contract" has centered issues of distributive justice. When to this is added a marketplace mentality, the tendency to invoke a social contract is reinforced. An entire social vocabulary is imported into the clinical situation from politics and commerce; quality assurance, consumer protection, fair pricing, cost/benefit.

Emblematically, the patient entering a U.S. hospital sees "Patient Rights" posted in corridors and examination rooms, and usually receives a copy with other admission documents. Of course, given the anxiety that accompanies hospital admission, "Patients Rights" are lost in the shuffle, just like most other documents. It is doubtful that much attention is paid to these proclamations except by institutional administrators, legal counsel, and patient advocates. But we are accustomed to such nods to virtue. To be sure, when a violation of duty occurs, "Patient Rights" seem to serve as evidence of a social contract, but are more likely to have the force of a secular contract between buyer and seller. Rights and their underlying contract lie dormant, as it were, until called into play (e.g., a marriage contract usually gathers dust until divorce becomes an issue).

Patient rights are neither "ideal" nor "claim" rights, to use Joel Feinberg's terms.[44] These are identified by what are variously called "God-given," "natural," or "human" rights or by a social contract. The proclamation of "patient rights" is misleading. Such rights are generated by caregiver institutions—such as the Joint Commission, the American Medical Association, the American Hospital Association—and can be amended unilaterally or even withdrawn at will. So they are not "rights" in the usual meaning of the term, although the language of rights fits with our cultural assumptions. Since they reflect a grant from one party to another in a transaction, they occupy ground somewhere between rights and privileges. But authority remains with the granting power except where limited by statute or case law. For patient rights properly so called, negotiation between equal parties has not occurred. And as between patient and caregiver, inequalities of knowledge and power make the notion of rights dubious.

To remedy this situation, a number of federal statutes like the Patient Self-Determination Act have been adopted in the last several decades, including those on living wills, refusal and withdrawal of treatment, informed consent.[45] In 1997 President Clinton appointed a National Advisory Commission on Consumer Protection and Quality in the Health Care Industry in order to account for the corporate environment. In November of that year it proposed a "Patient Bill of Rights." It called for the enactment of new laws and provided, among other things, for the right to full information, to emergency care, to confidentiality, to nondiscriminatory treatment, to an advocate. It is unsurprising, of course, that those opposed to legislative enactment of such a "Bill of Rights" urged relying on voluntary compliance. In other words, authority to grant and withhold should remain untouched. As George J. Annas, a member of the President's Commission, noted,

Attempts to transform the physician–patient relationship into a business transaction fundamentally threaten not just physicians as professionals but people as patients. This threat is real, frightening, and intolerable, which is why the new patients' rights movement aims not simply to preserve the physician–patient relationship in general but also to eliminate the financial conflicts of interest in managed care that are most threatening to that relationship. Thus, the new patients' rights movement seeks to shift power not from physicians and hospitals to patients but from managed care companies, insurance companies, and health care facilities to patients and their physicians.[46]

As Annas's comment reveals, the attempt to restore the practice community's traditions by means of an enacted bill of rights tells us how far we have moved into a secular and demythologized environment. The move toward enacted rights is not limited to the United States, just as the changes in the practice community do not stop at national borders. Thus, the Council of Europe adopted its own Convention on Bioethics and Human Rights.[47] That is, along with global diversity, a common transnational legal—if not moral—pattern is evolving.

For good or ill, the multiplication of rights gives no sign of slowing down, nor are the conflicts disappearing. A right to die is one example. But rights also entail duties. A consequent duty to assist in dying may well raise yet other violations, such as the conflict between a caregiver's duty to provide for the other and his or her duty to self. As addictive behaviors—alcoholism, drugs—have increased, the rights of the fetus enunciated in arguments about abortion have been asserted against the privacy rights of the mother in a number of states. These developments and conflicts occur within an already accepted universe of discourse, the discourse of law and justice. As that discourse evolves, we move from rules toward their explicit justification, just as we move from the traditions of the practice community toward the explicit enunciation of rules.

But this discourse raises issues of moral adequacy. For example, rights and the underlying notions of universality, equality, and autonomy attach to individuals. In the moral world, rights trump other moral categories. We are not to take moral account of special relationships or of particular biographies. In a rights world, neither stranger nor friend nor family is a relevant moral term; person qua person is. "Justice," we say, "is blind"— in principle if not in fact. Obligation is owed to anyone who is party to the social contract or who is a member of the species or who is a rational being. Obviously, this carries with it a certain view of human beings and of human society: the typical assumptions of individualism, the notion of self-interest, and so on.

A rights world is morally parochial. It would not do, however, to ignore its benefits. To take account of the person qua person leads to a livable civil society, particularly when it is no longer possible for its members to know each other. In such a society, we are expected to protect the other—another meaning of rights—whether or not we know or approve of the other. Of course, in the tradition, treatment was owed to the person in need whether or not he or she was lovable or hateful, hero or villain. Now it becomes an explicit right of the patient rather than an implicit duty of the members of the practice community. The shift in authority appears again.

At the same time, the inadequacies of individualism and contract are visible. As problems of access become urgent, we need some notion of the common good to complement the notion of fair distribution. We need to identify duties that are owed by caregiver and patient to society, and that do not arise only between persons or rely only on the consent of persons. An Israeli critic makes a similar point:

The conventional Western view says to competent people who wish to end their lives, "If that is your autonomous desire, we will not obstruct you in any way." . . . The traditional Jewish view says, "You are so valuable to us, beyond what you mean to yourself, that we simply cannot permit you to die. We care so much about you that we are willing even to violate your human rights in order to save your life." These two contrasting approaches represent, on the one hand, an individualistic view of society, and on the other hand, a perception of society more as a community, even a family.[48]

Longing for traditional and implicit relationships is not the only source of a critique of rights. Feminists, as Virginia Held writes, put "the criticism of rights from the perspective of care. . . . [It] is a criticism of the conceptually imperialistic role that law has played in moral thinking. . . . It is not directed at overthrowing rights in the domain of law, but at keeping legal thinking where it belongs . . . rather than supposing it to be suitable for all other moral problems."[49] Similarly, a communitarian movement challenges individualism.

Ideological debate, however, does not entirely convey the problems raised by transforming relationships into rule-guided conduct. At least as significant is the reliance of rights on the method of reason. Again, it is important not to throw away the values of rationality in order to account for criticisms of it. Coherence, consistency of judgment, and an effort to avoid special pleading or conflicts of interest are not mere luxuries. Absent rationality, the confrontation of intuitions or the assertion of authority can be adjudicated only by power and force. In the clinical situation, the power of the "secret" knowledge of the practice community would overcome any attempt to challenge it. More generally, without rationality the inequalities of clinical relationships would be incorrigible and inevitably legitimate master–servant relationships.

Nevertheless, the method of reason stirs concern. Feminists, among others, legitimately raise questions about the association of reason with gender-based politics and social authority. While it is not clear whether this association is only contingent or whether they are causally related, it is clear enough that the question cannot simply be ignored. As James Lindemann Nelson notes,

many feminists are dubious about moral theories that rely heavily on hypotheticals in an attempt to determine what is "required by reason"; to do so without careful attention to the influence of the historical and social forms in which reason makes itself manifest misconstrues reason's nature. Many feminists also place a good deal of emphasis on ethical reasoning, not only as situated, but also as a collaborative enterprise. . . . A related concern stems from what I take to be a widely shared feminist suspicion . . . about the use of intuition in moral reasoning. This concern arises from the conviction that our moral intuitions emerge . . . from the circumstances of our socialization, and those circumstances are, virtually without exception, shot through with misogynist and otherwise unacceptable practices of action, policy, and thought.[50]

A morality of rules, rights, and principles is not uncontroversial. It is useful that biomedical ethics has rediscovered the virtues of casuistry, that is, methods of doing ethics that include narratives, paradigms, analogies, and models. The dialectic of moral concept, method, and practice still awaits absorption into the habits of the practice community—the reconstruction, as it were, of tradition. That community, as we have seen over and over again, thinks with cases. This requires attention to the relationships, perspectives, and histories that particularize the actors in it and that call for imaginative and often unique judgments of relational and ambiguous experiences. It is striking, for example, that Tom Beauchamp and James Childress, who pioneered the development of a principled approach to biomedical ethics, add in the most recent edition of their seminal work the following statement:

Often, what counts most in the moral life is not consistent adherence to principles and rules, but reliable character, moral good sense, and emotional responsiveness. Principles and rules cannot fully encompass what occurs when parents lovingly play with and nurture their children, or when physicians and nurses provide palliative care for a dying patient and comfort to the patient's distressed spouse. Our feelings and concerns for others lead us to actions that cannot be reduced to the following of principles and rules, and we all recognize that morality would be a cold and uninspiring practice without various traits of character, emotional responses, and ideals that reach beyond principles and rules.[51]

I suspect that the move toward contract marked by rules, rights, and principles within a background cultural consensus is only a mediating step toward a new tradition. A return to the story and case makes sense as its strategy. But in that return, story and case need to be reperceived.

NOTES

1. Negligence has become a political and economic issue. However, it has been seriously overdrawn. For example,

... while it is reasonably easy for patients to threaten a suit ... the fact is that few negligently injured patients sue. For example, a recent Harvard Medical Practice Study of New York hospitals found that seven to eight times as many patients suffered negligent injuries as filed malpractice claims. Also, one of the investigators with the Harvard Study who compared hospital files with litigated actions found that fewer than 2 percent of negligent adverse outcomes resulted in claims. (Reference is to Harvard Medical Practice Group's report, Patients, Doctors, and Lawyers: Medical Injury, Malpractice Litigation and Patient Compensation in New York [Cambridge, Mass.: 1990]; citation is from Françoise Baylis, "Errors in Medicine: Nurturing Truthfulness," *Journal of Clinical Ethics*, Vol. 8, No. 4 [Winter 1997], p. 338.)

2. Gail Gazelle, "The Slow Code—Should Anyone Rush to Its Defense?" *New England Journal of Medicine*, Vol. 338, No. 7 (February 12, 1998), pp. 467–469.

3. Susan W. Tolle, "How Oregon's Physician-Assisted Suicide Law Spurs Improvements in End-of-Life Care," in *Physician-Assisted Suicide and America's Culture of Death* newsletter (New York: Grantmakers Concerned with Care at the End of Life, 1997), p. 3.

4. Linda Greenhouse, "Justices Uphold Laws Banning Assisted Suicide," *New York Times*, June 27, 1997.

5. Linda J. Romero, Robert D. Lindeman, Kathleen M. Koehler, and Andrew Allen, "Influence of Ethnicity on Advance Directive and End-of-Life Decisions," *Journal of the American Medical Association*, Vol. 277 (January 22/29, 1997), pp. 298–299.

6. Stanley Joel Reiser, "The Era of the Patient," *Journal of the American Medical Association*, Vol. 269, No. 8 (February 24, 1993), p. 1013.

7. Stanley Joel Reiser, "The Ethical Life of Health Care Organizations," *Hastings Center Report*, Vol. 24, No. 6 (November–December 1994), p. 29.

8. Nancy S. Jecker, Joseph A. Carrese, and Robert A. Pearlman, "Caring for Patients in Cross-Cultural Settings," *Hastings Center Report*, Vol. 25, No. 1 (1995), p. 12.

9. Annette Dula, "African American Suspicion of the Healthcare System Is Justified: What Do We Do About It?" *Cambridge Quarterly of Healthcare Ethics*, Vol. 3 (1994), p. 347.

10. For example, Marshall B. Kapp writes:

Nevertheless, placing too much reliance on empowerment of the elderly can lead, if we are not careful, to the implicit condoning of neglect of the elderly if they do not exercise their power sufficiently. Individualism and independence, if too rugged, may turn into health care nihilism. ... To blend autonomy and beneficence effectively, empowerment ideally should entail a negotiated sharing, as opposed to a sequential transfer of authority. ("Medical Empowerment of the Elderly," in Thomas A. Mappes and Jane S. Zembaty, editors, *Biomedical Ethics*, third edition [New York: McGraw-Hill, 1991], p. 199; citation is from *Hastings Center Report*, Vol. 19, No. 4 [July–August, 1989], pp. 5–7)

11. Edmund D. Pellegrino, "The Metamorphosis of Medical Ethics," *Journal of the American Medical Association*, Vol. 269, No. 9 (March 3, 1993), p. 1161.

12. A discussion of the debate between futility and patient autonomy includes the following:

The clash of values occurs when a patient (or his or her family) requests treatments that in the physician's judgment will not reverse or ameliorate the patient's condition. Although generally agreeing that treatment ought not to be provided, [R] Zussman documents in a study of intensive care units the fact that physicians, if requested, will almost always continue what [S. B.] Fiel labels desperate "end stage gestures." They do this in the belief that patient autonomy involves not only the right of patients and their families to accept or decline a proposed therapy, but also the right to whatever life-sustaining intervention they desire. (John J. Paris, Michael D. Schreiber, Mindy Statter, Robert Arensman, and Mark Siegler, "Beyond Autonomy—Physicians' Refusal to Use Life-Prolonging Extracorporeal Membrane Oxygenation," *New England Journal of Medicine*, Vol. 329, No. 5 [July 29, 1993], p. 354)

13. Ludwig Edelstein, "The Hippocratic Oath: Text, Translation and Interpretation," *Bulletin of the History of Medicine*, Supp. 1 (1943). Hippocrates was a fifth-century B.C.E. Greek physician born on the island of Cos and a member of a family that claimed to be descended from Asclepius, son of Apollo.

14. "Daily Prayer of a Physician" (Prayer of Maimonides), translated by Harry Friedenwald. The prayer is attributed to Maimonides, a twelfth-century Jewish physician in Egypt. Probably it was written by Marcus Herz, a German physician and pupil of Immanuel Kant and physician to Moses Mendelssohn. It first appeared in print in 1793. *Bulletin of the Johns Hopkins Hospital*, Vol. 28 (1917), pp. 260–261.

15. *World Medical Journal*, Vol. 3 (1956), pp. 10–12.

16. Translated by Zenonas Danilevicius, *Journal of the American Medical Association*, Vol. 217 (1971), p. 834.

17. Robert D. Orr, Norman Pang, Edmund D. Pellegrino, and Mark Siegler, "Use of the Hippocratic Oath: A Review of Twentieth Century Practice and a Content Analysis of Oaths Administered in Medical Schools in the US and Canada in 1993," *Journal of Clinical Ethics*, Vol. 8, No. 4 (1997), p. 384.

18. Error is by no means minor. For example:

Patients are harmed by medical error with surprising frequency. Brennan and colleagues, in a review of over 30,000 randomly selected charts from 1984, estimated that negligent adverse events occurred in 1 percent of hospitalizations; one quarter of those led to death. In a survey of 254 internal medicine house officers, 45 percent of whom completed an anonymous questionnaire regarding their mistakes, 90 percent reported that they had made errors related to serious adverse outcomes, including death in 31 percent of the cases. (Daniel Finkelstein, Albert W. Wu, Neil A. Holtzman, and Melanie K. Smith, "When a Physician Harms a Patient by a Medical Error: Ethical, Legal, and Risk-Management Considerations," *Journal of Clinical Ethics*, Vol. 8, No. 4 [Winter 1997], p. 331; reference is to T. A. Brennan et al., "Identification of Adverse Events Occurring during Hospitalization," *Annals of Internal Medicine*, Vol. 112 [1990], pp. 221–226)

19. Gina Kolata, " 'Passive Euthanasia' in Hospitals Is the Norm, Doctors Say," *New York Times*, June 28, 1997.

20. Tamara Lewin, "Ignoring 'Right to Die' Directives, Medical Community Is Being Sued," *New York Times*, June 2, 1996.

21. Nat Hentoff, "Duty to Die?" *Washington Post*, May 31, 1997.

22. Stuart Sprague, "Religious Reflections on Suicide, Assisted Suicide and Euthanasia," *Journal of the South Carolina Medical Association*, Vol. 92, No. 2 (February 1996), p. 58.

23. Edmund D. Pellegrino, "Ethics," *Journal of the American Medical Association*, Vol. 275, No. 23 (June 19, 1996), pp. 1777–1858.

24. Obviously, this account of "habit" owes much to John Dewey's *Human Nature and Conduct* (New York: Henry Holt, 1922). In particular, see Part One, "The Place of Habit in Conduct."

25. Bernard Gert, Charles M. Culver, and K. Danner Clouser, *Bioethics* (New York: Oxford University Press, 1997), p. 6. Italics added.

26. Gustav Niebuhr, "Cloned Sheep Stirs Debate on Its Use on Humans," *New York Times*, March 1, 1997.

27. "Cloning and Morality," *Minneapolis Star Tribune*, March 16, 1997, quoting Gilbert Meilaender, a theology professor at Valparaiso University.

28. Peter Steinfels, "Beliefs: Cloning as Seen by Buddhists and Humanists," *New York Times*, July 12, 1997.

29. See Alexander M. Capron (a member of the commission), "Slow the Rush to Human Cloning," *Los Angeles Times*, February 13, 1998.

30. Quoted in Peter Steinfels, "Beliefs: The Latest Advances in Cloning Challenges Bioethicists," *New York Times*, October 30, 1993.

31. Charles Marwick, "Scientists Flock to Hear Cloner Wilmut at the NIH," *Journal of the American Medical Association*, Vol. 277 (April 9, 1997), pp. 1102–1103.

32. Gina Kolata, "Geneticists Ask: When, Why Should Humanity Genetically Alter Itself?" *New York Times*, March 21, 1998.

33. Alan Meisel and Mark Kuczewski, "Legal and Ethical Myths About Informed Consent," *Archives of Internal Medicine*, Vol. 156 (1996), pp. 2521–2526. Reference is to J. Katz, *The Silent World of Doctor and Patient* (New York: Free Press, 1984), p. 60.

34. Rebecca D. Pentz, "The Vagaries of Informed Consent: Experience in Oncologic Care," *Clinical Ethics Report*, Vol. 9, No. 3 (Fall 1995), p. 1.

35. Jay Katz, "Informed Consent: Ethical and Legal Issues," in John D. Arras and Bonnie Steinbock, editors, *Ethical Issues in Modern Medicine*, fourth edition (Mountain View, Calif.: Mayfield, 1995), p. 93.

36. Martha Weinman Lear, "Should Doctors Tell the Truth?," *New York Times Magazine*, January 24, 1993, p. 17.

37. President's Commission on the Study of Ethical Problems in Medicine and Biomedical Behavioral Research, Vol. 1 (Washington, D.C.: Garlt Printing Office, 1982).

38. Paris, Schreiber, Statter, Arensman, and Siegler, "Beyond Autonomy—Physicians' Refusal to Use Life-Prolonging Extracorporeal Membrane Oxygenation," p. 356.

39. Albert R. Jonsen, Mark Siegler, and William J. Winslade, *Clinical Ethics*, fourth edition (New York: McGraw-Hill, 1998), p. 139.

40. John D. Arras and Bonnie Steinbock, "Moral Reasoning in the Medical Context," in John D. Arras and Bonnie Steinbock, editors, *Ethical Issues in Modern Medicine*, fourth edition (Mountain View, Calif.: Mayfield, 1995), p. 21.

41. Edmund D. Pelligrino, "The Place of Intention in the Moral Assessment of

Assisted Suicide and Active Euthanasia," in Tom L. Beauchamp, editor, *Intending Death* (Upper Saddle River, N.J.: Prentice-Hall, 1996), pp. 164–165.

42. Timothy E. Quill, Rebecca Dresser, and Dan W. Brock, "The Rule of Double Effect—A Critique of Its Role in End-of-Life Decision Making," *New England Journal of Medicine*, Vol. 337 (1997), pp. 1768–1771.

43. Charles Marwick, "Medical Records Privacy a Patient Rights Issue," *Medical News and Perspectives* (American Medical Association), December 18, 1996. Denise M. Nagel is president of the National Coalition for Patient Rights, Lexington, Massachusetts.

44. See Joel Feinberg, *Social Philosophy* (Englewood Cliffs, N.J.: Prentice-Hall, 1973).

45. The seminal activity for such statutory developments was the work of the President's Commission for the Study of Ethical Problems in Medicine and Biomedical and Behavioral Research. Its reports, issued in the 1980s, addressed special areas of concern.

46. George J. Annas, "A National Bill of Patient Rights," *New England Journal of Medicine*, Vol. 338, No. 10 (March 5, 1998), pp. 695–699.

47. Povl Riis, "Council of Europe Convention for the Protection of Human Rights with Regard to the Application of Biology and Medicine," *Journal of the American Medical Association*, Vol. 277 (June 18, 1997), pp. 1855–1856.

48. Shimon M. Glick, "Unlimited Human Autonomy—A Cultural Bias?" *New England Journal of Medicine*, Vol. 336, No. 13 (March 27, 1997), pp. 954–956.

49. Virginia Held, "Rights and the Ethic of Care," *APA Newsletters*, Vol. 94, No. 2 (Spring 1995), p. 40.

50. James Lindemann Nelson, "Measured Fairness, Situated Justice: Feminist Reflections on Health Care Rationing," *Kennedy Institute of Ethics Journal*, Vol. 6, No. 1 (March 1996), p. 57.

51. Tom L. Beauchamp and James F. Childress, *Principles of Biomedical Ethics*, fourth edition (New York: Oxford University Press, 1994), p. 462.

CHAPTER 6

Being and Denial

ABANDONMENT

In trying to make moral sense—and medical sense, too—we leave the story behind. We move on to case, to common sense, to rules and rights, and ultimately to theory and metatheory. Each move seems an advance, seems to get us closer to the truth of things. But as this happens, the temptation to wash out the details, to forget the persons and players, is very great. Like the Platonist, we are given to scientific models and to comprehensive abstractions. We search for the one inclusive explanation, as it were. Like the "Theory of Everything" in physics, this becomes our ideal. It is reinforced when, as in medical practice and in ethics, tradition encourages us to reduce the clinical situation to manageable concepts and easily retained simplifications. With the move toward rules, rights, and theories, other practice communities—philosophy, religion, law— enter the arena. But nontraditional communities expect admission, too. New players, often anonymous players, are introduced into the clinical situation. Their members now claim a stake, an ownership, in the case. So to the ordinary cast of characters—patient, family, physician, nurse, chaplain—is added a nearly indefinite number of participants. Interests are pluralized around different and, often, contradictory ends-in-view. Conflicts of interest thus inhere in the emerging situation as such, and are not just instances of villainy, cupidity, or blindness.

Traditionally, the move away from the story and toward the case served the treatment purposes of the practice community by connecting patient and practitioner. Not least of all, it served the teaching purposes of the community by, in turn, connecting practitioner and apprentice. The case also connected the participants to what was being done in the present and to the doings of past and future, that is, to other cases. This move was necessary for the survival of the practice community itself. The clinical situation needed quick and decisive actions for the sake of the patient in need and for the sake of those not yet attended to. The habit of "thinking with cases" is an acknowledgment of the usefulness, the inevitability, and the dangers of this move.

Cases, as I have noted, mediate between the particularities of the story and the universalities of the practice community. But in the condition of technocratic habit and market orientation, cases come to subvert the story. Thinking with cases becomes less than thinking and more like sorting, collecting, and reporting data. This may, more charitably, be described as "thinking with kinds." It is, of course, useful as populations grow, discoveries multiply, and resources shrink. But, as the Hastings Center report *The Goals of Medicine* warns:

Fragmenting the patient. The most glaring deficiency of the "diagnose and treat" model as with the biomedical research paradigm on which it rests, is that when simplistically interpreted it fragments the patient as a person into a collection of organ and bodily systems. Sometimes such fragmentation does not matter, as with emergency surgery, but often it fails to capture the full psychological and spiritual dimensions of a patient's illness. Too frequently, it alienates patients from physicians, who can seem only concerned about patients as the bearers of pathologies to be eliminated. A rich and strong doctor–patient relationship, historically at the core of medicine, remains a basic and enduring need. It is both a point of departure for medical education and a focal point for an understanding of the patient as a person.[1]

The clinical situation faces many ways at once. The members of the practice community must pay attention to the patient here and now, to the needs of next patients, and to their own needs as well. But the situation is also muddied by developments within and around the practice community, by the claims of other practice communities, and by society itself. It is caught, then, in a modern ambivalence. It must defend its own needs and interests, and at the same time attend to the interests of other and numerous practice communities as coclaimants on skill, resource, and duty.

Ambivalence and urgency nurture the art of deliberate forgetting. To be sure, forgetting may be a mark of sanity. Many details must be suppressed, else the doctor–patient relationship would become an exercise in endless description, perhaps finally only a literary exercise. At the same time, figuring out what is and what is not to be forgotten returns us to case and story. Thinking with cases includes learning how, what, and why to forget in order to attend. This ability to remember and forget depends on trained recognitions. Remembering and forgetting emerge from a tutored intuition that is both individual to the practitioner and characteristic of the practice community. Deliberate forgetting is, then, a skill that is learned through cases. At some remove from clinical forgetting, although not unrelated to it, is scientific forgetting. Often intuitive, simplifications, correlations, and probabilities are necessary for any disciplined inquiry and for any effective practice. So a certain epistemic legitimacy underlies both clinical and scientific forgetting.

But there is another face of forgetting that is neither constructive nor generous. In the modern clinical setting, proper names are deliberately forgotten. Borrowing its legitimacy from scientific forgetting, diagnosis, disease, and prognosis become, as it were, independent beings. To be sure, that replacement was always a part of clinical forgetting. At times crude, as in the reference to the patient as the "pneumonia" in room Y or as the "appendectomy" in room X, at other times less charitable, as in reference to the "zombie"—the comatose patient—in room Z. This kind of naming provided for a quick and ready reference at the bedside. It also allowed for humor and anger, and for the relief of anxiety and frustration that could not be confessed to the outsider but nevertheless was surely present. But we formalize a language of nonpersonality, use a functional language that turns proper names into items in a database and subsumes personal stories within diagnostic categories. Since traditional and scientific forgetting, each problematic in its own way, reinforce this development, modern forgetting looks like an extension of what was "always" done or of what makes medicine scientific.

Of course, the practice community attends to the business needs of its members, to patient fees and costs of practice. But modern forgetting elevates values and practices alien to the clinical situation, that is, practices of political and market calculation. Traditional forgetting was still personal, even humorous at times, and could always be recalled to the particular through the case and the story on which it relied. So it was joined to the ever-present possibility of remembering. But the new forgetting is much more deliberate and insistent. Indeed, not to forget in this new way is to risk survival in the practice community itself, as with overspending for a given patient in an HMO or, under Medicare and Medicaid rules, taking more time for a consultation than is permitted by statistical norms or prescribing medications that exceed standard budgetary allowances.

Like forgetting, which is its psychological and behavioral accompaniment, we hear more and more about abandonment. Within the patient's experience, to be abandoned is to experience forgetfulness on all sides. Typically, then, talk of abandonment appears in the context of the lost

story, and more and more stories are lost. This is situational abandonment. Seldom admitted—the busyness of machinery and chemistry and
the routines of care continue—situational abandonment is typical in
cases of terminal or deteriorating illness where little can be done medically to change the outcome. No doubt less than praiseworthy, it is an
understandable response to helplessness. The conclusion "I can do no
more" invites it, particularly where the practice community is so deeply
embedded in the notions of the "war against disease" and the "victory"
of cure. To admit abandonment, after all, is to surrender; the enemy has
won, death has won.

The doctor summoned us into the "family room," . . . It was the place where doctors told families their loved one was dying. . . . "He has an infection," the doctor
said carefully. He made deliberate eye contact with each of us as he spoke. "He's
dying."
    "Antibiotics won't help?" I said. The word, infection, brought me false relief. I
imagined bottles of pink amoxicillin in my refrigerator, bought to cure my children's myriad infections. "They might," the doctor said. "But in a few days or a
few weeks he'll just get another infection."
    "So what do we do?" one of us asked. Now the doctor turned his gaze on my
mother. "We can make him comfortable," he said. "You want to kill him!" my
mother shrieked.
    "I'm not in the business of killing people," the doctor said. "I'm in the business
of healing. And I cannot heal him."[2]

The physician, of course, is not the only one to walk away. Family and
friends sooner or later walk away, too. In fact, nearly everyone does. The
article continues,

I struggled with the fact that my father was certainly going to die, and soon. . . .
I was alone in my struggle. The thing about serious illness is, we cannot escape
it. Close friends and relatives who have been spared so far did not want to talk
to me about what I was experiencing. They did not want to glimpse their own
futures.[3]

To be sure, the nurse and the chaplain remain at the bedside. But even
they, as I have heard over and over again in discussions of "futility,"
cannot help but surrender to the angers of hopelessness. They appear
attentive, caring, responsive, and they visibly struggle to be attentive, caring, and responsive. But in the hallway and office, they confess the pointlessness of it all. The "responsible" family member remains behind as
well—there always seems to be a "responsible" family member left
behind—but often resentfully, complaining of those who have abdicated
and who have imposed an unfair burden. Inevitably, the patient—unless
in a coma or PVS (persistent vegetative state) or heavily sedated—catches

on. He or she knows that he/she has become only an excuse for the unwilling presence of others and that he or she has ceased to count for very much.

Of course there is sadness everywhere, but there is also impatience and annoyance and guilt. The desire to escape is overpowering. The visitor is out the door almost before he or she enters the room. Soon enough, the patient would rather be forgotten than feel the angers of those around him or her. A culture of denial invites abandonment.

If they can't be whole, they are somehow less than human. The dying are too often marginalized in this way. When they start looking weird or ugly, when they smell bad or don't make sense, when they need intimate personal care, they may be abandoned by most of their family and friends who do not want to be in the presence of such unpleasantness. It is uncomfortable to just "be" in the presence of one who is suffering and whose illness and symptoms we cannot fix.[4]

Of course, there is that rare breed who stays with the patient, the nurse who has chosen to be with the dying, the clergyman whose vocation expresses a "pastoral" sensibility. And there is, too, the physician who remains behind. In fact, most physicians remain behind, sometimes. Save for the saint, however, remaining behind relies on a relationship marked by thickness of personal knowledge—the continued presence of the nurse at the bedside, for example—the truth behind the mythic doctor–patient relationship. Thus, Timothy Quill describes his experience of his patient Diane, who was dying of acute myelomonocytic leukemia.

The next several months were very intense and important for Diane. Her son stayed home from college and they were able to be with one another. . . . Her husband did his work at home so that he and Diane could spend time together. She spent time with her closest friends. . . . There were emotional and physical hardships as well. She had periods of intense sadness and anger. Several times she became very weak, but she received transfusions as an outpatient and responded with marked improvement of symptoms. . . . After three tumultuous months, there were two weeks of relative calm and well-being, and fantasies of a miracle began to surface.

Unfortunately, we had no miracle.[5]

I recall reading Quill's essay to my class. He pictures Diane's last moment.

Diane's immediate future held what she feared most—increasing discomfort, dependence and hard choices between pain and sedation. She called up her closest friends and asked them to come over to say good-bye. . . . As we had agreed, she let me know as well. . . . Two days later her husband called to say that Diane had died. She had said her final good-byes to her husband and son that morning and asked them to leave her alone for an hour. . . . They found her on the couch, lying very still and covered by her favorite shawl. There was no sign of struggle. She seemed to be at peace.[6]

Once again I was transported to the bedside, saw the shawl spread over her body, felt Diane at peace, Quill's relief, the silent sadness of husband, son, and friends. My voice broke. My students were very quiet. For some reason I thought of the Buddha emptying himself of ego, renouncing Nirvana, and willingly taking on the suffering of the other as his own. The members of the class were still and then, as if shaking themselves free, began slowly to describe their feelings. The experience of being-with and being-for became tangible for us. We, too, were thinking with cases. But, after a while, the ordinary discourse of the classroom— the safe discourse of forgetfulness and abandonment—reappeared.

Special relationships, which are norms of the clinical situation, are vanishing. Functionalism and functionary replace being-with and being-for. It is not incidental, then, that abandonment has become a theme. Nor is it only the doctor–patient relationship that alters. Under managed care, nursing staffs are reduced. Nurses are caught in excessive patient loads and administrative duties. In other words, they cannot be nurses. Families, too, lose their purpose. Geography fragments intimacy. People just live longer. These developments strain and then fracture relationships, making demands for which we are personally and socially unready.

Embedded attitudes and feelings toward sickness and dying do not prepare us. We learn to deny that we feel pain, lose control, grow weak, get old, inevitably die. Our norms are youth, energy, health, and our mood is battle against anything that subverts these. Of course, we know that this is an unwinnable battle, but that only leads us to intensify denial, leads us to the *heroism* of "against the odds" and "in spite of." The abortion controversy, the AIDS epidemic, and physician-assisted suicide have renewed discussion of death and dying, posed the need for acceptance. Yet for most of us these discussions remain only an abstraction.

When talk shows signs of becoming personal, we tend to withdraw, to become silent. I recall one of my students presenting a paper about fetal tissue research. A Roman Catholic, she could not help but associate it with abortion, and so with the moral status of the fetus. Try as she might, she was caught in her own memories and values. Finally, unable to continue, she abruptly left the classroom without explanation or comment. The other students and I were surprised, even shocked. The academic agreement to keep experience and issue apart had been violated. A phone call to her that evening confirmed the memories that led to her departure. Ironically, the student reported surprise at her own feelings and responses.

In fact, we rarely transform issues of discourse into matters of experience. Existential anxieties lead us to build a wall between them. The clinical situation is particularly vulnerable to this habit of isolation. For example,

An examination of the records of the patients who died at Beth Israel by *The New York Times* suggests that the intensive public debate over issues surrounding the dying process has generally not trickled down to discussions between patients and their families, and patients and their doctors. The price of that silence can be steep. . . . Patients endure treatments they may not have wanted. Families who never discussed the end of life agonize over decisions about care, then live with the gnawing guilt that they may have made the wrong choice. Doctors and hospital staff members worry that they could be penalized for withdrawing care or prolonging it.[7]

Of course, silence is broken by events. The clinical situation, given the inevitability of pain, helplessness, suffering, and death, cannot help but be broken into. The connection between discourse and experience is made, albeit unwillingly. Thinking with cases institutionalizes the connection. But the case is all too often swallowed by the kind. Against this, other institutions respond to the challenge. Hospice, comfort care, and palliative care try to make dying as gentle as possible and to replace abandonment with connection. However, most patients still die attached to machines and tubes, and often alone and in pain. A follow-up to the SUPPORT study reported, "Most elderly and seriously ill patients died in acute care hospitals. Pain and other symptoms were commonplace. . . . Family members believed that patients preferred comfort, but life-sustaining treatments were often used."[8]

This reminds us of another kind of abandonment, another form of forgetting. The surround of the case and story is situational, but the more likely appearance of abandonment these days is structural. We are isolated, alienated in the midst of abstract presences. A crowd is at the bedside but it is no longer peopled by family, physician, nurse, pastor. The members of that crowd—a growing number—are identified by role and not by personality. They do many useful and well-intentioned things, but they are anonymous, invisible, and yet imperative.

So a sad irony engulfs abandonment. Never have so many participants been engaged in caring for the patient; never has the patient been more alone. To be sure, we die alone. This is the existential core of abandonment—I am dying; I am on the way to abandoning myself; I already model the certain absence to come. Family, friends, physician, nurse, and chaplain try to reconnect, to remind even as they withdraw and deny. Of course, they do not succeed, but they persist. In that persistence they create yet other connections for the survivors, connections that confirm the patient is still to be accounted for. They create memories. So, when a patient has no family or friends, their absence is almost tangible. But the anonymous members of the crowd have other ends in view. Their task is goal-oriented. Despite the rhetoric of patient-centered care, they are concerned with institutional and collective purposes. Conversation yields to decision-making, implicitness to formalism, memories to record-keeping.

This second forgetting is much more frightening than the first. With proper names and actual relationships, it is possible to retell the story and so to address situational abandonment, to complain of it, to resist it, even in the midst of dying to feel the vitalities of anger. But functionaries have a different being and a different agenda. Theirs is not an abandonment of denial but an abandonment of purpose. The authorship of the story is transferred. The original author and the story all but vanish. The vocabulary of invisibility grows; the moral vocabulary deteriorates. The language of autonomy, informed consent, and confidentiality feeds this invisibility. The patient with a proper name is no longer teller and told-to, but done-to. And the doing relies for its effectiveness on the invisibility of the doers in the crowd. The named members are put to one side—consulted, perhaps, but within the protocols of alienation. Thus, the physician, the nurse, the family member, and the friend become a minority at the bedside, and with the impress of function, tend toward role-playing, too. They have the right to speak within a patterned discourse whose rules are set elsewhere. Like the invisibilities and accusations in Kafka's *The Trial*, abandonment is a move—a move typical of our culture—from person to object, now in the name of virtue.

SUFFERING

Abandonment stirs questions about and for the other, about myself as other. I struggle unsuccessfully to be present, turn away from the patient, depart. And in that turning away, like the patient, I rehearse over and over again the death to come that ends the dying. Unable to help myself, I know what I am doing, and yet I go on doing it. Thus abandonment also raises the question of myself as other, myself as the one who is also suffering. It is something that is happening to me, too. I suffer from my helplessness at my helplessness, my anger at my anger, my annoyance at my annoyance. I suffer because I am relieved that I am not the one dying, and that relief makes me feel unworthy, somehow diminished in my compassion for the one who is dying. I also know that mine is a derivative suffering, dependent on someone else's story. And much as I may be a character in that story, even an author in some retelling of it, I am yet a creature of another's creation. So as other, I want to escape this dependency, and again this desire to escape adds to my feeling of unworthiness, and thus to my suffering.

I all too easily block the emotionality of the hospital room, the mix of pain, suffering, depression. I watch the visitors conversing with each other, exchanging gossip and interests. The patient lies there, nearly unseen. In the examining room, too, the patient—particularly the older patient—is present but not a presence, is talked about and not to, not with. I recall being in the examining room during my parents' visits to their doctor. The physician "seeing" my father or mother spoke to me and not to them. Of course, I, too, was addressed in the grammar of the "third person." Presence was quite literally denied, as if the patient already did not exist. I remember challenging the physician. Shamefacedly, he respoke his comments to them. But by the next visit, the habit of third-person talk returned. I remarked on this to others and heard the reply, "That's happened to me, too." Partly, but only partly, this is an understandable strategy of self-protection. We are all at risk. We are all dying, all soon dead.

Meanwhile, the patient is other and self, too. Knowing abandonment, he or she is confirmed in unworthiness, becoming an object prematurely, so to speak. And, unworthy, the patient soon abandons himself or herself. This is to know oneself as abandoned: to understand abandonment's reasons, even to agree with them, and to grasp that the other who abandons me is also myself as the one who abandons others. Indeed, my sickness and my dying are already evidence of my fault, my imminent abandoning of others. I feel that knowledge inescapably; I feel it as an intense knowing without words. The demanding patient, the indifferent patient, the happy-faced patient—all the many ways we show that we feel abandoned—tell the story of this agreement to my disappearance. "Why do you bother with me, it isn't worth it; I'm not worth it," and "I must be a nuisance," and still the hidden plea of anger, "Pay attention to me, even if only for a little while more."

Abandonment, which is rooted in the ultimacies and intimacies of human experience, was a religious idea long before it became a biomedical idea. Damnation is, after all, being turned away—the believer from his or her god, god from his or her creation, the creature from his or her being. Scripturally, dying is pictured as abandonment: "he turned his back to them, turned his face to the wall and died." The inevitable dance of other and self around the theme of departure is, of course, the seed of suffering. Little wonder, then, that religious imagery is also filled with portraits of suffering: the "suffering servant" of the Christians, the compassion of the Buddha, the homelessness of the Hebrew, the eternal return of the Hindu. But in a secularized society, this religious wisdom disappears along with the theologies that have outlived their meaning.

As with forgetting and abandonment, there are kinds of suffering. The first is, if you will, the experience of presence and departure. Suffering thus is radically subjective. Each of us can know only his or her own suffering; each of us can speak only to his or her own suffering; each of us can touch only the externalities of the suffering of another. At the same time, we are not entirely blind to the suffering of the other. There is a connection between us through suffering. Compassion and empathy, the overcoming of the loneliness of suffering, are not mere sentimentalities. Thus, the subjectivity of suffering does not tell a story of entire separation. I cannot really know the ways the other suffers. But I can catch the other in me.

It is death and dying that help us take hold of the meanings of suffering and the response of compassion. It is possible, then, to speak with each other of suffering. Thus,

[M]any of the people who oppose assisted suicide *feel* that we have an *absolute* ethical obligation to preserve life at any cost. . . . The sustaining value . . . the overriding value is that life is precious, death irrevocable, and human knowledge, power, and wisdom are severely *limited*. . . . Proponents of assisted suicide also affirm that life should be respected. But this "respect for life" takes on a very particularly meaning. . . . For these physicians, respect for life means respect for *this* life as *this* living person understands her or himself. . . . These admittedly scant summaries are presented to highlight certain themes. The first is that the best proponents of both positions are motivated primarily by compassion. Physicians on both sides of the issue *experience* or *feel* an *ethical call* that is, at least on some level, *absolute* enough to compel action.[9]

Traditionally, suffering may be understood as atonement for wrong done or evidence of redemption still to come. It may be understood as sacrifice, taking on the suffering of another as one's own, or it may be a sign of injustice, as in the suffering of the innocent.[10] To the clinical situation, we bring these memories of suffering and its meanings. We struggle to absorb them into the language and norms of the practice community. For example,

[T]here is now a large body of data on the components of suffering in patients with advanced terminal disease. . . . There are three main factors in suffering: pain and other physical symptoms, psychological distress, and existential distress (described as the experience of life without meaning). It is not only the patients who suffer but also their families and the health care professionals attending them. These experiences of suffering are often closely and inextricably related. Perceived distress in any one of the three groups amplifies distress in others.[11]

No doubt, the religious, moral, and emotional thickness of suffering is a puzzle to the practice community, particularly in its more positivist incarnation. In response, reductive strategies seek to set limits to what suffering is permitted to mean. As Kathleen Foley, a leader in the struggle to develop palliative care, reminds us in the above article, suffering begins with pain that is definable, describable, even treatable. First questions in the clinical situation are "Where does it hurt?" and "What is hurting you?" Pain is thus a doorway into story and case; it is biologically and morally useful. It alerts us to matters gone awry, motivates us to risk becoming a patient. Pain tells its story to the practiced eye and ear and hand. And pain's memory continues.

We respond to pain hesitantly, slowly, and inadequately. Thus the tardy arrival of pain management and the fear of "overdosing" the dying patient, as if drug addiction were really a worry at such a time. No doubt a puritan impulse in us still sees virtue in suffering, interpreting it as deserved, pedagogical, or redemptive. To seek to defeat pain, then, is to minimize suffering, to confess weakness of will or failure of moral understanding. Once upon a time, we would tell someone to "be a man" or "not to be weak as a woman." If this gendering of pain is less acceptable these days, the meaning lingers, the connection of pain and suffering and virtue. We hear in this praise of suffering—for that finally is what it comes down to—an acknowledgment of some cosmic purpose, as in "God's plan" or atonement for "original sin," or, less theologically, "no pain, no gain." Paradoxically, it seems that just by accepting pain, that suffering is reduced; by rejecting pain, that suffering is increased. Pain is not just had. It means and serves.

To be sure, much of this cosmic and cultural baggage is unspoken. But it is yet another form of forgetting. Pain is to be fought, conquered, denied, ultimately borne. And yet, in the having, pain becomes reality. Suffering it thereby loses its possibilities.

The English poet, John Keats . . . wrote simply, "Until we are sick, we understand not." That is so true—until we are the ones who are feeling the pain, until we are the ones who are on the sick bed, we cannot fully appreciate what the other person is going through. And even having been there myself, today I cannot fully appreciate what someone is going through on the burn ward. . . . When I was in the hospital, there were many reasons I wanted to refuse treatment, but one was overriding—the pain. The pain was so excruciating, it was so far beyond any pain that I ever knew was possible, that I simply could not endure it.[12]

But while pain is overpowering for the self in pain, it is not for the other, and this not just from lack of care or absence of feeling. Cruelty does not explain our resistance to treating pain or the belated arrival of palliative care. Something more than utility is at work.

Of course, pain is not sufficient to explain suffering. The discussion of physician-assisted suicide has forced attention to a cognate theme, depression. "In one study, for example, Dr. Harvey Max Chochinov, a psychiatrist at the University of Manitoba . . . found that among suicidal cancer patients who expressed a consistent, unequivocal desire for death, more than half were clinically depressed. In a New York study of 378 AIDS patients, the strongest predictor of a personal interest in doctor-assisted suicide was the presence of depression."[13] As those who report the experience tell it, to be depressed is to find life and world pointless, hopeless, dark, without relief, to be unable to feel pain. But this "finding" is not the pessimist's reflection on the state of self or universe. Depression is a way of being in which being itself is denied and for which no relief is felt possible. Nothing is untouched, uncolored; nothing permits joy or even toleration.

What we call depression used to be called melancholy. And though it has had many other names as well . . . there is reason to believe that it felt the same to sufferers in the past as it does today. One hundred and fifty years ago, Ralph Waldo Emerson wrote in his great essay, "Experience," about what it is like to be caught in a midlife trance from which he could not be roused: "We wake and find ourselves on a stair, there are stairs below us, which we seem to have ascended; there are stairs above us, many a one, which go upward and out of sight. But . . . we cannot shake off the lethargy now at noonday."[14]

Unfortunately, in the cool of diagnosis, we lose depression's existential tonality. For example, "Depression is a feeling of intense sadness; it may follow a recent loss or other sad event but is out of proportion to that event and persists beyond an appropriate length of time."[15] But sadness is, after all, a feeling, and in depression feeling itself is lost. To be sure, in the clinical situation sadness is to be expected. No one joyfully enters into treatment. At best, there may be a sense of relief; something can be done about my troubles. Sadness, however, is also a confession, in our culture, a confession of inadequacy. So sadness moves us toward depression, signals the lessening of our being, and begins to teach us depression as a way of being. Certainly sadness, with greater or lesser intensity, colors life and relationship. But it may be fractured by other moments, compete with other senses of things. Ultimately, then, "sadness . . . is not the same as [clinical] depression. . . . Sadness does not rule out hope, whether it is the hope of seeing a new grandchild or enjoying a movie. Depression does. Sadness does not render a person helpless. Depression does."[16]

Neither pain nor sadness tells the entire story of depression, which is also a "loss of meaning." While this may seem a philosopher's category, this loss is felt before it is understood, and as depression takes hold of us, it is not understood at all. What once fitted together now falls apart; what once was enjoyed finds no place in some lost scheme of things. Even what once was regretted or hurtful is now only itself, disconnected from memory and future, only regret and hurt. Above all, with that loss of meaning, connection itself become empty. So even suffering—which

permits the connection of compassion and so, in part, warrants its virtue—vanishes.

But loss of meaning need not rely on existential or theological poetry
for our grasp of it. It has its behaviors. The patient, a short while ago
about life's tasks, lies there waiting for the attention of others and at the
same time not caring about that attention. Purposes are put to one side,
perhaps to be returned to in recovery, perhaps never to be retaken.
Relationships grow tenuous and break. Routines, going-through-the-
motions, replace activity. Of course we protest, but even that notices our
loss. And soon enough protest grows mute. Sooner or later, we cease to
struggle. I recall the bedside of the dying patient, more than a few dying
patients. I knew—the nurses knew, the physicians knew—that he or she
was ready to die. With the apparent peaceableness, caring itself vanishes.

Ironically, even the "miracle" becomes a challenge to meaning, even
"hope" becomes a difficulty. Thus, the response of AIDS patients to the
"cocktail" that for many delays death indefinitely:

"It's like being resurrected," said Robert, who spoke on condition that he not be
fully identified because he feared prospective employers had misperceptions
about AIDS. "I feel like a child."[17]

And

"For many people who are dealing with a terminal illness, death can become a
major safety valve," said Frank . . . 43, an artist with AIDS. . . . "It promises a release and a cessation of pain. On the other hand, you might find out that you're
going to be fine for the indefinite future and say, 'What am I going to do now?' "
. . . "Such news can throw people off balance," said Dr. Robert P. Cabaj, a psychiatrist. . . . "Suddenly, all the emotional work involved in getting ready to let go
has to reverse itself."[18]

The confrontation between structural abandonment and suffering initiates today's more inventive responses. Thus in a different way, hospice,
comfort care, and pain management enter the clinical situation. In part,
these are efforts to gain control where no control is finally possible, to
bring death and dying within the ambit of cure when, paradoxically, cure
is ruled out. So these might be seen as further instances of the "medicalizing" of suffering. But these inventions are deeply countercultural.
We get a hint of difference in the following:

You could argue that my sister, mother and husband died from the advanced
stages of terminal illness and not from morphine. My sister, the first to die, had
bravely fought breast cancer for more than a year, but it was the morphine that
hastened her death. My mother astonished her doctors time and again by hanging
on in the face of all odds. Maybe she would have rallied again had I not asked

her doctor to put her on a regular schedule of morphine injections to ease her acute pain. She died within 24 hours of my request. . . . By the time my husband became seriously ill, I knew it would be the morphine, not his metastasized cancer, that actually made him stop breathing. . . . I cried, mostly from exhaustion but also from a sense of failure, thinking that I had somehow made the wrong decisions. Morphine-induced death isn't pretty. . . . It, too, is a struggle. Dying is as hard as birth.[19]

Hospice, comfort care, and pain management are ways of humanizing the medicalized experience, shifting from struggle to acceptance, retaking the story. They respond to a problematic sociology and demography, the sociology of individualism and nuclear families and communities of strangers, the demography of large numbers and an aging population. Hospice and comfort care are modes of overcoming abandonment, denying denial, and attending to subjectivity. In describing the relationship of Ira Byock, president of the American Academy of Hospice and Palliative Medicine, to one of his patients, a reporter wrote:

Mike Morris [the patient] had planned a huge garden, his family had bought a new minivan and they had begun to visit places that Mike wanted to see once more. Mike's sessions with Byock were a high-speed emotional roller coaster, with talk of suicide one week and the next week a firm conviction to live his life fully until the end. . . . Byock's progress notes read: Mike talked more determinedly about mending his relationships with his wife and four children. His pain was reasonably well controlled, but it would only get worse in the days ahead. . . . Increasing pain medication and a continually weakening system would also bring other symptoms. It was time to take the next step.[20]

With suffering acknowledged, the wall between discourse and experience is broken. As Timothy Quill, also a hospice physician, wrote, "Dying patients need more than prescriptions for narcotics or referrals to hospice programs from their physicians. They need a personal guide and counselor through the dying process."[21]

DECEPTION

Deception[22] is no stranger to the clinical situation. There are the comforting lies we tell in order to avoid adding to the pain of an already suffering patient. These are the lies we know as lies. Behind them is the thought—praiseworthy, on the face of it—that nothing is lost by telling them, and much might be gained by easing the patient's final days and hours. I recall a conversation with a group of caregivers in the Soviet Union some years ago. Our commitment to patient autonomy and informed consent did not move them very much. Unanimously, they regarded our commitment to telling the patient the truth in "hopeless situations" as "cruel" and "unnecessary." This response was typical. For example, "According to an international survey, oncologists in Africa, France, Hungary, Italy, Japan, Panama, Portugal and Spain estimated that fewer than 40 percent of their colleagues would tell their patients the truth if they had cancer."[23]

Individualism enables a way of thinking that makes autonomy a moral and legal priority. But, at least through the 1970s, our conduct was closer in behavior, if not in language, to international practice. And we are still caught with mixed motives. As a physician wrote,

As a radiologist who has been sued, I have reflected earnestly on advice to obtain informed consent but have decided to "take the risks without informing the patient" and trust to "God, judge, and jury" rather than evade responsibility through a legal gimmick. . . . In a general radiological practice many of our patients are uninformable and we would never get through the day if we had to obtain their consent to every potentially harmful study.[24]

Another source of deception is the tension between egalitarianism and paternalism. For example, for a very long time a diagnosis of "cancer" was not even mentioned. Patients were left to their anxieties in the name of kindness. Informed consent, however, has moved from research protocol to medical practice, and is now a matter of law as well as morality.[25] Thus, the direct lie is likely to be avoided. But deception is not. Truthful but misleading language or the telling of partial truths replaces the lie. Technical jargon is still the habit. "There's always hope" is an unspoken hedge in most communications, and "it's hopeless," if spoken at all, is reserved for last moments when speaking itself becomes irrelevant. Extraordinary efforts to continue life at nearly any cost are still the rule, however, and the fact in itself conveys hope. The bedside is a very busy place even at the last moment. Appearances are preserved.

Patients, of course, hear what they want to hear. So they also participate in deception. At the same time, a large majority of patients (about 80 percent in most studies) say that they would prefer to know both diagnosis and prognosis.[26] But this preference is prospective. Things grow muddier in the event. More often than not, however, deception doesn't deceive. In fact, it is a good bet that many patients already know they are dying. But they are not permitted, do not permit themselves, to share that knowledge with family and friends who also know they are dying. So, as it were, deception breeds deception. Even more problematic, patients who can recover suspect the worst, particularly in the face of a silence that does not distinguish between truth and kindness. Failure to tell the truth thus sustains denial for the dying and increases anxiety for the living. It further infantilizes the patient by blocking actions he or she could still be taking to announce that life persists until death—for instance, practical actions having to do with economic arrangements and last wishes, symbolic actions having to do with saying good-bye. And as the anxiety of dying grows, infantilization is even welcomed. As it were, with deception, death comes early and often.

Family and friends want and do not want to know what is going on. Thus, they receive the well-intended report of the physician that "there is one chance in a thousand" as saying the patient will recover. They are able to hear only the promise. Hence, the repeated responses "do everything you can" and "miracles do happen" and "hope is important" are not only cries of desperation. It is not quite fair, then, to blame the family for their "unreasonable" demands, although we do that often enough. True, the physician's statement is accurate, or as accurate as he or she can get. But probabilities are used to mask our unwillingness to say the thing that is so. Psychological, if not logical, meaning changes when the numbers are put in reverse order, that is, "There is a 999 to 1 chance that the patient will die." But that is not what we say.

Science, as everyone knows, solves problems, and dying is only a problem! So talking with numbers, talking "scientifically," is comforting. However, this does not avoid deception and even strengthens it. Cool communication is a defensive move, too, a method of self-protection for the physician and an offer to share deception's benefits with others. Thus, even while knowing its falseness, the family holds on to hope, hearing the "one favorable chance" and not the 999 unfavorable chances. This encourages the family to participate in self-deception, to enter into a psychological conspiracy in order to benefit from the protection that is available to members of the practice community. In a sense, then, deception is a strategy of choice on all sides.

To be sure, deception must finally fail. Recognizing that, programs on death and dying have become significant projects for hospitals, organized medicine, even a few medical schools. But, given what has gone before, these efforts have trouble succeeding. Moving from a failed reliance on persons—to be honest, to face realistic choices—we attempt to put structures in place that guard us against personal failure. Inevitably, these structures are caught in ambivalence. They are intended to sustain persons, which they often do, and yet they invite us to avoid persons. In other words, they cannot by themselves overcome a culture of denial. The process of institutionalization continues to evolve. For example, without noticing its paradoxical formulation, we hear calls for "compassionate clinical management." But the issue is cultural and not only medical.

The virtue of benevolence would seem to grant pardon to both lie and deception. This, however, is to read morality in a single dimension, as good intentions. But deception opens wide a moral and psychological gulf between patient, family, and physician. The urgency of connection, when all connection is threatened, has been betrayed. Trust erodes. Sooner or later the angers that accompany chronic debilitating sickness and prolonged dying turn support into hostility. Acceptance and peaceableness vanish. Bitter denial and frantic activity take their place in the face of the outcome that cannot be admitted or talked about. Along with the guilts of regret, suffering and dying are filled with guilts of deception. What could have been done to ease pain, to do final things, to interpret life, to celebrate connections is not done. As a physician described it,

There were many similarities between this patient's clinical history and the story of Ivan Ilych. For Mrs. R. L., as for Ivan Ilych, her final illness occurred at what felt like the wrong time. . . . Again like Ivan, Mrs. R. L. and her family went through a time when their sole focus was on finding a cure for her illness. At the end, Mrs. R. L. had to face death alone, while her family and I went on refusing to acknowledge her impending death in her presence. The death of Mrs. R. L. had a devastating effect on me. . . . I felt tremendous guilt for my participation in deceiving a patient about her condition and great frustration with my inability to facilitate thoughtful and empathetic acknowledgment and discussion of her impending death, while trying to accommodate the strongly held desires of a family that I did not know well. I feel I neglected my moral responsibility to my patient.[27]

Benevolence tempts yet other deceptions. The move away from paternalism thus hides its own moral dangers, the dangers of autonomy. To be sure, collectivities and authorities have historically been dangerous for persons. Against these, autonomy deserved its welcome. It is the patient who is to decide whether to accept treatment or not, whether to cease treatment or not. In that way, the patient continues as a responsible being, a person. He or she is presumed to respond with his or her entire experience, his or her entire "life plan," in mind. Authority is defeated. But its conqueror, the autonomous person, may be as problematic.

Although things are changing, it is rare in our society to suggest the legitimacy of sacrificing a personal good for the good of others; to save a family's wealth or a society's resources, for example, instead of expending these for futile treatments or minimal benefits. Articulating the need for a more inclusive sense of what is best, Daniel Callahan calls for "standards . . . established collectively, by joint bodies of lay people and physicians":

What would be the pertinence of such a development. . . . It would be valuable if in coming years some consensus were achieved about futile treatment. "Futility" needs, however, to be understood in two senses: futile because no benefit whatever can be achieved from treatment and futile because, given resource limitations, the treatment is economically unjustifiable. Thus, we must have a general social agreement on the right of physicians to withhold medical treatment from persons in the persistent vegetative state, and an agreement on the forms of medical treatment that would be considered futile for those faced with imminent death from an acute or chronic illness or from the slow death of dementia.[28]

A radical individualism only seems truthful to experience. In reality, it carries the burden of hidden choices, often social and cultural choices. Deception, in other words, is deeper in us than we acknowledge or, perhaps, than we can acknowledge. For example, Carl Elliott writes:

In his essay, "Madness and Religion," . . . [M. O'C.] Drury confesses his own self-doubts. . . . He tells the story of a Catholic priest he treated for depression, a man once considered very gifted by his parishioners but who had lost his faith. . . . he became convinced that he had cancer. When a work-up showed otherwise . . . the priest became resentful, saying that his problem was spiritual, not medical, and that he himself was to blame. Today, such a priest might be prescribed anti-depressants. Drury gave him electroconvulsive therapy (ECT). [After seven treat-ments] the priest's insomnia and stomach pain immediately disappeared. . . . A therapeutic success? Perhaps. . . . For Drury, it is clear that mental and physical health, while important, are not the supreme human goods. The question for a psychiatrist, says Drury, is when to say, "This man is mad and we must put a stop to his raving," and when to say, "Touch not mine anointed and do my prophet no harm."[29]

The decision to refuse or withdraw treatment is based on what are called "quality of life" issues—more bluntly, on whether life is worth living when attached to machinery or when the mind is going or when pain is intolerable or when the things that gave meaning and pleasure are no longer available. No doubt, personal values and needs, desires and dreams shape the choice. But these do not come out of nowhere. Or, to put this in Aristotelian terms, we are "social animals." But that means we not only are shaped socially but we survive on sociability.

I recall a visit with an old friend. In his early eighties, "B" had never known major illness. Still active in the community, widely read, he participated regularly in my classes at the university, enjoyed a good dinner with friends, kept up with local and national events, about which we argued vigorously and often. He shared his memories about his life as a very successful business executive and effective public citizen. And when we sat together at a local restaurant, he still managed to flirt innocently with the waitress. He had an eye, as he put it, for a "pretty face and figure." Of course, his memory was not as good as it had once been. For all that, he had his circle of friends and activities, however, he was also lonely. His wife had died some years earlier, and his children and grand-children lived hundreds of miles away. Now he was in a hospital bed, having suffered a heart attack. A difficult surgery and a painful but likely recovery could, he told me, prolong his life for a few years. Without it, he would probably "be dead within the year." But he added that he had never before experienced the kind of pain that went with the attack, and that he could not contemplate actually opting for such pain again.

We talked through the silences. Then he turned to me and asked, "If you were me, would you have the operation?" I didn't have a ready answer. I knew that this was a genuine question—he did want my answer— and a false question—he already knew what his answer would be. Finally, I told him that I would choose the surgery, although I did not urge it in a forceful way. But as we talked further, I realized that prolonged life was not what he wanted . . . and not just because he could not stand the pain or the thought of the pain. *He* was ready to die, although he did not say so directly, but *I* was not ready for him to die. Pain was the excuse for our unwillingness to talk about suffering.

The temptation to try to persuade was very great. I think he wanted me to try to convince him so that he could tell me why he wouldn't, couldn't, agree with me. In part it was a game—to be sure, a very serious game—for both of us. We sat quietly for a while longer. He had a twinkle in his eye when he said, "Think about it, we'll talk more." He left the hospital a few days later, lived for a few months, and then quietly died. In that interval, we continued to see one another, to talk about many things. Only once, however, did he talk about his coming death, and then in order to ask my views on his funeral plans. For the rest, death was simply a background for us, present but unspoken.

The choice of refusing or withdrawing treatment seldom comes in a timely way or as a calculation of cost and benefit. It is never as rational as that. Fear mingles with anxiety. Worries about impoverishment color the situation, although no one wants to talk about costs—except, ironically, the patient. "I don't want to be a burden" is heard often enough. No doubt, finding echoes in the listener, these echoes are not confessed aloud and so strengthen the strategy of deception. Fatigue is not unknown, a tiredness with life itself, which expresses itself as "enough already."

More often than not, the decision to refuse treatment is not what it seems. Indeed, as appears in the commentary around physician-assisted suicide, at times the right to refuse treatment seems actually to moralize deception.

"We have a well-established underground practice" of physicians hastening death of the terminally ill, declared one lawyer arguing for the new constitutional right. Justice Ruth Bader Ginsburg then asked Solicitor General Walter Dellinger who opposed the proposition, whether that didn't mean the whole court battle is "a great sham, because physician-assisted suicide goes on for anybody sophisticated enough to want it." "We looked and we don't know," responded Mr. Dellinger. "There is no evidence."[30]

But in fact the evidence is emerging. For example, a recent survey of 1,902 physicians (out of 3,102 asked) reported that of 320 doctors who had received requests for assistance and 196 who had been asked for lethal injections, "sixteen percent . . . reported that they had written at least one prescription to be used to hasten death, and 4.7 percent . . . said that they had administered at least one lethal injection."[31] Further, it is not simply physicians who are encouraged to deceive. As N. Ann David writes,

Patients who really prefer death . . . may achieve their end by exaggerating . . . their aversion to the proposed life-saving treatment . . . to prevent people . . . from reaching the conclusion that the . . . refusal of treatment [is] . . . tantamount to suicide. If we assign . . . priority to agents' representation of their . . . intentions and motivations, it is clear that we are licensing deception, self-deception, and abuse.[32]

In the context of deception, the "rule of double effect" becomes even more problematic. It is not just a matter of whether the intention to relieve pain but not to cause death is truthfully reported, but of whether the rule can be authentic. Intention, which is at the core of the defense of "double effect," may itself be a deception, a self-deception. In the midst of the drama of dying, intention is unavoidably mixed with motivation and desire. Looking back, it may be possible to separate out intention's variousness. Yet, in the event, it remains difficult if not impossible to say whether we are dealing with rationalization, justification, or explanation. Certainly, the rapidity with which "double effect" has entered the language of the clinical situation suggests that we have seized upon it to help us accommodate to unresolvable circumstances.

Double effect also relies on a distinction between "letting die" and "causing death." Thus, in assisted suicide and euthanasia we are said to be the *agents* of death, while in aggressive relief of pain it is the disease that is said to be the *cause* of death. No doubt, the tempo of dying slows when opiates are given for pain relief rather than to hasten death's arrival. But whether duration itself can carry the burden of distinguishing moral from immoral conduct is problematic. In fact, only a particularist argument sustains the difference, an argument based in an essentialist ethics.[33] "Let nature take its course" is its representative statement. It is possible to defend the position that it is the disease which is the cause of death and that it is the action of a moral agent which diminishes pain. But it is also possible to defend the position that the notion of causality may itself be misleading, exhibiting what Alfred North Whitehead identified as the "fallacy of misplaced concreteness." Thus, to name something a "cause" and something else an "effect" is already to interpret an event on the grounds of some specific moral and metaphysical commitment.

But that commitment is hidden behind the rule which becomes, as it were, a convenience. Adopting the rule includes adopting its foundation, but this is not scrutinized. As it were, a type of philosophic deception comes into play.

As with abandonment and suffering, there are other kinds of deception that are less innocent. Structural changes, particularly those connected to the invasion of the practice community by marketplace and society, also encourage deception. "Gaming" the system to take advantage of the ambiguities of law may benefit both patient and physician, but inevitably at a cost to other patients and physicians. The more obvious kinds of deception are evident enough, such as the manipulation of diagnostic categories in order to increase payments. No doubt not alone, and in the process of making drastic changes in its practices, the difficulties in the past several years (1997–1998) of Columbia/HCA Healthcare Corporation, the largest for-profit health care company in the United States, are illustrative. A *New York Times* investigative report noted the following:

Under Medicare rules, outpatient treatments like home care are reimbursed on a formula based on cost. Prosecutors are investigating whether Columbia improperly shifts hospital costs onto its home care agencies. . . . A computer analysis by *The New York Times* . . . found sharp differences between Columbia and its competitors in the amount paid by Medicare for outpatient services. . . . For example, the *Times* analysis of Medicare data from Texas showed that care provided after hospitalization . . . cost Medicare 23 percent more at Columbia hospitals than the state average even after adjusting for differences in severity and conditions of illness.[34]

As with all deceptions, language both conveys and hides reality. As needs for medical care increase and resources remain static or even shrink, some form of rationing is already taking place, but we do not admit it. For example, we are careful to say that we are making what are called "allocation" or "sharing" decisions, and by and large, these do not stir anger and resistance. A sense of fair and fairly administered procedures makes for acceptance.[35] Even where suspected favoritism is reported, it is met with the feeling that these are exceptions to the rule. And where there have been policy questions, as in the recent debate over unequal, and so unfair, access because of regional differences, underlying confidence is by and large unchallenged. No doubt, the fact that sharing is administered by a not-for-profit system and priorities are rationalized as medically indicated sustains our confidence.

Admitting that we are "rationing" health care on economic grounds, however, is taboo. When, in the rare instance, this admission is allowed to surface, it interrupts deception and stirs controversy. For example, the

Oregon plan for increasing Medicaid coverage by establishing treatment priorities initially tried to address the question of rationing directly.

At first the Oregon plan made repeated headlines and provoked strong criticism. "The Oregon plan will target a new group for discrimination—the seriously ill," wrote one physician in a letter to the editor of the [New England] Journal [of Medicine]. "It denies care only to the politically powerless poor," commented health analyst Emily Friedman. "Oregon's decision to ration health care to its poorest women and children," charged Al Gore, "is a declaration of unconditional surrender just as the first battles are being fought over the future of our health care system." . . . Oregon had openly embraced the "R" word: rationing—worse, rationing for the poor.[36]

Of course, the market already rations. The ability to pay determines access to health care, and in many instances the quality of care, too. But admitting this is unacceptable. Rationing means assigning a dollar value to life and death. We are caught between economic constraints and our sense of the innate "worth" of the human being. The fact that we already assign such values in negligence and accident claims, as we do in setting wages and welfare benefits, is conveniently forgotten.

Deception is encouraged by our institutions. Illustrative is the development of genetic screening in the context of a for-profit insurance system.

Around 1970, it came to be feared that people with the sickle cell trait—that is, who possess one of the recessive genes for the disease—might suffer the sickling of their red blood cells in the reduced-oxygen environment of high altitudes. They were prohibited from entering the Air Force Academy, restricted to ground jobs by several major commercial air carriers, and often charged higher premiums by insurance companies. Recently, a couple whose first child suffers from cystic fibrosis became pregnant and sought to have their fetus diagnosed prenatally for the disease. Their medical insurer agreed to pay for the test so long as the mother would abort the second child if the results were positive. Otherwise, the company would cancel the family's health plan. (The company relented, but only under threat of a law suit.)[37]

Screening, like other modern institutional forms, encourages the illusion of secrecy in a society where secrets cannot be kept. Deception, and not simply at the bedside, becomes everyone's game.

NOTES

1. Daniel Callahan, *The Goals of Medicine*, special supplement, *Hastings Center Report*, Vol. 26, No. 6 (November–December, 1996), p. S21.

2. Ann Hood, "Rage Against the Dying of the Light," *New York Times*, August 2, 1997.

3. Ibid.

4. Elizabeth Oettinger, "The Way of Compassion," *Reflections* (newsletter, Department of Philosophy, Oregon State University), special ed. (October 1997).

5. Timothy E. Quill, "Death and Dignity," *New England Journal of Medicine*, Vol. 324, No. 10 (1991), p. 693.

6. Ibid.

7. Esther B. Fein, "Gift to a Dying Daughter: Orders to Spare Her Pain," *New York Times*, March 6, 1997.

8. Joanne Lynn et al., "Perceptions by Family Members of the Dying: Experience of Older and Seriously Ill Patients," *Annals of Internal Medicine*, Vol. 126, No. 2 (January 15, 1997), pp. 97–106 (abstract).

9. Francis Dominic Degnin, "Levinas and the Hippocratic Oath: A Discussion of Physician-Assisted Suicide," *Journal of Medicine and Philosophy*, Vol. 22, No. 2 (April 1997), pp. 100, 101. Italics in the original.

10. For a discussion of suffering that catches this "of" and "about" of the theme, see William R. Jones, *Is God a White Racist?* (Boston: Beacon Press, 1998). As with feminist scholarship, African-American scholarship exposes matters too easily subsumed under standard categories and languages, and so too easily ignored.

11. Kathleen M. Foley, "Competent Care for the Dying Instead of Physician-Assisted Suicide," *New England Journal of Medicine*, Vol. 336, No. 1 (January 2, 1997), pp. 54–58.

12. "'Confronting Death: Who Chooses, Who Controls?' A Dialogue Between Dax Cowart and Robert Burt," *Hastings Center Report*, Vol. 28, No. 1 (January–February 1998), pp. 16, 17.

13. Jane E. Brody, "Depression May Lead Dying Patients to Seek Suicide," *New York Times*, June 18, 1997.

14. Andrew DelBanco, "The Anatomy of American Melancholy," *New York Times*, May 30, 1998.

15. Robert Berkow et al., editors, *The Merck Manual* (Whitehouse Station, N.J.: Merck Research Laboratories, 1997), p. 403.

16. Brody, "Depression May Lead Dying Patients to Seek Suicide."

17. Lynda Richardson, "When AIDS Loosens Grip, It's Back to the Job Market," *New York Times*, May 21, 1997.

18. David W. Dunlap, "Death Deferred: New AIDS Drugs, New Dilemmas," *New York Times*, July 1, 1996.

19. Christina Walker Campi, "When Dying Is as Hard as Birth," *New York Times*, January 5, 1998.

20. Paul Wilkes, "Dying Well Is the Best Revenge," *New York Times Magazine*, July 6, 1997.

21. Timothy Quill, "Doctor, I Want to Die. Will You Help Me?" *Journal of the American Medical Association*, Vol. 270, No. 7 (August 8, 1993), p. 872.

22. See Sissela Bok, *Lying: Moral Choice in Public and Private Life* and *Secrets: On the Ethics of Concealment and Revelation*, both reprinted by Vintage Books (New York, 1989).

23. Theresa Tamkins, "Doctors Hide Diagnoses, Study Finds," *Dallas Morning News*, August 12, 1995.

24. Nicholas Demy, Letter to the Editor, *Journal of the American Medical Association*, Vol. 217 (1971), pp. 696–697.

25. See *Patient Self Determination Act*, part of the Omnibus Budget Reconciliation Act of 1990, Stat. 1388, Sec. 4206 (a). It went into effect in December 1991.

26. Donald Oken, "What to Tell Cancer Patients," *Journal of the American Medical Association*, Vol. 175 (1961), pp. 1120–1128. See also Robert Veatch, *Death, Dying, and the Biological Revolution* (New Haven, Conn.: Yale University Press, 1976), pp. 229–238.

27. Rita Charon, Howard Brody, Mary Williams Clark, Dwight Davis, Richard Martinez, and Robert M. Nelson, "Literature and Ethical Medicine: Five Cases from Common Practice," *Journal of Medicine and Philosophy*, Vol. 21, No. 3 (July 1996), Dwight Davis IV, "Lessons About Patient Deception," p. 257.

28. Daniel Callahan, "Pursuing a Peaceful Death," *Hastings Center Report*, Vol. 23, No. 4 (July–August 1993), p. 37.

29. Carl Elliott, "Bad Philosophers and Slum Landlords," *Hastings Center Report*, Vol. 28, No. 1 (January–February 1998), p. 39. Reference is to M. O'C. Drury, *The Dangers of Words and Writings on Wittgenstein*, edited by David Berman, Michael Fitzgerald, and John Hayes (Bristol, U.K., Thoemmes Press, 1996).

30. Eugene H. Methvin, "A Compassionate Killing," *The Wall Street Journal*, January 20, 1997.

31. Diane E. Meier, Carol-Ann Emmons, Sylvan Wallenstein, Timothy Quill, R. Sean Morrison, and Christine K. Cassel, "A National Survey of Physician-Assisted Suicide and Euthanasia in the United States," *New England Journal of Medicine*, Vol. 338, No. 17 (1998), p. 1193.

32. N. Ann David, "The Right to Refuse Treatment," in Tom L. Beauchamp, editor, *Intending Death* (Upper Saddle River, N.J.: Prentice-Hall, 1996), p. 118.

33. The presumption of "double effect" is the objectivity of moral acts, their independence from preference, desire, and circumstance. While this would seem to suggest a Kantian basis for the rule—nothing is finally good but the good will— it is clear, on analysis, that a Kantian, although not Kant himself, could read the good will as both forbidding and permitting assisted suicide. To treat a person as an "end-per-se" leaves open the question of what counts as a person, obviously a matter of debate these days. Behind "double effect," however, is a specific metaphysics of morals that is quite different from Kantian phenomenology, a critical metaphysics that severs the connection between cosmology and morality.

34. Kurt Eichenwald, "Hospital Giant Under Attack Plans a Shake-Up of Practices," *New York Times*, August 7, 1997.

35. As Albert R. Jonsen writes:

In addition, the United Network for Organ Sharing was established in the 1980s. UNOS is a private nonprofit corporation with a contract with the federal government to operate a registry of transplant recipients and a system of organ procurement and distribution. The system, set up in accord with the National Organ Transplantation Act of 1984 (Public Law 98–507), attempts to effect an efficient and equitable access to transplantation for all who are medically suitable. In this system, all patients are entered in a single coordinated waiting list for all organs, and each patient is given priority in terms of length of time on the list, histocompatibility, urgency, and so forth. (Albert R. Jonsen, "Ethical Issues in Organ Transplantation," in *Medical Ethics*, second edition, edited by Robert M. Veatch [Boston: Jones and Bartlett, 1997], p. 265)

36. Thomas Bodenheimer, "The Oregon Health Plan—Lessons for the Nation," *New England Journal of Medicine*, Vol. 337, No. 9 (August 28, 1997), pp. 651–655, and No. 10 (September 4, 1997), pp. 720–723.

37. Daniel J. Kevles and Leroy Hood, editors, *The Code of Codes* (Cambridge, Mass.: Harvard University Press, 1992), p. 322.

CHAPTER 7

Back to the Beginning

IN SUMMARY

In these pages, I've tried to share my journey between clinic and class-room. At first glance, thinking with cases seemed self-evident. But it didn't turn out that way. I was led backward to the story and forward to the practice community. Together, these opened up issues of personal and professional moral values. They pointed me to the not so hidden assumptions and attitudes that guide us through the clinical encounter. They exposed the existential side of things—suffering, denial, depression—that shapes that encounter. At the same time, they pointed to the new agenda of medicine and biomedical ethics. Thus the rapid diffusion of science and technology, and the rise of market rationalization to resolve issues that were ignored when third-party payers made costs invisible.

While exploring the ethical side of clinical experience, I have tried to keep on eye on the possibilities it might have for moral education. Of course, a direct transfer from the clinical encounter to the classroom makes no sense. The teacher is not confronted with the urgency of cure, although it is not far-fetched to understand teaching as the "cure of souls." Nor is the teacher equipped—or likely to be equipped—with the armory of tools, skills, resources, and traditions that make the practice community effective. Teaching does not enjoy the support of a well rooted practice community, although its traditions reach back to the

Sophists, the rabbinate, the Confucian, and the guru. Nor does teaching benefit from an elevated social status as medicine does.

Like medicine, teaching learns from the sciences, but without the critical empiricism that characterizes the clinical situation. Absent are community supports for research as a worthy activity for teachers. Like the clinician, the university professor must leave classroom for research, which is clearly more prestigious than mere teaching. But unlike the clinician, the connection to practice is, at best, tenuous. The elementary and high school teacher is neither expected to make, nor supported in, disciplined inquiry into his or her teaching. In fact, discoveries in teaching are all too quickly buried in ideological debate, as in the conflict over reading methods or the "new" math. And self-criticism is muted by an understandable defensiveness in light of the vulnerability of schools and teachers. Absent from teacher training is the extended apprenticeship that converts abstract considerations into instructed experience. So there is much to be learned from thinking with cases for teaching and especially for moral education. The deficiencies that show up suggest an agenda for educational reconstruction.

In a macabre way, the clinic can learn from the classroom. What has happened to teaching is a cautionary tale for the practice community as it shifts from "community to contract" and as the number of physicians who are corporate employees grows.[1] Professions, in the modern world, converge around a single sociology, an administrative and rationalized existence. The dialectic between trade and calling is collapsed into careerism. To be sure, a hierarchy marked by status, trust, and wealth persists. But even that is under challenge as profession is demythologized and ultimately devalued. So the clergy is less likely to be trusted and the law is met with cynicism. Physicians are not exempt. Corporate organizations—governments, insurance companies, HMOs—transfer authority to themselves and redesign roles and responsibilities. Clinically, physicians contend with alternative therapies that, for good or ill, subvert their power and authority. As a historian summed it up:

The range of alternative therapies on offer is now enormous: osteopathy, acupuncture, aromatherapy, Alexander technique, homeopathy, massage, shiatsu, iridology, chiropractic, herbalism, meditation, transformational workshops, holistic reflexology, kinesiology, colonics and hypnosis—to name only the most popular. What is even more remarkable is that, in the UK, two in five GPs now refer patients to complementary therapists, while in the Netherlands 7 percent of the population now visits unorthodox healers each year. In 1990 Americans made 425 million visits to unconventional healers compared with 388 million to primary care physicians.[2]

Generally, the transformations of the profession may be read as a victory for democracy. But it is a strange victory as the art of the professional comes to be dominated by bureaucracy. It is revealing that just as, if not because, professions are devalued, nursing comes closer to professional status. Yet, reflecting the fact that nursing was and still is a "woman's" occupation, nurses remain subservient to the physician and, by and large, remain anonymous to the patient. Everywhere the professional becomes an employee, a manager, and a functionary. Indeed, the very idea of a profession—a calling that integrates transcendent, civic, and personal virtues—is on the way to surrender.

I have also tried to keep an eye on the import of biomedical ethics for the development of ethics as a field of inquiry. After all, a precondition of moral education is a coherent content and method, an answer to the question "What is ethics all about?" In searching for reply, the history of biomedical ethics recapitulates in recognizable ways the evolution of ethics itself, the move from a Socratic concern with clarity of language and reference, the emergence of principle, the need for some transcending secular or nonsecular justification, and then the reemergence on new ground—such as a plurality of ideas, cultures, and traditions—of a concern for what is going on in all its richness and confusion.

With its bewildering rapidity, biomedical ethics truncates this evolution. Centuries are reduced to decades. This has its advantages. We can see the ways in which what comes later benefits from what has gone before. In that sense, biomedical ethics is a more progressive discipline than its parent. I recall, for example, a presentation on the history of biomedical ethics. That history included the work of many of the people sitting in the session. They, in turn, were able to comment directly about events to which they were witnesses and in which they were participants.[3] The pace of biomedical ethics has its problems, too. It is almost impossible to absorb the ideas and methods that spring up so quickly and that are so quickly amended or even replaced. The leisurely move from Socrates to Thomas to Spinoza to Kant to Mill to Dewey vanishes. Pace itself becomes a problem to be mastered. Biomedical ethics is thus a revealing study in moral discovery, invention, and adaptation under modern conditions.

It is in this context that I come back to the spaces between knowing and doing, ought and is, reason and passion, and to the way in which story, case, and practice community bridge those spaces. We can, of course, treat story, case, and practice community as distinct levels of discourse—which is possible—but that is to miss their import. Thus the story is authored by the patient. In the telling, a world is, as it were, created that is bracketed, set apart as *an* experience. Yet it also points to the case, which in turn locates the story within a variety of connections. The story is reauthored by others. Time, which is encapsulated in the story, is stretched out by the case in the search for causes, treatments, and prognoses. The story is transformed by memory into predictions and actions. It connects with other cases and with traditions that specify what does and does not count for inclusion. The story, becoming the case, also becomes part of the institutional memory of the practice community.

Story, case, and practice taken together can be appreciated aesthetically, used pedagogically, and treated analytically. It is this threefold characteristic that identifies the deficiency of moral education, the lack of an articulated and embedded narrative and of a well-founded practice community. The attempt to reduce the three to a single dominant mode— such as the moral dilemma in the classroom, treating the disease but not the patient in the clinic—ensures moral failure. Thus, the moral educator hears echoes:

In my experience, teaching medical residents and students in clinical setting, the pressure is great and the temptation strong to reduce complexity, to sheer off the rough edges and smooth out the wrinkles of a patient's story in order to get a clear bead on the source of a patient's presenting complaint. But with many conditions—certainly with grave illness or injury, but also with ordinary ailments of ambiguous or unknown origin—the rough edges and wrinkles are part and parcel of what ails the person. To eliminate from consideration what may seem at first blush to be incidental or extraneous factors is to risk misdiagnosis and mistreatment. . . . Paying attention—attending—is both a means of discovery (diagnosis) and the outward and visible form of what T. S. Eliot called "the sharp compassion of the healer's art."[4]

Story, case, and practice are not simply distinguishable as more or less primitive. The story is a persistent reminder to case and practice of the happening—the pain, the fear, the anxiety—that initiates them. The case in turn seeks to capture the story, even to tame it, but it never finally succeeds. And as the tradition of the practice community evolves, the case is absorbed into its memory. The interaction of these three modes of experience is not always evident. That tells us why, for all its reliance on the sciences, caring remains a personal art. But then, science can be understood as an art, too, and not simply as disciplined inquiry into causes and consequences. As A. R. Luria put it, in what he called "romantic science":

They [romantics] do not follow the path of reductionism, which is the leading philosophy of the classical group. Romantics in science want neither to split living reality into its elementary components nor to represent the wealth of life's concrete events in abstract models that lose the properties of the phenomena themselves. It is of utmost importance to romantics to preserve the wealth of living reality, and they aspire to a science that retains this richness.[5]

Biomedical ethics reflects this aesthetic and so, despite resort to principles and models, finally resists codification. The interaction of story, case, and practice reveals itself as a dialectic transaction. However, it is also possible to say a kind word for reductionism. Whether in the classroom or the clinic, there is never time enough for an endless conversation. Of course, questions are asked over and over again, and answers are pondered over and over again. But endless conversation would require our translation into another world, residence in the eternal dialogue pictured critically and prophetically by Socrates in the *Phaedo*. But we are Earthbound and ethics is Earthbound, too. The anxieties of decision need the therapy of simplification. Else, we would be paralyzed into inaction, unable to meet the ultimate demand of ethics: do what ought to be done when it ought to be done and have good—but never perfect or final—reasons for it. Risk and doubt are encountered and overcome, too, and certainly nowhere more dramatically than in the judgments of life and death that shape the clinical situation. So another dialectic, the tension between the ever-not-quite and the immediacy of the ought.

It is not just the substance of story, case, and practice that teaches, but the experience of them as orchestrated movement. Thinking with cases is an exercise of the moral imagination, the play and replay of what-if. Simplification stands at one pole in the process, context at the other. Moving between them, we see ourselves seeing, experience a temporary and temporal suspension of our natural passions, which is quite distinct from detachment as a type of depersonalization. Thus, the daily teaching rounds at the bedside and the grand rounds of the practice community.

The passions are never entirely suppressed. Dispassion is only a moment in the process. It is the pause that allows us to judge our judgments and recoup our energies. But it is only a pause. Made normative, the pause of dispassion turns into the illusion of neutrality.[6] As Carol Gilligan puts it, "As a framework for moral decision, care is grounded in the assumption that . . . detachment . . . is morally problematic, since it breeds moral blindness or indifference—a failure to discern or respond to need."[7] Imagination drives us back into the passion of the story. The pause is embedded in an invitation to what one critic calls a "sentimental re-education." Discussing a distanced and indifferent son's response to his mother's Alzheimer's disease, he notes:

What is needed then, is to *install* a set of feelings in Robert that will make him alive to the call of the needs of his mother and his siblings. And in the less-hyperrational Roberts of the world—those who haven't rationally killed inconvenient inclinations, but whose inclinations are too weak to motivate them effectively—we need to make such feelings more vivid and forceful. And this in turn suggests a strategy for Jane and Suzanne [Robert's sisters] and their allies.

What Robert lacks is not arguments, because there is no place for them to engage him. Instead, he requires a sentimental (re)education, or better, retraining.[8]

In that move from judgment to pedagogy, biomedical ethics reveals the possibility of a radical re-construction of moral education. It allows us the realism of an anti-moralism.

PERFORMING ETHICS

The story is a place marker for the lived-through experience. It is, however, bivocal, still a transaction between teller and told-to. In that sense, it distorts the moral situation, in which there are many voices often speaking all at once. To capture its thickness, the story needs to be enacted and reenacted by actual persons. This, too, is the work of moral imagination, the dialogue within that replays the event, the dialogue between that exposes the event. Everyone will be playing roles. These will leave persons at some remove from each other and from the event. Even so, that event—the primitive event, the happening—is made more adequately present to us when it is, as it were, re-presented. Thus, the movement of story, case, and practice is illuminated when theater is its metaphor. As such, it becomes its own event, another lived-through experience modeled on the initial enactment, yet unable to replicate it. There remains an epistemic distance between the primitive event and the reenactment.

Ultimately, that distance is unbridgeable. We may argue about whether or not having an experience may be unmediated—philosophers and psychologists do all the time—but remembering, telling, and sharing are in fact mediations. As such, any lived-through experience is evanescent, very quickly layered over, only to be re-presented by someone to someone. This is why the performance of the "same" play—or the "same" musical score, the "same" poem—is unique despite the familiarity of its script. It is why we can attend performances of the "same" play, the "same" music, the "same" opera and still find them fresh, original. Very soon, however, the vividness of performance pales, too. We surrender to memory. With another reenactment, mood, tone, and color return again, no longer *the* original yet still original. Without that return, for all its inadequacy, thinking with cases becomes unintelligible and moral education remains abstract. Of course, as *the* original is lost, the adequacy of any reenactment to its subject is problematic. Theater is not re-production. It is interpretation and commentary—hermeneutics, if you will. It appears within the drama, its emerging script, and yet distanced from it as in perspective-taking. Thus the soliloquy, the aside.

In short, theater is a metaphor for re-construction, richer than the case, to be sure, but a re-construction nevertheless. The effort to complete story, case, and practice in the reenactment, then, cannot escape illusion, the illusion of actual recurrence. For moral education as for biomedical ethics, this entails the permanent inadequacy of its method and the permanent skepticism of its epistemology. Acknowledging imperfectibility of "fiction" at the heart of ethics is a token of "good faith," a reprise of the classical instruction: know thyself. As Tod Chambers remarks, "Reading cases with attention to their fictional qualities, that is, their constructedness, in turn reveals how dilemmas are framed in ways that conceal as well as reveal other ways of seeing. To ignore the narrative characteristics that the bioethics case shares with fiction is to confuse representation with the thing it represents."[9] And, I add, to ignore those characteristics is to indulge in moralism of one sort or another.

Using tradition, the case shapes the story through action and connection. But its root in the story makes even the most obvious of cases problematic. The report closest to the happening is not an unclouded mirror. The story represents but cannot present. Its author—and later its coauthors—is equipped with memories, individual and collective, so the story is told in a certain way with a certain vocabulary and a certain trajectory. The event is, to be sure, original as experienced and yet of a genre as played. Story, case, and practice, then, are outcomes of habits, pressures, and interests. So the clinical situation evokes a certain kind of theater, the existential drama. With it, another happening—not just story, not just case, not just practice—stands in the place of the vanished original, only now it is a re-constructed happening, a new original.

In the existential drama, past and future are subordinated to an expressive present. Time, in other words, is had both as duration and as simultaneity. Other durations and other simultaneities—happenings elsewhere and elsewhen—are exteriorized as vague backgrounds. The scene is framed not simply by setting and stage—the classroom, the clinic—but by having, as Aristotle put it with seductive simplicity, a beginning, a middle, and an end. But in the existential drama, these are only retrospectively understood as having led from one to the next. Looking forward, the drama is surprising, unpredictable, disorderly, accidental. Both disorder and connection are truthful, which is why the existential drama is not an in-itself only but an outcome of viewpoints and perspectives, many dramas all at once. Living-through is, as it were, both in process and interrupted. Waiting, thinking back, looking forward happen all at once.

The ordinary features of drama are present, too: story line, conflict, tension, resolution. The players, however, do not read from a script. They are caught in the situation, sometimes not even knowing they are players. Passions are at work, and doubts and surprises. The script is written down after the fact—the patient's history, the case notes, the lesson plan. Yet the players are not free to write just anything at all. They are who they are, which is why it is possible to say, as we can of Oedipus or Hamlet, that "character is destiny." And yet, they are also becoming in the reenactment. So we cannot be sure that destiny is all, or better, cannot be sure about what is destined. Of course, we know how the drama, even the existential drama, will turn out—the patient will die, let us say, or the lie will be told—and yet we hesitate: Will it really turn out as it has before, and will it really turn out in the way that it has before? Death is not one but many; lies are not one but many. Again, the what-if.

This aesthetic of reenactment seems a far distance from clinic and classroom. The complexities of presentation seem unavailable in the hurly-burly of doings and judgings that is the clinical situation amid the busy classroom. But presentation is not a luxury. It occurs, however, in the midst of things. This implicit interpretation of meanings in clinic and classroom is the validation of thinking with cases, its completion. It is why this kind of thinking works out, or else we could simply reduce biomedical ethics to principles, practices, and rules of procedure, and the classroom to mere moralism. If thinking were not also doing, we could not account for the rough-edged maturations emerging out of lived-through experiences. If it were only habit, we could not account for real distinctions, say between the brilliant and the ordinary diagnostician or teacher, or between insight and routine.

Principles and procedures, of course, are not to be dispensed with. Reason and science have certainly moved modern medicine from quackery and chaos to disciplined and effective care and cure. The Enlightenment project is corrected but not dismissed by narrative.

The [French] Revolution and its aftermath removed hospitals from the hands of the Church into those of the nation. . . . This hospital milieu bred new priorities. Clinical practice had always leant heavily on traditional bookish teachings and the physician's personal sagacity; but yesterday's authorities went the way of the *ancien regime* as the revolutionary doctors put bodies before books, prizing the hands-on experience gained through indefatigable examinations of the diseased and later of their cadavers. Endorsing the Enlightenment empiricism of the philosopher, Pierre Cabanis (1857–1808), Paris medicine's golden rule was "read little, see much, do much."[10]

The clinical situation is an embedded situation. Seeing, doing, and reasoning are not enough to grasp it any more than "bookish teachings" are. Persons are situated within and by it. Location—of person, place, and time—is at work but it is seldom brought to consciousness.[11] It is just this task of consciousness, of locating persons, that is the obligation of biomedical ethics and moral education. They have the perplexing task of being and of being conscious of their being. Consciousness—almost, I think, mere consciousness—is turned into awareness, that is, directed, selected consciousness, self-consciousness. Without it, the needs of urgency could not be met. At the same time, awareness is dangerous because it is so easily transformed into authority or into freestanding rules of practice. Personal location is lost in the anxieties of cause and cure, as in the anxieties of moral insecurity. The complaint against the reduction of the professional's art to technique—the quantifications of testing in the classroom, for example—recognizes the suppression of the personal situation. This is invited by conversion of awareness into habit of thought, a conversion that is reinforced by the sciences, by the market, and by the devaluation of the professional. Once again, we encounter the imperfectibility of the moral task.

Personal location arises from the interplay of expectation and surprise that characterizes the clinical situation. It is not just a literary or philosophic illusion—the invasion of the practice community by alien beings like philosophers, poets, and novelists. For example, a psychiatrist describes his responses to a patient diagnosed with a "widely disseminated stomach cancer."

There was nothing to be done. . . . Fairly quickly, both she and her husband began to ask for a quick death. I argued for life. . . . Although I had been tested this way with other patients, none had ever been quite as poignant, as deeply moving, or as involving as this case. . . . I went home that night in a total turmoil, struggling with the question. After a great deal of internal debate, I decided that I would help her die. I called the hospital room. My patient's husband answered . . . I told him of my decision. He wept with relief. He turned the phone over to his wife and she too was extremely grateful. They went to sleep, and I did not.[12]

Finally, personal location characterizes the roles to be played in the existential drama. The names are familiar enough—doctor, nurse, patient, family. But the names are only preliminary, only preliminaries to attention. They come alive when we use the proper names that signal the presence of actual persons. The protagonist is this person in pain; the advocate is this person's voice and action; the agent is this member of the practice community. The roles enacted are both imminent and distanced. We become the roles we play, and the roles we play become ourselves. When, as happens, the gap between role and being grows too wide, doing ethics becomes an unconvincing exercise. But when the gap disappears, doing ethics becomes impossible. It is no longer possible to use language and idea—the practice community, the history and tradition of ethics—to cross boundaries from one event to another.

As with any drama, it is the audience, too, whose passions are enacted and whose lives are engaged. I recall, once again, my work with the ethics committee. I read the case report; listen to the patient, the family, the doctor, the nurse; hear the comments of the social worker, the chaplain, the friend. At first, the language is technical, abbreviated, sparse. The committee unpacks the language, deliberates, makes its recommendations, writes its report. Later, I look back, noticing the differences made by the particular story, case, circumstance, time, noticing the departures I have made—we have made—from a common beginning. I see myself at first as the interested and helpful citizen. But I realize that only at the beginning was I part of an audience watching the clinical situation play out before me. Sooner or later, I enter the reenactment; others enter the reenactment. The committee's members individuate as story and case resonate differently for each of them. We become a radically active audience. In fact, we are transformed; the audience becomes the chorus of classical theater. I react, reflect, respond, comment. With the reenactment I sympathize, feel pain for the pain of another and empathize, experience the pain of another as if it were my own. Sympathy and empathy are unique transactions. A newly arrived actor, I puzzle at my role and myself.

I struggle for perspective, try to recapture the role in the guise of searching for objectivity. At that point, I encounter the drama of deception and unmasking, my deception, my unmasking. I realize that I am not transparent, a neutral medium of response and transmission. Of course, I feel the pain of some, but not of all, others as my own. As the told-to, I respond to some stories and not to others. I select without admitting that I select. Some of the players, unwelcome thought, are not sympathetic; some—the recalcitrant patients, the stubborn family members—"deserve" what is happening to them; some stories are just not interesting. Yet I am reminded that I suffer and die, that I, too, will be selected by some other but not by all others. I know the "pity and terror" of identification and desertion that Aristotle names the genius of tragedy.

The existential drama has hidden specters that haunt the conversation. I am the fortunate self, too. I know that right now and just here, it is not I who is suffering, dying. I feel relief that it is not I, not my lived-through experience, that has brought us to this meeting. And yet, I feel not a little bit of guilt at my escape and not a little bit of guilt at not having the feeling for all and not just for some. These feelings are tinged with judgment on myself, shame at my indifference, relief at my escape. Discrimination, which is aesthetically expected and encouraged, becomes morally problematic as selection appears where it is not supposed to appear. I understand in a new way the benefits of what is called professional objectivity, the values and temptations of dispassion. This objectivity, however, is not simply on behalf of the patient, but on my own behalf. The existential drama reveals not just the moral ambiguity of situations but the moral ambivalence of the self.

I am an arena of becomings; reenactment is a personal act. I am many persons, am both inside and distanced from the scene all at once. I know that remembering uninterrupted would make my life unlivable and would make judgment inaccessible. But I know, too, that I can be distracted by these conclusions. They become my alibi. I defend myself against the blindness these bring with them. I realize that moral blindness takes many forms. The reenactment becomes a moral education, becomes my moral education.

OF SELF AND OTHER

To round out the metaphor of existential drama, I need to say something more about the nature of the players, in particular the players whose characters are mapped by names like doctor, nurse, family, consultant, counselor, surrogate. Experience in clinic and classroom is a way of unmasking the self-deception of the roles we play and the existential anxieties that attach to them. Right at the start, this raises a question: Can I say *the* and *our* ethics committee experience, or am I permitted to say only *an* and *my* ethics committee experience, and in the same way *the* classroom or *a* classroom? At first glance, I am not mistaken in using generic language. Yet it is inadequate and misleading. I bring with me my own story. Together, we have our story, too, and it is not quite the story of other collectivities. We are, as it were, both *the* cast of characters—the typical members of a committee—and *a* cast of characters. This becomes evident as I meet the persons at play in the existential drama; it becomes all the more evident as I meet my fellow committee members one by one; it becomes most evident as I meet people from other places. They reconstruct me and, I suppose, I reconstruct them. We are not interchangeable and, as anyone who has moved from place to place can attest, our locations are not interchangeable either. The layering of the moral situation continues.

In the clinical setting, self is deliberately suppressed, just as it is in moral education. The intent is beneficent; the need for impartiality, fairness. But the move away from the subject is never really successful. I am actually present. I am not some abstract person—the moral agent, the rational being, the impartial observer of ethics talk; the instructor, the facilitator, the discussion leader of classroom talk—nor am I some abstract participant in a biomedical ethics consultation. But even this is an imperfect correction. My presence is not just a given, as if I were morally completed. But I act and am expected to act the part as if I were. Yet I, too, am in moral motion. But again, I do not admit it and I am not expected to admit it. In other words, I treat the patient and family as developing, but myself and other members of the committee as already developed. And, more significantly, I treat my role and title as if they were morally transparent, serving only as instruments of legitimation.

Again, it is the aesthetic of the moral situation that enables self-consciousness. This is not an aberrant suggestion, another deception, perhaps. More and more frequently, we recognize but do not necessarily act upon the importance of the humanities for the practice community and in biomedical ethics.[13] The humanities are, after all, a task of the consciousness of self and other. They are moved by a consciousness of particularity: the need to account for actual persons.[14] Thus, a comment about the place of literature in medical ethics:

Robert Coles, who uses novels such as George Eliot's *Middlemarch* and Sinclair Lewis's *Arrowsmith* in his classes, says bluntly that the purpose of teaching literature in a medical humanities course is "ethical reflection." For Coles, ethical reflection means more than analytic medical ethics; it means pursuing "moral inquiry of a wide-ranging kind" that requires "intense scrutiny of one's assumptions, one's expectations, one's values, one's life as it is being lived or as one hopes to live it." He does not believe that professional ethics can be discrete from a person's general moral sensibility. Coles's broader vision of medical ethics requires the larger scope of a novel, but the novels that work for his purpose do so because of their realistic representation of human psychology and behavior.[15]

Before particularity emerges, we are only strangers—ethicist, doctor, nurse, chaplain, community representative, quality assurance officer. To be sure, we are armed with the skills of analysis, the perceptions of discipline, the recollections of experience, the commitment of care. These are what sanction our presence and what we bring to situations. Quickly donning the costume of the practice community, we think of ourselves as consultants. We are present to observe, inquire, and recommend but not to participate. Like the others, I move easily, more or less, into my role. Its specifications take over. In a sense, I am not present. I am not the person who plays with his grandchildren, who enjoys a good meal, who struggles with an abstract idea. I am not the person who fears death, who feels pain, who knows doubt. I realize this when I hear the before-and-after reports we occasionally get of the physician, the nurse, the ethicist who has been a patient. I realize this when I recall that I have been a patient. Nor am I even the person who sat with the committee in other consultations, other discussions. In a sense, I vanish and a generalized "I" takes over. But this "I" of the role is an illusion.

The conversation proceeds, the case is presented, the voices are heard, the story is probed, the connection is identified. Listening, observing, asking are my opening gambits. In this, I am not unsympathetic, not mechanistic—roles and rules can be orderly without being mechanistic. After all, I do care, or I would not be here. The setting—the hospital, the conference room—has its impact, too, both as *hospital* and as this hospital. It generates expectations, conveys mood and style. Soon enough, however, I look for reminders of other reenactments, other stories. I begin the process of location: Where does this case fit? What kind of case is it? And I begin the canvass of outcomes. But I am not yet reflective. The busyness of it all is like a noise that blocks coherence. Yet, ironically, I do not know this because the noise—the categories and memories and setting—seems coherent.

As I note this interplay of noise and intelligibility, I recall three brothers. Two of them entered quietly, saddened by the soon-to-be death of their comatose mother, who was suffering from untreatable cancer. The oldest son, living far away, could not be present but had written a long and impassioned letter. He wanted "everything done." Life itself was "sacred," its preservation under any conditions and at any cost, a "moral" duty. The youngest wanted only to make his mother "comfortable." The middle brother wavered between the two. Caught in the middle, too, was the physician. He described the medical situation, the unavailability of treatment, the inevitability of outcome. This was, I thought, an obvious case of "futility" and an equally obvious story of guilts and regrets. A certain impatience appeared among us. One of the clergymen present grew vehement about the "dogmatism" of the oldest son and the "wishy-washy" character of the middle son. It was all so obvious to us. As was also obvious, the youngest son was really being "sensible." By implication, the others weren't. The question, then, was not what was to be done for the patient, but rather what was to be done to deal with the stubbornness of ignorance and dogmatism. The issue seemed essentially tactical. And that was the way it went, with, finally, a telephone call to the oldest son delivering our recommendation for palliative care and against heroic measures. But that outcome was already present in the beginning and unchallenged from the beginning.

As I drove home, I felt a certain satisfaction. We had done our work, served the interests of the patient, supported the physician, relieved the hospital of liability. Common sense had prevailed and wasteful effort had been avoided. Looking back, I have no fault to find with the outcome. But, looking inward, I realize that anger had entered the room with us, had been reenacted before us, and finally had included us. Our language— "dogmatism," "wishy-washy," "sensible"—was revealing. Of course, that language was part of our private discussion and did not appear in our report. I ask myself: Did we take account of the actual persons, the actual situation, or had category overwhelmed us? Was the older brother absent by necessity or by intention? Was he simply making the gesture in writing the letter, knowing the outcome? I don't know, and I didn't try to find out or see a reason for finding out. At the time, this didn't bother me. And the middle brother. Was he simply weak-willed, or was he trying to avoid raising yet one more wall between his brothers? Again I don't know. What of the sensible brother? Was he just tired or seeking relief or really sensible?

"Families matter," James Lindemann Nelson writes.

Their variegated forms notwithstanding, familial and other intimate relationships are typically crucial for attaining or protecting much of what is widely valued about human beings. . . . Families aren't simply more or less efficient means to some independently specified good ends. . . . On this point we have the testimony not only of our intuitions . . . but also of reflection which reveals something uncomfortably close to a paradox: if we think of families *exclusively* as of *instrumental value*, we greatly attenuate their ability to produce that instrumental value.[16]

On reflection, this family—the three brothers—was treated as instruments toward a clinical judgment. The mother was absent, but perhaps she was absent in more than one way. The outcome was satisfying, but what were we satisfied about? The what-if had been truncated. Our rapid consensus hid our separate stories. We had not served each other well, not corrected the subjectivity we each brought to the scene. The brothers remained angry and apart. The latent anger of the committee was not exposed. And the sadness of death was not well served by anger.

These reflections trouble me. I can, of course, hear my colleagues, were they to read this, complain of the obtuseness of the philosopher-critic and the luxury of hindsight. Yet if the moral encounter is to qualify as moral, the way the outcome is arrived at is as significant as what the outcome is. And, in any event, whose outcome—the patient's, the brothers', the physician's—was to count, and for how much? I cannot help but ask what might be called institutional questions, too: Were we anxious to help the hospital avoid an unpleasant, perhaps a costly, situation? And I ask authority questions: Was our attentiveness to the physician's concern for his patient unmixed with acceptance of his authority? I recall the physician. He was not insistent, not dominating. In fact, he conveyed a sense of care and doubt not unmixed with frustration. He did not know what the patient wanted and had no way of finding out. There was then an unconfessed sadness in him that I know is shared by many physicians in similar circumstance. But this sadness had to be hidden by the mask of professionalism. Like the rest of us, most physicians are untutored in the expressive dimension and, in fact, instructed in its opposite. It is rare, for example, to hear a physician say, as Timothy Quill does:

From her deathbed, Mrs. Martinez asked if I still loved her. Although I don't believe it is possible or desirable to love all my patients, this term of affection is clearly accurate for some, and Mrs. Martinez was one of those. Love in this context describes a special friendship, characterized by deep affinity, that can develop over time between doctor and patient. This bond of personal commitment and connection supplements the more professional requirements of the doctor–patient relationship such as integrity, confidentiality, informed consent, and medical competence. The doctor comes to know the patient as a friend as well as a patient and what happens to him or her takes on an emotional and existential complexity that enriches the practice of medicine. This more intimate approach to patient care is a powerful antidote to the remoteness of excessive professionalism.[17]

Remoteness is the peril of any profession. It guards, to be sure, against wishful thinking and sentimentality, which is why canons of medical ethics advise the physician against treating a family member and why, less exaltedly, the cliché "A lawyer who defends himself has a fool for a client." It is the teacher's admonition: Don't play favorites. It is why the moralist struggles against self-serving judgment. At the same time, these impulses to objectivity mislead. It is all too easy for remoteness to be self-protection, all too easy to avoid the paradoxical role of intimate stranger.[18]

In today's clinical situation, the traditional role of advocate—the model that suggests the intimate stranger to me—has taken on new meanings. Once advocacy was a feature of medical paternalism. The patient surrendered to the physician. Now, as corporate organizations, economic constraints, scientific sophistication, and functional relationships become the rule, advocacy is attached to a plurality of "strangers at the bedside" and ultimately institutionalized as the "patient representative." Someone is assigned to speak for the patient in ways the patient as patient cannot. And yet, if paternalism is not simply to reenter, disguised as specialized knowledge, advocacy cannot be simply another name for surrender to function. The advocate is the voice of the patient in language the patient cannot master. That, on the surface, seems clear enough. In that sense, the advocate is the patient in another guise. The advocate's knowledge, then, is not simply professional but personal. But personal knowledge is vanishing, and this turns advocacy into a puzzle. Of course, personal knowledge is always elusive. Now it becomes even more elusive.

For advocacy, there is more than one kind of knowledge at play: the knowledge of the caregiver, of what is and what is not possible; the knowledge of the patient, of his or her interests and desires; the knowledge of the institution, of its possibilities and limitations. Each of these knowledge is shaped by the personal story, such as the physician who cannot, on conscientious grounds, perform an abortion; the patient for whom another moment of existence, even if in pain, is precious. Personal knowledge is informed by recognition and not limited to cognition. The advocate appears as, and not simply for, the patient. At the same time, he or she appears as, and not simply for, the practice community. Knowledge, then, is embedded in histories and roles. It is inherently conflicted.

Perhaps nothing illustrates this complexity of knowledges better than the role of the surrogate decision maker, a role that becomes more and more dramatic as life-prolonging technologies evolve. The notion of the surrogate carries greater emotional and moral weight than do cognate notions like representative, attorney, or agent. Thus a surrogate will have to make decisions in the absence of clearly stated intentions or an unambiguous record of what the patient "really wants done." The surrogate's burden is increased by the fact that the decision is typically unrecallable—a decision to withdraw treatment, for example. And finally, the surrogate will decide without hope of checking his or her judgment against the judgment the patient might have made. Most decisions, after all, are made for patients who will not recover. Seeking relief, nonpersonal collective criteria are invented, and biomedical moral language reflects the attempt. Thus, the appearance of terms like "quality of life," "best interests," and "substituted judgment." Attempts to ease the burden are reflected in "living wills," "advance directives," and "durable powers of attorney."

Yet the language of surrogacy is ambiguous. Discussions of "quality of life" move beyond matters of medical fact and function. Other matters of quality demand attentiveness: commitment and dignity and freedom, pleasure and response to being cared for and the vanishing ability to care. "Quality of life" is not a given. Today, I enjoy a good book, a film, a walk in the woods. Tomorrow, I will be unable to do these things, appreciate these things. I may then experience a different but no less worthy "quality of life." Of course, I may become comatose, unable to respond, to know, to feel. Yet the quality of life of the other—the parent, spouse, child, friend—may enter the consideration. We may be autonomous but we are not, most of us, isolates. The story returns and the surrogate must know the story. At the same time, he or she can only retell it, only reenact it imperfectly.

The statement of intentions, as in a living will, is not unambiguous. No document can capture all possible conditions or judgments for the unexperienced future. Multiple agendas are nearly always present in the clinical situation—and that, too, complicates the surrogate's life. To be sure, the surrogate is not to pay attention to the intentions of others. But in the event—the distraught wife or husband, the quarreling children, the insistent doctor—that is easier said than done. Nor is "best interests" a self-evident guideline.

If the right decision is thought of as a matter of "discernment," or "seeing what's called for" in the situation, the concept of best interests could be understood as a "lens" through which all the other factors related to the particular decision should be "viewed" or "filtered." The concept would function primarily as a method for focusing the process of decision making. The concept of "focus" also informs the "aural" metaphor of the tuner. If making the right decision is thought of as a matter of hearing and respecting the voices of those with a stake in the decision, the concept of best interests . . . can function primarily to "tune" or "shape the ethical discourse . . . a method for "hearing" the . . . [voiceless one].[19]

The surrogate is expected to listen but is caught in the problem of whom to listen to. A surrogate is not simply a representative person, a designated functionary. He or she must make the effort—never success-ful—to be present as the other when the other cannot be present. Yet no one can be expected to really be another or even as another, and yet the surrogate is expected to be. He or she is required to move from personal knowledge to personal being. The surrogate is caught in the role. He or she is the paradigmatic hero—the Hamlet of the soliloquy—of the existential drama that unfolds the clinical situation.

PARADIGM AND PRINCIPLE

It is all too easy to lose ourselves in the existential drama and the search for particularity. The story tempts us. We love gossip, the latest news, whether in Herodotus' *History* or the pages of today's newspaper. So we are trained, perhaps overtrained, against the story and its distrac-tions. In moral education, we denude the story of its detail, sacrificing its richness for the sake of making things "clear and distinct." It is even more likely, then, that the urgency of the clinical situation will force us toward rules and habits. Yet both story and decision make legitimate moral claims. The former exhibits particularity and evokes participation. The latter leads to judgment and action. Both, of course, respond to the event.

The very fact that someone is sick . . . creates a moral claim on our attention. The person's condition cries out for diagnosis and treatment, because phenomena such as fever, nausea, vomiting, or pain are essentially value-laden. Recognizing that the language of sickness and illness essentially involves such mixed judg-ments does not, however, rely on a specific theoretical commitment or under-standing. . . . They arise in a specific practice domain and are based on the commonsense pretheoretical experience of the clinical phenomena themselves. . . . Pain is not merely a physical fact that is value neutral . . . rather maxims such as "pain demands relief" have a pretheoretical moral ultimacy because "the fact" and "value" aspects of pain are themselves inseparable, though they can be distin-guished.[20]

In the lived-through experience, reflection seems to be—and some-times is—a luxury. Thus, it is neglected or postponed. The impatience of the clinician with "too much talk" is its symptom. Symptomatic, too, is the escape to moralist maxims. Yet it is also clear that in the lived-through experience, connections are present to be discovered. We not only react but recognize. We use a common language that is not invented for the event. In some sense, then, reflection is going on. If it were not, then each event would stand entirely by itself. We would, of course, not be able to talk to each other. But situational atomism is not truthful to experience. The story remembers and leads, and the outcome, over time, is a progress of skill and comprehension. That, in fact, is a precise re-statement of what happens when we think with cases. The lived-through experience is inquiry and education all at once.

The case exposes a special kind of reflection, one that is historical and simultaneous. But what kind of reflection does the case exhibit? It is natural to turn to the law and its language of cases as a conceivable sibling to the clinical situation. But we quickly discover that the legal case is deeply embedded in precedent and standardized practices. In princi-ple, it denies its existential qualities: "Justice is blind," Judgment is im-partial, and so on. Indeed, the much-praised and misnamed "Socratic method" in legal education reveals the departure. As the appeals process illustrates, the case serves the law. Perhaps for good reasons, reasons of the polity, legal reasoning becomes an end in itself. All too often, the legal case is a joust between lawyers. The client becomes a bystander. In the criminal case, where the existential drama is close to the surface, the story is finally made invisible by plea bargaining. The urgency and the story that force reenactment in the clinical situation are further diluted by the tempo of the law. Time is attenuated by crowded calendars, so the legal case seems to lack urgency. It is marked by discontinuities and alienation, not least of all the alienation of class and caste. The story and the case are radically separated.

Thinking with cases is not philosophic reflection, nor is it scientific inquiry. Philosophy is a discursive discipline. It returns to repeated themes—the great themes—ponders and analyzes meanings, suggests criticisms. It is found in time and place, to be sure, but it is also imagined as standing apart from time and place. So it is instructive to return to the Platonists, to the Thomists, to the Cartesians, to the Kantians, and all the rest with profit. And it is why philosophic reinterpretation and recon-struction can take place anywhere and anywhen. Scientific inquiry, on the other hand, is progressive, is empirical and deliberately ahistorical. Idea displaces idea. It would be a strange science indeed that did not discard Ptolemaic astronomy or phlogiston theory, or that envisioned the embryo as homunculus. It would be a strange philosophy that ignored Plato and Aristotle. But, however they may differ, both philosophic and scientific inquiry step aside from the event. They reflect for the sake of adequacy to whatever is meant by reality. The end is intelligibility.

To be sure, experiences of comprehension rely on more primitive ex-periences. And the test of adequacy is ultimately to be found in matching in practice constructed and lived-through experiences. Utility is not a justification but a verification. Even for the pragmatist, outcomes are veri-fications despite our misunderstanding of William James's comment that "the truth is what works." Philosophy and science are, as it were, explo-rations within pseudo worlds where error does not pay the price of risk. Of course, mistakes may be psychological or intellectually painful. And, at times, their cost can be very great, particularly when, as ideologues or technocrats, we forget that world and pseudo world are not the same.

In thinking with cases, however, we do not step aside. Thus, the distinction between clinic and laboratory. Reenactment is then more suitable than discourse. But before that could become visible, biomedical ethics struggled for leverage. Assigned its task by the radical pace of the clinical agenda, it lacked a relevant history, its own role in the practice community. The traditional language of codes and rules did not address the event. Quinlan and Cruzan, for example became icons and not just "landmark cases." The urgency of certain kinds of stories demanded response. Biomedical ethics was forced to borrow habits of thought from religion, philosophy, and the law before new habits had time to form. But habits do not come unencumbered. With them, biomedical ethics also stepped aside without meaning to, without wanting to. And so, as it were, we acted before we knew. Thus,

Clinical bioethics—embedded in real cases, real stories—was a response to the complaints of clinicians . . . that the kinds of analyses and justifications of philosophers working in medical ethics were not relevant to real-life experience. I sometimes call this the "trolley car problem." Philosophers analyze hypothetical cases and offer elaborate justifications for their positions. But the cases . . . were simply not compelling. The point of the exercise is justification of one's argument. From the perspective of the social scientists or nurse, philosophers have an uncanny ability to talk about cases that have absolutely no basis in "real life," easily debating the side effects of drugs or surgical procedures that couldn't possibly exist . . . John Fletcher and Howard Brody argue that "clinical ethics strengthens the conceptual underpinnings of bioethics with experiential data, and helps motivate clinicians to reform their practices."[21]

With thinking with cases, reflection takes a new turn. It occurs in the midst of things, simultaneously lived-through and distanced. But while we know it when we see it happening, we are not yet sure what it is and what counts as its relevant object. Ideas do not simply amend other ideas. Cases are not just instrumental to some nonclinical end. And while theory creation continues in biomedical ethics—the arguments about deontology, about utilitarianism, for example—these are reserved for some small corner of the field. We are doing ethics in vivo, so to speak. Terms like "pain" and "wound" are more than symbols of discourse. They are a presence in our thinking and not just in our doing.

At present, biomedical ethics lacks security. Its symptom is the near sudden explosion of variations on old themes and the introduction of new ones. This pluralism is disturbing. It seems to undermine the moral foundations just when we need them most, just when the either/or of decision must be faced. To tame this variety, we resort to patterned thinking. As it were, history becomes foundational, such as the near ritualistic reference to Hippocrates and "do no harm." We are participants in a tug-of-war between dispassion and connection. The discussion of what biomedical ethics is and does and talks about reflects our uncertainty.

This is not the place to rehearse in any great detail the arguments for and against different claimants. There is an accessible and growing literature on the subject. But, for good or ill, that literature does not lead to a definitive end. In fact, in reviewing the proposals for making moral sense, I typically find myself agreeing and then, sooner or later, adding, "But . . ." Nor is my reaction unusual. It is instructive, then, to enumerate in a paragraph or two some of the ideas that are put forth. The enumeration itself is instructive.

Ideas—theories, concepts, criteria—are recognized in use. But the attempt to isolate and define them distorts. So the process is better captured in narration, a fit companion to story and theater.[22] Analysis is, as it were, stepping aside, an epiphenomenon, the stuff of meetings and journals but not of thinking with cases. We move from the "principlism" that early on captured biomedical ethics, to amending principles with stories and cases, thus acknowledging the need for interpretation and not just application. In another part of the forest, proponents of "care" theory shift away from the so-called impersonality of justice and rights. Caring entails actual relationships, relationships between "caring for" and "being cared for."[23] The language of caring is not so much reflective as an attempt at mirrored reference in language of particular kinds of lived-through experiences, almost literally an attempt at reflection. The impulse to find patterns continues. So "care theory" becomes problematic—is it theory, approach, point of view, orientation?[24]—and it is in any event not without precedent. As Robert Veatch reminds us, "In the 1960s this dispute [between justice and care] was referred to as the 'rules-situation' debate. . . . More recently, similar issues have been discussed under the rubric of moral particularism. . . . It is possible that care theorists are staking out a position in some 1990s version of that debate."[25]

For many feminists, the mother–child relationship is a normative model. Given its biological university—at least until now—it is presumed to be immediately recognizable. Of course, with in vitro fertilization, surrogate motherhood, and cloning, its universality becomes problematic. The relationship also varies with time, culture, and personality. So nurturing and caring acquire a specific content within a recognizable form. As such, then, the mother–child model evokes a critique of abstract universalism—the language of any person and all persons—and yet finds a way into its own universalism. Feminism thus calls attention to "situatedness" and what is called "standpoint theory."[26] At the same time, nurturing and caring carry a transcultural meaning that, so to speak, is known preconceptually. Hence, our response to the weeping mother holding the sick or dying child, the sense of violation we feel when mothers and children are victims—innocent victims, we say.

Still others, in the struggle to find their way to thinking with cases, adapt the notion of a "paradigm," which is

an abbreviated story that has few but striking details. It also incorporates a moral value that can be expressed as a principle . . . its elements can be sorted out in such a way as to show their relationship to each other. One way to parse a paradigm is to set out the "claims," . . . offered for general acceptance, the "grounds," . . . offered to make good the claim, the "warrants," . . . that authorize the rational moves between claims and grounds and, finally . . . the body of reasoned experience relied on to validate the warrant.[27]

The notion of paradigm leads to casuistry, yet another borrowing from religious tradition. In place of an orderly set of a priori principles—whether transcendent or not—we do ethics historically and culturally, and finally personally. Opinions are set against each other in Thomist fashion in order to reason toward a more adequate resolution of the differences between them. It should also be noted that opinions are held by named individuals; they are signed. Thomas, for example, is scrupulous in identifying particular persons in particular theological environments. At the same time, persons and environments are representative. Underlying casuistry, then, is a latent universalism. Thus the possibility of identifying similar cases across time and space and confidence in rational analysis as the means for building a bridge between them.[28] Yet other traditional resources are brought into the debate these days. "Virtue" theory, for example, is a rediscovered Aristotelianism, and the role of moral character rather than right action becomes central to moral thought.[29] At the same time, the meaning of moral character varies with location. So, yet again, the pattern forces return to the concrete and the modes of conveying it.

In a sense, the age-old quarrel between Platonists and Aristotelians is replayed in the clinical situation. At first, this explosion of views recalls Aristotle's moral empiricism, the notion of *phronesis* (practical wisdom).

Matters concerned with conduct and questions of what is good for us have no fixity, any more than matters of health. The general account [of practical knowledge] being of this nature, the account of particular cases is yet more lacking in exactness; for they do not fall under any art or precept, but the agents themselves must in each case consider what is appropriate to the occasion, as happens also in the art of medicine and navigation.[30]

This explosion of views, however, reflects a common enterprise. In one way or another we are thinking with cases. To be sure, the proponents tend to make exclusive claims. And it is risky indeed to settle for an uncritical eclecticism, turning enumeration into menu and the pattern of reconstruction into norm. So a language of conversation appears in biomedical ethics in the search for commonality. In part, this reflects the attempt at foundation in the midst of an unsettled state of things. But it points to a permanent state of things, too. The clinical situation is both particular and recurrent, story and genre, case and practice community. Thus, the Aristotelian insight is corrected by the Platonic, the struggle between them remains dialectical.

The consequence is a necessary, perhaps even desirable, moral opportunism. The event will be served even at the sacrifice of the idea.

In the real world, moral actions must confront complexities and practical constraints. For example, every American jurisdiction permits death to be defined by whole-brain criteria as well as traditional respiratory criteria. It is also the case that conceptual disagreement over the definition remains. To view the widespread adoption of whole-brain criteria as mere "political" consensus would surely underestimate the resonance that this definition has with diverse moral and religious views about personhood and death held by many persons.[31]

For example, debates about abortion and physician-assisted suicide are both in themselves and paradigmatic. The dialectic between trade and calling is another instance. The clinical situation does not validate reduction to a single interpretation, to a single moral theory or point of view. As Paul Lauritzen remarks, "the appeal to experience is like an invitation to conversation; it is the beginning and not the end of moral deliberation."[32] This is unsatisfying to that in us which loves the elegant solution. But it is our lot. On a more affirmative note, this normative pluralism is consistent with the move toward democratic community that now reaches into the practice community in a helpful and constructive way. Ethics becomes another way of thinking with cases.

Deliberative democracy goes beyond proceduralism and constitutionalism by not only tolerating but encouraging continuing discussion of fundamental values in all phases of the democratic process. Deliberative democracy is the opposite of soundbite democracy. . . . Soundbite democracy suffers from a deliberative deficit. The din and deadlock of public life—where insults are traded, slogans proclaimed, and self-serving deals are made and unmade—certainly reveal the deep disagreements that pervade public life. . . . Democracies cannot avoid disagreement . . . but can deliberate about their disagreements in a way that contributes to the health of democratic society.[33]

Epistemologically, thinking with cases marks the difference between sciences, where a unified theory may be dreamed of, and humanistic practices, where a single moral wisdom is chimerical. In short, thinking with cases is a communal activity; its patterns are rooted in philosophic dialogue and parliamentary practice.

NOTES

1. It is not surprising that delegates to the AMA's 1998 meeting in Honolulu called for the organization to "do more to foster collective bargaining" (*AM News*, January 4, 1999). I could not help but recall arguments between the NEA (National Education Association) and AFT (American Federation of Teachers) about "professionalism and unionism," and similar debates in the AAUP (American Association of University Professors) about the inappropriateness of collective bargaining for "professionals." By now, NEA and AAUP are engaged in collective bargaining and compete for "union" members with the AFT.

2. Roy Porter, *The Greatest Benefit to Mankind* (New York: W. W. Norton, 1997), p. 688.

3. LeRoy Walters, "The Top 206 Events Related to the Birth of Bioethics, 1925–1975," presented at the 10th Annual Bio-Ethics Retreat, Brewster, Mass., June 17–21, 1998.

4. Roland A. Carson, "Thinking About Cases as Stories," *Journal of Clinical Ethics*, Vol. 5, No. 4 (Winter 1994), p. 347.

5. A. R. Luria, *The Man with a Shattered World* (Cambridge, Mass.: Harvard University Press, 1987), p. 6. Steven R. Sabat, "Voices of Alzheimer's Disease Sufferers: A Call for Treatment Based on Personhood," *Journal of Clinical Ethics*, Vol. 9, No. 1 (Spring 1998), pp. 35–48, called my attention to Luria's work.

6. See Ruth Groenhout, "Care Theory and the Ideal of Neutrality in Public Moral Discourse," *Journal of Medicine and Philosophy*, Vol. 23, No. 2 (April 1998), pp. 170–189.

7. Carol Gilligan, "Moral Orientation and Moral Development," in *Women and Moral Theory*, E. F. Kittay and D. T. Meyers, editors (Totowa, N.J.: Rowman and Littlefield, 1987), p. 24.

8. James Lindemann Nelson, "Reasons and Feelings, Duty and Dementia," *Journal of Clinical Ethics*, Vol. 9, No. 1 (Spring 1998), p. 64.

9. Tod Chambers, "From the Ethicist's Point of View," *Hastings Center Report*, Vol. 26, No. 1 (January–February 1996), p. 32.

10. Porter, *The Greatest Benefit to Mankind*, p. 306.

11. Feminist theory addresses the notion of "standpoint." Thus,

. . . unlike liberal feminists, most other feminists believe that it will take more than accurate facts and attentive ears to make medicine and science objective. Existentialist, multicultural, global Marxist, socialist, cultural, radical, and ecofeminists all adopt some version of standpoint epistemology. Feminist standpoint epistemologists believe that liberal feminists' quest for gender neutrality, for sameness with him, and for the articulation of impartial and objective "human" standards is misguided. They argue that it is a major error to assume that men's and women's interests are fundamentally the same, since the differences between men's and women's interests are quite apparent. (Rosemarie Tong, *Feminist Approaches to Bioethics* [Boulder, Colo.: Westview Press, 1997], pp. 87–88)

12. Samuel C. Klagsbrun, "Physician-Assisted Suicide: A Double Dilemma," *Journal of Pain and Symptom Management*, Vol. 6, No. 5 (July 1991), p. 326.

13. For example, a discussion of this theme appeared in *Journal of Clinical Ethics*, Vol. 5, No. 4 (Winter 1994). See Anne Hunsaker Hawkins, "Literature, Medical Ethics, and 'Epiphanic Knowledge' " (pp. 283–290); Mark Kuczewski et al., "Make My Case: Ethics Teaching and Case Presentations" (pp. 310–315); Ronald A. Carson, "Thinking About Cases as Stories" (pp. 347–348). The drama of medical ethics is revealed in those "cases" which are historic and precedent-setting. It is not incidental that the legal rhetoric in such cases can be appreciated as narrative. A useful collection can be found in Gregory A. Pence, *Classic Cases in Medical Ethics*, second edition (Boston: McGraw-Hill, 1995).

14. Increasingly, conferences and seminars in biomedical ethics include extended discussions of novels, short stories, poems. The fine arts are not yet attended to. No doubt this is a reflection of the verbal bias of the field, but I suspect it will change under the influence of cultural pluralism and of the styles of changing generations. The interest of "medical humanities" is epistemological and methodological and ultimately, too, clinical. The humanities are not just a therapeutic tool, as in art therapy, nor only a pedagogical device, as in the story with a moral. No doubt these discussions reflect the growing influence of feminist theory as well as the revival of virtue theory in ethics.

15. Anne Hudson Jones, "Literature as Mirror or Lamp?" *Journal of Clinical Ethics*, Vol. 5, No. 4 (Winter 1994), p. 341. Reference is to Robert Coles, "Medical Ethics and Living a Life," *New England Journal of Medicine*, Vol. 301, No. 8 (August 23, 1979), pp. 445–448.

16. James Lindemann Nelson, "Taking Families Seriously," *Hastings Center Report*, Vol. 22, No. 4 (July–August, 1992), p. 7.

17. Timothy E. Quill, *A Midwife Through the Dying Process* (Baltimore: Johns Hopkins University Press, 1996), pp. 64–65.

18. For a discussion of the "intimate stranger," see Howard B. Radest, *Community Service, Encounter with Strangers* (Westport, Conn.: Praeger, 1993), Chapter 7.

19. Bill Bartholeme, letter to Medical College of Wisconsin discussion group, July 6, 1998.

20. George T. Agich and Bethany J. Spielman, "Ethics Expert Testimony: Against the Skeptics," *Journal of Medicine and Philosophy*, Vol. 22, No. 4 (August 1997), p. 391.

21. Barbara A. Koenig, "The Power (and Limits) of Proximity," *Hastings Center Report*, Vol. 26, No. 6 (November–December 1996), p. 30.

22. "Narrative ethics" is a particular approach to ethics. But I am using "narration" in its generic sense, as a way of conveying any number of approaches to the field. Included are drama and dialogue—which have been part of the philosophic tradition—as well as novel and poetry. The motive for this sense of narration is the imperative of the happening and its story, the ensuing enactment and reenactment.

23. The sources for "care" theory are Carol Gilligan's seminal work, *In a Different Voice* (Cambridge, Mass.: Harvard University Press, 1982), and Nel Noddings, *Caring: A Feminine Approach to Ethics and Moral Education* (Berkeley: University of California Press, 1984).

24. For a discussion of the status of "care theory," see the special issue of *Journal of Medicine and Philosophy*, Vol. 23, No. 2 (April 1988), titled "The

Chaos of Care and Care Theory," Margaret Olivia Little and Robert M. Veatch, editors.

25. Robert M. Veatch, "The Place of Care in Ethical Theory," *Journal of Medicine and Philosophy*, Vol. 23, No. 2 (April 1998), p. 212.

26. On this point, see Mary Mahowald, "On Treatment of Myopia: Feminist Standpoint Theory and Bioethics," in *Feminism and Bioethics* Susan-Wolfe, editor (New York: Oxford University Press, 1996), pp. 95–115.

27. Albert R. Jonsen, "Criteria That Make Intentional Killing Unjustified: Morally Unjustified Acts of Killing That Have Been Sometimes Declared Justified," In *Intending Death*, Tom L. Beauchamp, editor (Upper Saddle River, N.J.: Prentice-Hall, 1996), p. 49.

28. In *Ethics in Clinical Practice* (Boston: Little, Brown, 1994), Judith C. Ahronheim, Jonathan Moreno, and Connie Zuckerman describe casuistry as follows (p. 68):

Casuists contend that moral beliefs arise as the result of particular experiences. These experiences are by no means limited to those of a single individual, but rather embrace those of whole cultures and societies over many years. Certain of these experiences do stand out, however, as paradigmatic. The paradigm cases of ethics function much like the historically important cases in the law, in the sense that they provide valuable precedents that can guide us through subsequent situations. There are skill and ingenuity involved in finding the right analogies to our current experience from among the paradigm cases, and in analyzing and comparing the "fact pattern" of the paradigm case to the current case. Just how the facts between the two cases are similar and contrasting will determine how directly applicable the conclusion of the paradigm case will prove to be with regard to the current one.

29. The modern locus classicus of "virtue theory" is Alisdair MacIntyre's *After Virtue* (Notre Dame, Ind.: University of Notre Dame Press, 1981).

30. Aristotle, *Nicomachean Ethics*, Book II, part 2, 1104a4–9, in *The Works of Aristotle*, translated by W. D. Ross, Vol. II (Chicago: Encyclopaedia Britannica Press, 1952).

31. Patricia A. King, "Embryo Research: The Challenge for Public Policy," *Journal of Medicine and Philosophy*, Vol. 22, No. 5 (October 1997), p. 446.

32. Paul Lauritzen, "Ethics and Experience, the Case of the Curious Response," *Hastings Center Report*, Vol. 26, No. 1 (January–February 1996), p. 13.

33. Amy Gutmann and Dennis Thompson, "Deliberating About Bioethics," *Hastings Center Report*, Vol. 27, No. 3 (May–June 1997), p. 39.

Postscript . . . and Moral Education

Biomedical ethics raises useful and interesting questions for the class-room. However, there is a certain cruelty in asking them. In the clinical situation, thinking with cases demonstrates an inventive epistemology and a supportive history and culture. The pain of disease is its shared imperative; the tradition of a practice community, its resource. Parallels are evident in the classroom: learning by doing, school as community, concern for students. Remedies—participation in and through a practice community, moral realism, improved social status, and so on—are obvi-ous. Yet the obvious is not put into practice. The rhetoric of education— such as the talk of "community"—does not meet reality. Society only pretends to concern. Perhaps, then, the effort to put what we learn from biomedical ethics to work in the classroom is futile! But even if it only grounds a future critique, it is worth a look.

The absence of a practice community is felt. To be sure, there are professional associations, endless faculty meetings, codes of conduct. But the paraphernalia of institutions does not sum up as communities. In fact, the teacher as teacher is found alone and behind closed doors. The classroom is an isolated entity. The symbolism of this escapes us, al-though here and there efforts like team teaching and the "open class-room" try to take its meaning seriously. In the absence of a communal culture, however, these efforts cannot succeed. The relationship between biomedical ethics and the practice community is instructive. This prob-lematic is addressed, imperfectly, to be sure. For the classroom, however, the language of address is hardly invented.

Typically, administration leads faculty even where faculty governance is claimed, for instance, administration controls budget and policy. The hierarchy of the classroom is replicated throughout the institution. Admittedly, this has its reasons, or perhaps its excuse. The classroom is a more complicated psychological and political environment than the clinic. Its boundaries are less easily defined. Yet, as the agenda evolves, the clinic encounters threats much like those found in the classroom. The clinical situation could then become less and less clinical, the practice community could lose its special characteristics. The pattern is repeated elsewhere: in law, in governance, in professions generally. At some point, then, a mutual exchange of models is forecast, a search for the reconstruction of traditions. But that is another subject and for another time.

Biomedical ethics is self-conscious in ways that moral education is not. This shows up in its response to stories, in the formation of cases, and in the evolution of institutional memory. This shows up, too, in the problems and ambiguities it encounters and in the ways in which these are responded to. Above all, this appears in the evolution of its mode of addressing clinical events. Biomedical ethics is on the way to thinking with cases, and so to a relationship between master and apprentice in an environment of genuine and urgent demands. In turn, master and apprentice connect to the practice community, a collective mastery that transcends them both. This suggests a classroom where actual persons meet each other, identify actual needs, and have actual purposes.

Of course, the student is still the student; the teacher is still the teacher. But both are unfinished projects, and so another obstacle appears. It is difficult to admit to ourselves and to each other that we are incomplete. So the classroom uses the language of development without meaning it, a type of bad faith. Development is for the student but not for the teacher. We talk of child development, adolescent development. Even "stage theory," despite its claimed universality, is rarely addressed to adults except in special environments like prisons and medical schools. As such, it remains a focus of research. Its practice, however, is not in itself a subject matter. Of course, the good teacher learns and knows that he or she learns, but the classroom does not expect or honor that learning. And, in the absence of a practice community, that learning remains, as it were, idiosyncratic and does not enter the construction of institutional memory. Thus the formalism of continuing education requirements, the habit of advancement by seniority, and so on. Similar things, of course, can be said of continuing education in medicine and the law. But the clinical situation is its own deliberate education; the formalism of continuing education—certificates of attendance and the like—is, for the most part, only that.

The classroom acts as if moral development were a relationship of superiors and inferiors. But development relies on a moral geography, on differences of location and biographical moment and not on differences of status. In the interaction of location and biography and an authority of competence, development enacts moral equality. But this is felt as an abdication of status. How, then, is a sense of incompletion to be confessed when the teacher is under attack and needs the authority of the role? And how is the student to be convinced that he or she can actually be responsible for the classroom when taught the opposite: the arrogance of authority, the student as object?

Thus, teacher and student are located in a common enterprise but not in a shared enterprise. To be sure, the classroom talks endlessly about sharing. And the teacher does care for his or her students. But, typically, student and teacher are alienated from one another by the way their roles are formulated and by the expectations that these roles embody. This alienation grows as the student moves through the grades from the community of kindergarten to the atomism of graduate study. There are other sources of alienation, too: differences of class, caste, gender, and race for example.

At the same time, alienation is surely a legitimate moral subject matter, much as biomedical ethics instructs the practice community. Its study can be an opening to self-consciousness and particularity. Within it are the problems of ethics: integrity, trust, respect, toleration, truth-telling, and the like—a curriculum, if you will. But to reach to these as personal knowledge is, of course, risky, as all personal knowledge is risky.

Instead, the classroom exhibits a dyadic pattern, a "to" and "from" pattern reminiscent of a clinical paternalism that has been delegitimized. The classroom lacks the impulse of an equivalent to biomedical ethics. Yet, if teacher and student are to reconstruct commonality from accident to essence, that pattern is to be reshaped as shared relationship, even as collegial relationship. Teaching, after all, is the best way to learn, and each of us has something to teach and something to learn. Seen from the perspective of the clinical situation, teacher and student are, as it were, simultaneously patient and caregiver. Together, they reflect but seldom reflect on their particular environment. Their experience is formulated as stories, and so potentially is a subject matter of moral education. But the stories are told in private, as it were, and are ruled out of the public space, the classroom.

Particularity is difficult to reach over our habits and defenses. It authorizes telling personal stories just as the patient tells his or her story. Given the psychological complexity of the classroom—difference of age and maturity and not just of status—the personal story, particularly among adolescents, is told, if at all, as if it had happened to another. Students hide from teachers—the special languages and signals of childhood are an example. Teachers hide, too, using role as mode of concealment. But the story will not be denied. Like the symptoms of the patient, the noises of the classroom are the sounds of stories being told. The costumes and music students enjoy, the notes and whispers passed between them, the outbursts of anger, even the terrors of classroom violence are embedded stories. The school yard, the cafeteria, the faculty lounge, the athletic field, the corridor are their scene. In the classroom, however, stories are suppressed as both student and teacher "get down to business." Indeed, in the "well-ordered classroom," stories are "discipline" problems, are treated as mere noise, as disruptions. Thus misidentified and ignored, resentment is inevitable. Anger becomes another unheard story.

Attention to stories calls for cognate stories, that is, reformulating story as case and so as connection to the experiences of others. In fact, this is the mastery of the master teacher, to be a storyteller, to articulate memory, and in the process to build a practice community. Stories are the doorway to history, literature, art, and poetry as lived-through experience and not as mere genre and criticism.

Biomedical ethics encounters its own difficulty with stories, as we have seen, but it cannot exclude them. As George Annas reminds us:

We normally do not look to novels for scientific knowledge, but they provide more: insights into life itself.

This failure of imagination has been witnessed repeatedly, most recently in 1997, when President Clinton asked the National Bioethics Advisory Commission to make recommendations about human cloning. Although acknowledging in their report that human cloning has always seemed the stuff of science fiction rather than science, the group did not commission any background papers on how fiction informs the debate. Even a cursory reading of books like Aldous Huxley's *Brave New World*, Ira Levin's *The Boys from Brazil*, and Fay Weldon's *The Cloning of Joanna May*, for example, would have saved much time and needless debate. Literary treatments of cloning inform us that cloning is an evolutionary dead end that can only replicate what already exists but cannot improve it; that exact replication of a human is not possible; that cloning is not inherently about infertile couples or twins, but about rights as persons that we grant any other human being; and that personal identity, human dignity, and parental responsibility are at the core of the debate about human cloning.[1]

Like biomedical ethics, moral education looks to the arts. These are, as John Dewey put it, both "consummatory" and "instrumental." They appear as responses to felt experiences and as appreciations. They remind us that moral education is both purposive and appreciative—the moral decision, to be sure, but also the story of moral hero or villain. The arts engage the moral imagination, the play and interplay of what-ifs. As Patricia Werhane writes:

Moral judgments are the result of a delicate balance of context, evaluation, the projection of moral minimums, and the presence or absence of moral imagination. The process takes into account context and tradition, a disengaged view from somewhere and minimum moral standards. . . . The lynch-pin [sic] of this process is a highly developed moral imagination that perceives the nuances of a situation, challenges the framework or scheme in which the event is embedded and imagines how that might be different.[2]

Above all, thinking with cases is a turn to experience. Not incidentally, it reminds us of progressive education: the "core curriculum," learning by doing. A critical empiricism is its guide.[3] But in fact progressivism is lost, a totem for some, an enemy for others. Learning by doing becomes a slogan, its own abstraction, and misses its re-creation as thinking by doing. It becomes a hobby, a pastime, a project that lacks the realism of the actual. For thinking with cases, something genuine and genuinely felt must be at stake. The classroom, however, turns to problems where little if anything is at risk. Thus, moral rules are presumed to operate independently of events. Learning them—or in more sophisticated places, learning their arguments and background principles—is said to be the task of moral education. That is the moralism of the classroom and, not surprisingly, it invites a deserved indifference. Students and teachers confront moral problems in their actual relationships. By and large, these are not addressed but converted. They appear as "discipline" problems, as "guidance" problems, as "administrative" problems. They leave the classroom and are referred elsewhere. In that way, we set moral education apart from the classroom.

The curriculum suggested by thinking with cases unfolds by its very absence. I have no illusions about its likelihood. We are, after all, trapped in an educational mood where everything must be measured and where status authority must be maintained. Hardly anyone notices, however, that we can measure only what is measurable, that status authority is not moral or intellectual authority. Against this, as Nel Noddings writes:

We live in a time when everyone seems to be looking for quick and sure solutions . . . in every branch of education, including moral education, we make a mistake when we suppose that a particular batch of content or a particular teaching method or a particular configuration of students and space will accomplish our ends. The answer is both harder and simpler: we, parents and teachers, have to live with our children, talk to them, listen to them, enjoy their company and show them by what we do and how we talk that it is possible to live appreciatively or, at least, non-violently with most other people. Even if we do all this, there is no guarantee that our children will become good people. After all, there is no guarantee that a person who has been reasonably good for forty or seventy years will finish his or her life as a good person.[4]

Finally, another question: In using the model of biomedical ethics for moral education, do we sacrifice too much? After all, the value of thinking with cases in biomedical ethics is still unproven. Does thinking with cases leave us with unmanageable and ultimately unintelligible moral judgments? Are we trapped in particularity, like the professor in Gulliver's voyage to Balnibarbi?

... since words are only names for things, it would be more convenient for all men to carry about them such things as were necessary to express the particular business they are to discourse on ... many of the most learned and wise adhere to the new scheme of expressing themselves by things; which hath only this inconvenience attending it; that if a man's business be very great, and of various kinds, he must be obliged in proportion to carry a greater bundle of things upon his back, unless he can afford one or two strong servants to attend him.[5]

Skepticism—an array of questions—is, for the moment, the final word. In the effort to make moral sense, it is perhaps more salutary than certainty. Hence, thinking with cases suggests its lesson, an offering of humility that is the lasting benefit of doubt. So we are left with the skeptic's question: Is what we learn in the clinical situation transferable, and if so, ought it to be transferred? The answer awaits the effort.

NOTES

1. George J. Annas, "Why We Should Ban Human Cloning," *New England Journal of Medicine*, Vol. 339, No. 2 (July 9, 1998), p. 118.

2. Patricia Werhane, "Moral Imagination and the Search for Ethical Decision-Making in Management," in *The Ruffin Lectures in Business Ethics* (Charlottesville, Va.: 1994), p. 33.

3. See John Dewey, *Democracy and Education* (1916) (New York: Free Press, 1966).

4. Nel Noddings, "Conversation as Moral Education," *Journal of Moral Education*, Vol. 23, No. 2 (1994), p. 116.

5. Jonathan Swift, *Gulliver's Travels* (1726, 1735) (London: The Folio Society, 1994), p. 170.

Selected Bibliography

Ackerman, Terence F., and Carson Strong. *A Casebook of Medical Ethics*. New York: Oxford University Press, 1989.

Ahronheim, Judith C., Jonathan Moreno, and Connie Zuckerman. *Ethics in Clinical Practice*. Boston: Little, Brown, 1994.

Anders, George. *Health Against Wealth*. Boston: Houghton Mifflin, 1996.

Annas, George. "The Prostitute, the Playboy, and the Poet: Rationing Schemes for Organ Transplantation." *American Journal of Public Health*, Vol. 75, No. 2 (1985), pp. 187–189.

Arras, John D., and Bonnie Steinbock, editors. *Ethical Issues in Modern Medicine*. Fourth edition. Mountain View, CA: Mayfield, 1995.

Battin, Margaret P., Rosamond Rhodes, and Anita Silvers, editors. *Physician Assisted Suicide*. New York: Routledge, 1998.

Beauchamp, Tom L., editor. *Intending Death*. Upper Saddle River, NJ: Prentice-Hall, 1996.

Beauchamp, Tom L., and James F. Childress. *Principles of Biomedical Ethics*. Fourth edition. New York: Oxford University Press, 1994.

Bok, Sissela. *Lying: Moral Choice in Public and Private Life*. New York: Vintage Books, 1989.

———. *Secrets: On the Ethics of Concealment and Revelation*. New York: Vintage Books, 1989.

Briscoe, C. C. *Abortion*. Bryn Mawr, PA: Dorrance, 1984.

Brody, Baruch. *Life and Death Decision Making*. New York: Oxford University Press, 1988.

———. *The Ethics of Biomedical Research: An International Perspective*. New York: Oxford University Press, 1998.

Brody, Howard. *The Healer's Power*. New Haven, CT: Yale University Press, 1992.

Brooks, Tim. *Signs of Life: A Memoir of Dying and Discovery*. New York: Times Books, 1997.

Callahan, Daniel. *What Kind of Life?* New York: Simon and Schuster, 1990.

————, project director. *The Goals of Medicine*. Special supplement, *Hastings Center Report*, Vol. 26, No. 6 (November–December 1996).

Caplan, Arthur. *Moral Matters*. New York: John Wiley, 1995.

Cassell, Eric J. *The Nature of Suffering and the Goals of Medicine*. New York: Oxford University Press, 1991.

Chambliss, Daniel F. *Beyond Caring*. Chicago: University of Chicago Press, 1996.

Cleaveland, Cliff. *Sacred Space: Stories from a Life in Medicine*. Philadelphia: American College of Physicians, 1998.

Coles, Robert. *The Call of Stories*. Boston: Houghton Mifflin, 1989.

Davis, Courtney, and Judy Schaeffer, editors. *Between the Heartbeats: Poetry and Prose by Nurses*. Iowa City: University of Iowa Press, 1995.

Delury, George E. *But What if She Wants to Die*. Secaucus, NJ: Birch Lane Press, 1997.

Donagan, Alan. *The Theory of Morality*. Chicago: University of Chicago Press, 1977.

Drury, M. O'C. *The Dangers of Words and Writings on Wittgenstein*. Edited by David Berman, Michael Fitzgerald, and John Hayes. Bristol, UK: Thoemmes Press, 1996.

Dworkin, Ronald. *Taking Rights Seriously*. Cambridge, MA: Harvard University Press, 1977.

————. *Life's Dominion*. New York: Alfred A. Knopf, 1993.

Emanuel, Ezekiel. *The Ends of Human Life: Medical Ethics in a Liberal Polity*. Cambridge, MA: Harvard University Press, 1992.

Engelhardt, Tristram. *The Foundations of Bioethics*. Second edition. New York: Oxford University Press, 1996.

English, Dan C. *Bioethics: A Clinical Guide for Medical Students*. New York: W. W. Norton, 1994.

Ethical Issues and Patient Rights. Oakbrook Terrace, IL: Joint Commission on Accreditation of Health Care Organizations, 1998.

Ethical Issues of Managed Care. Charleston: Medical University of South Carolina, 1995.

Filene, Peter G. *In the Arms of Others: A Cultural History of the Right-to-Die in America*. Chicago: Ivan R. Dee, 1998.

Fletcher, John C., Charles A. Hite, Paul A. Lombardo, and Mary Faith Marshall. *Introduction to Clinical Ethics*. Frederick, MD: University Publishing Group, 1995.

Fletcher, Joseph. *Situation Ethics: The New Morality*. Louisville, KY: Westminster John Knox Press, 1997.

Gert, Bernard, Charles M. Culver, and K. Danner Clouser. *Bioethics*. New York: Oxford University Press, 1997.

Gervais, Karen G., et al., editors. *Ethical Challenges in Managed Care*. Washington, DC: Georgetown University Press, 1999.

Gilligan, Carol. *In a Different Voice*. Cambridge, MA: Harvard University Press, 1982.

Gordon, Suzanne. *Life Support*. Boston: Little, Brown, 1997.

Haley, Kathleen, and Melinda Lee, editors. *The Oregon Death with Dignity Act*. Portland, OR: Center for Ethics in Health Care, 1998.

Handler, Evan. *Time on Fire: My Comedy of Terrors*. New York: Owl Books, 1996.

Harraway, Donna. "Situated Knowledges: The Science Question in Feminism and the Privilege of Partial Perspective." *Feminist Studies*, Vol. 14 (1988), pp. 575–599.

Heifetz, Milton D., with Charles Mangel. *The Right to Die*. New York: Berkley, 1975.

Humphry, Derek. *Final Exit: The Practicalities of Self Deliverance and Assisted Suicide for the Dying*. Secaucus, NJ: The Hemlock Society, 1991.

Humphry, Derek, and Mary Clement. *Freedom to Die*. New York: St. Martin's Press, 1998.

Jaggar, Alison M. *Feminist Politics and Human Nature*. Totowa, NJ: Rowman and Allanheld, 1983.

Jones, James H. *Bad Blood: The Tuskegee Syphilis Experiment*. New York: Free Press, 1981.

Jonsen, Albert R. *The Birth of Bioethics*. New York: Oxford University Press, 1998.

Jonsen, Albert R., Mark Siegler, and William J. Winslade. *Clinical Ethics*. Fourth edition. New York: McGraw-Hill, 1998.

Jonsen, Albert R., and Stephen Toulmin. *The Abuse of Casuistry*. Berkeley: University of California Press, 1988.

Kevles, Daniel J., and Leroy Hood, editors. *The Code of Codes*. Cambridge, MA: Harvard University Press, 1992.

Komesaroff, Paul A. *Troubled Bodies*. Durham, NC: Duke University Press, 1995.

Koop, C. Everett, and Timothy Johnson. *Let's Talk*. Grand Rapids, MI: Zondervan, 1992.

Kramer, Peter. *Listening to Prozac*. New York: Viking, 1993.

Lantos, John D. *Do We Still Need Doctors*. New York: Routledge, 1996.

Laster, Leonard. *Life after Medical School*. New York: W. W. Norton, 1996.

Levi, Benjamin H. *Respecting Patient Autonomy*. Chicago: University of Illinois Press, 1999.

Lyon, Jeff, and Peter Gorner. *Altered Fates*. New York: W. W. Norton, 1995.

MacIntyre, Alisdair. *After Virtue*. Notre Dame, IN: University of Notre Dame Press, 1981.

Mappes, Thomas A., and Jane S. Zembaty. *Biomedical Ethics*. Third Edition. New York: McGraw-Hill, 1991.

May, W. F. *The Patient's Ordeal*. Bloomington: Indiana University Press, 1991.

McCullough, Laurence B. *John Gregory and the Invention of Professional Medical Ethics*. Boston: Kluwer Academic, 1998.

McCullough, Laurence B., James W. Jones, and Baruch A. Brody. *Surgical Ethics*. New York: Oxford University Press, 1998.

Mill, John Stuart. *On Liberty*. New York: Bobbs-Merrill, 1956.

Munson, Ronald. *Intervention and Reflection*. Fifth edition. Belmont, CA: Wadsworth, 1996.

Nelson, Hilde Lindemann, editor. *Stories and Their Limits*. New York: Routledge, 1997.

Nelson, Hilde Lindemann, and James Lindemann Nelson. *The Patient in the Family*. New York: Routledge, 1995.

Noddings, Nel. *Caring: A Feminine Approach to Ethics and Moral Education.* Berkeley: University of California Press, 1984.

Nuland, Sherwin. *How We Die.* New York: Alfred A. Knopf, 1994.

Nussbaum, Martha C. *Poetic Justice: The Literary Imagination and Public Life.* Boston: Beacon Press, 1995.

Pence, Gregory E. *Classic Cases in Medical Ethics.* Second edition. Boston: McGraw-Hill, 1995.

———. *Classic Works in Medical Ethics.* Boston: McGraw-Hill, 1998.

Perlin, Terry M. *Clinical Medical Ethics: Cases in Practice.* Boston: Little, Brown, 1992.

Porter, Roy. *The Greatest Benefit to Mankind.* New York: W. W. Norton, 1997.

President's Commission for the Study of Ethical Problems in Medicine and Biomedical and Behavior Research, 15 volumes. Washington, DC: U.S. Government Printing Office, 1983.

Quill, Timothy E. *Death and Dignity: Making Choices and Taking Charge.* New York: W. W. Norton, 1993.

———. *A Midwife Through the Dying Process.* Baltimore: Johns Hopkins University Press, 1996

"Quinlan: A Twenty Year Retrospective." Paper presented at Conference, Princeton University, April 12–13, 1996.

Rawls, John. *A Theory of Justice.* Cambridge, MA: Belknap Press, 1971.

Regan, Tom. *The Case for Animal Rights.* Berkeley: University of California Press, 1990.

Reich, Warren, editor. *Encyclopedia of Bioethics.* Second edition. 5 volumes. New York: Simon and Schuster, 1995.

Rodwin, Marc A. *Medicine, Money, and Morals.* New York: Oxford University Press, 1993.

Rosenthal, Joel H., editor. *Moral Education V.* New York: Carnegie Council on Ethics and International Affairs, 1995.

Ross, W. D. *The Right and the Good.* Oxford: Clarendon Press, 1930.

Rothman, David J. *Strangers at the Bedside.* New York: Basic Books, 1991.

Sherwin, Susan. *No Longer Patient: Feminist Ethics and Health Care.* Philadelphia: Temple University Press, 1992.

Shilts, Randy. *And the Band Played On.* New York: St. Martin's Press, 1987.

Silver, Lee M. *Remaking Eden.* New York: Avon Books, 1997.

Singer, Peter. *Animal Liberation.* New York: New York Review of Books, 1975.

———. *Practical Ethics.* Cambridge: Cambridge University Press, 1979.

Snyder, Lois, editor. *Ethical Choices.* Philadelphia: American College of Physicians, 1996.

Steptoe, Patrick and Edward Robert. *A Matter of Life: The Story of a Medical Breakthrough.* London: Morrow, 1980.

Theories and Methods in Bioethics: Principlism and Its Critics. Kennedy Institute of Ethics Journal, September 1955.

Thompson, Larry. *Correcting the Code.* New York: Simon and Schuster, 1994.

Tong, Rosemarie. *Feminist Approaches to Bioethics: Theoretical Reflection and Practical Application.* Boulder, CO: Westview Press, 1997.

Toulmin, Stephen. "How Medicine Saved the Life of Philosophy." In J. R. DeMarco and R. Fox, editors, *New Directions in Ethics*. Boston: Routledge and Kegan Paul, 1986.

Veatch, Robert M., editor. *Cross Cultural Perspectives in Medical Ethics: Readings*. Boston: Jones and Bartlett, 1989.

————. *Medical Ethics*. Second edition. Boston: Jones and Bartlett, 1997.

Verghese, Abraham. *My Own Country*. New York: Vintage Books, 1994.

Webb, Marilyn. *The Good Death*. New York: Bantam Books, 1997.

Whittemore, Kenneth R., and James A. Johnson, editors. *Dying in America: Choices at the End of Life*. Charleston: Medical University of South Carolina, 1995.

Williams, Bernard. *Moral Luck*. New York: Cambridge University Press, 1981.

Wills, Christopher. *Exons, Introns, and Talking Genes*. New York: Basic Books, 1991.

Wolf, Susan M., editor. *Feminism and Bioethics: Beyond Reproduction*. New York: Oxford University Press, 1996.

Women's Health Issues. Charleston: Medical University of South Carolina, 1996.

Index